Poverty Alleviation in Tanzania:
Recent Research Issues

Poverty Alleviation in Tanzania: Recent Research Issues

Edited by

M.S.D. Bagachwa

DAR ES SALAAM UNIVERSITY PRESS

Published by

Dar es Salaam University Press
P.O. Box 35182, DAR ES SALAAM.

In Collaboration with

Network for Research on Poverty Alleviation (REPOA)
P.O. Box 35121, Dar es Salaam, Tanzania

First Published 1994

Bagachwa (Mboya, S.D.)

Poverty Alleviation in Tanzania: Recent Research Issues

ISBN 9976 60 248 0

Contents

iv

List of Tables

List of Figures

Notes on the Contributors

BAGACHWA, M.S.D. - Associate Research Professor, Economic Research Bureau; and Associate Dean (Research and Publications), Faculty of Arts and Social Sciences, University of Dar es Salaam.

CHUNGU, A.S. - Development Engineer, Institute of Production Innovation, University of Dar es Salaam.

COOKSEY, B. - Secretary, Tanzania Development Research Group (TADREG)

MANDARA, G.R.R. - Senior Consultant Business Care Services Limited.

MASCARENHAS, A. - Research Professor, Institute of Resource Assessment and Director of Postgraduate Studies, University of Dar es Salaam.

MBUGHUNI, P. (Ms) - Senior Research Fellow, Institute of Kiswahili Research, University of Dar es Salaam.

MKAPA, B.W. - Minister of Science, Technology and Higher Education.

MTATIFIKOLO, F. - Senior Lecturer, Department of Economics, University of Dar es Salaam.

OMARI, C.K. - Professor of Sociology, Department of Sociology; and Associate Dean (Academic) Faculty of Arts and Social Sciences, University of Dar es Salaam.

SEMBOJA, J. - Associate Research Professor and Director, Economic Research Bureau, University of Dar es Salaam.

YZERMANS, J.L. - Counsellor, Royal Netherlands Embassy, Dar es Salaam, Tanzania.

Acknowledgements

First of all I would like to acknowledge and thank the contributors of the papers in this volume for providing the necessary material which has made the publication of this book possible. Secondly, I would like to thank members of the Workshop Organizing Committee specifically Y. Kohi, A. T. Makenya and J. Rugumyamheto for the effective organization of the January 11-12, 1994 Workshop at which the papers in this volume, were initially presented. All along I have benefitted from the logistical support, valuable assistance and comments from Dirk Bol and J. Semboja. I am equally indebted to the overall editorial advice provided by Brian Van Arkadie; the technical editing provided by A.F. Lwaitama; and the secretarial assistance provided by M. Kassanga and G. Kiwia.

Both the organization of the Workshop and the publication of this book have been sponsored by the Government of the Netherlands. I would like to express my sincere thanks for this generous assistance. Special thanks should go to Marie Hulsman - Vesjova' for her tireless efforts and encouragement to get things moving. However, the views expressed in this book are those of the respective authors and do not necessarily represent those of the University of Dar es Salaam or the Government of the Netherlands.

M.S.D. Bagachwa

Prelude

Opening Address by
Honourable Benjamin W. Mkapa, MP,
Minister for Science, Technology and Higher Education

Mr. Chairman,
Your Excellency The Ambassador of the Netherlands,
Distinguished Guests,
Ladies and Gentlemen,

I feel deeply honoured to have been asked to open this important workshop on research on poverty.

It is as recently as four weeks ago that I was invited to officiate at a similar function, a workshop organised by the research group TADREG. That workshop had for its focus, Education. The focus of this workshop is on poverty alleviation.

It seems to me that there is a dynamic link between the two issues of education and poverty - if not causal then certainly reinforcing. Education is perceived as a tool for mastering the environment for production and self-preservation. In many countries the poor are often also the uneducated. I suggest that the findings and recommendations from the one workshop will help in strengthening the deliberations and conclusion of the present one. And I am delighted to see that a number of participants in the one are also among us today.

There is an additional reason for satisfaction that these two workshops should take place within weeks of each other. This fact indicates that we are taking a hard look at the state of affairs in the social services sector of our national life. In turn this suggests that there is a crisis in this field and that there is need to review the assumptions, strategies and weaponry of the War against Poverty.

There is a saying in one of the Holy Books to the effect that the poor are always with us. But need they be? In spite of all the advances in knowledge, science, technology and systems organisation?

The government of independent Tanzania decided from the outset to minimise the numbers of the poor and the extent of the poverty with us. The post-independence clarion call has been Freedom and Hard Work to eradicate hunger, ignorance and disease. The word poverty is often substituted for hunger, but I have not done so deliberately. For it seems to me that ignorance and disease are not only inseparable from poverty, they are almost synonymous with it. In any event the number one agenda of independent Tanyanyika, Revolutionary Zanzibar and the United Republic of Tanzania became the eradication of Poverty - the removal of hunger, ignorance and disease. Government recognised that Poverty is incompatible with freedom and stability; that the inevitable consequence of poverty is dependence.

The country embarked on an ambitious goal of development with successive development plans. It established an extensive and successful infrastructure of social services - especially in education and health. It established a comprehensive network of agricultural extension services to boost agricultural production. It established a network of agricultural research institutes to serve the cause of revolutionising rural production in terms of both methodology and technology. In all these areas we were and remain the envy of many a developing country - *from the infrastructural point of view.*

The outburst of energy and the massive infusion of resources of the early years yielded great fruits. Incomes both rural and agricultural, of the employed and the self-employed, rose visibly. The health of the people improved - as evidenced by the rise in the average life expectation from 33 to 51 years. The number of children in schools swelled. Agricultural exports rose - leading to substantial reserves in crop price stabilisation funds. The successes were many and undisputed.

But it cannot also be disputed that these early dramatic achievements and successes have been very difficult to sustain in the last fifteen years. Indeed there have been real declines in some of them. The goal of accruing seventy per cent of the export crop price to the farmer has not been achieved, and because of exogenous factors, especially the decline in world agricultural commodity prices, farmers' real incomes have been declining. Wages, both in the private and public sector but especially in the public sector which is the largest employer, are to-day less than fifty per cent of what they were in the late 70s *in real terms.*

In the field of education, enrolment and completion rates in primary education are declining. In health, rates of maternal, infant and child deaths are still high and malnutrition is widespread. Access to clean and assured water is becoming more difficult because of the cost of sustaining the improved water supplies. In my own district for example by 1990 lack of pump spares and high operation and maintenance costs had made water schemes so difficult to run that less than half the hand pumps installed were functioning. The situation has only marginally improved in the meantime.

Let me state unequivocally that I believe our basic development policies to be sound. I cite these examples not as an illustration of failure of basic policies but to underscore the problem of sustainability of achievements in the war against poverty. I do so also to emphasise that problem solving should not allow us the luxury of burying our heads in the sand or closing our eyes and ears to realities. You will have read recently that Tanzania was placed last but one among the poorest countries in the world. When this same statistic was given two years ago there was a wave of indignation and a political furore. But let us accept that however disputable the grading system, the criteria or the definitions used to describe poverty may be, our country remains, in truth, one of the poorest in the world, much poor than we would like it to be.

Now the questions that come immediately in mind are: where are we going wrong? Or are we not doing enough? Or are we not doing things the right way?

I believe that the war against poverty has slowed down because in the flourish of the early successes we may have attacked on too many fronts at all at the same time with inadequate preparation for intervention. I believe that in planning, strategising, executing, supervising, monitoring, coordinating and setting out specific sectoral goals we may have been poorly informed and hasty of decision and action. Interventions were well-intentioned and called for. But the ground may not have been well set and the implementation may have been impatiently pursued.

This is where the role of research in policy making and implementation becomes very important. Important in the seance that it provides the opportunity to prepare the ground, review the assumptions, to re-evaluate the strategies and to correct the approaches to making the interventions in social development. For research provides for analysis of past action. Through research findings we can learn what went wrong, or what is going wrong with plans. And we can use the research findings to make adjustments or change course realistically and scientifically.

Mr. Chairman, Workshop Participants,

I hazard the proposition that there has been, and there continue to be, insufficient researched studies as firm background to the plans and interventions for the eradication of poverty by government, NGO's and Donor agencies in developing countries such as ours. One reason undoubtedly is the urgency with which the plans and projects are demanded and drawn up in the face of debilitating poverty. More often than not we politicians demand quick results and high profile. And in this characteristic I dare say aid administrators are no different!! But researched decisions require time and patience which we do not much allow ourselves. I believe however that the many workshops that have been held for the purpose of taking a second look at the grand schemes of change would have driven home the importance of research in making right decisions towards laying the foundation of sustainable achievements.

And yet this cannot be the whole story. Where there may have been an inclination not to solicit researched findings before decision, there has not been a lack of these findings. I referred earlier to the network of agricultural research institutes and extension services centres to support a revolution in rural production. That we have not witnessed such a revolution is not because these networks have not produced researched findings or that the findings have not been made available. It is just that people have not cared to use them to evolve policy. Scientific knowledge still idles at the periphery of policy dialogue and practical planning. And this is a serious obstacle to fast development.

There must clearly be a change of attitude and I ask your Workshop to discuss how to tackle this problem. Furthermore, because research is costly and yet a critical component in the process of effective decision making, I hope you will put together recommendations on how research funding can be mobilised in viable amounts. There are of course always competing needs for public funds; but research can continue to be given low priority only at the cost of undermining the commitment to eradicate poverty expeditiously.

Mr. Chairman, Ladies and Gentlemen,

There is much research funding which is undertaken by donors. Quite a considerable amount of it is however in support of consultancy type of studies rather than case studies. Understandably consultancies are quicker to conclude, and they address ad hoc situations. A balance needs to be struck so that a sufficient amount is allocated to the kind of studies that will address long term policy intervention.

In looking at the array of topics during this workshop I am gratified to note that they comprise factors which cause social stagnation. I hope that a serious agenda will emerge from the discussions of the workshop, not only in terms of research subjects but also in respect of the links between research on the one hand and public policy formulation and implementation on the other. I do want to reiterate that research can be of practical value to society only if it is appreciated and is utilised in determining public policy.

Mr. Chairman, Ladies and Gentlemen,

Allow me to express my special appreciation of the fact that included in the topics of the workshop is a subject central to the mission of my Ministry, namely the role of science and technology in the eradication of poverty. Those of you who recall my ministerial budget speech last July will remember that I pointed out that for a very long time we had stuck to the truism adumbrated in the Arusha Declaration to the effect that in order to develop country needed four factors: land, people, good policies, and good leadership. I said while this truism still held true it was time to add a fifth factor: Science and Technology.

There is great merit to the observation that: We are poor because we are unscientific in outlook and backward in the technology we use for production. People who use their heads for transporting goods and crops must remain poor. People who walk long distances to find water and then carry it on their heads must remain poor. People who do not know fertility limits of their soils, the yield capacities of their seeds, the likely vagaries of the weather, must remain poor: they will produce little and eat little. People who lose a third of their crop harvest because of bad storage capacity will remain poor. I need not belabour the point; I want to stress that without placing scientific knowledge, and tested appropriate technology at the centre of the process of change it will take decade upon decade to win the war against poverty.

The other topic of great importance which the workshop will address is the element of gender in research on poverty. Development and poverty research must take into account the social context. It is wishful thinking to imagine that poverty can be eradicated without considering the role of women in production and their access to social welfare. There may be debate as to whether rural production and their access to social welfare. There may be debate as to whether rural production is overwhelmingly undertaken by women, or just substantially undertaken by them. But that they are a decisive factor in household unit production and the well being of the family cannot be in dispute. How much and how is poverty related to the degree of access by women to resources and technology for production? What is the impact of socio-cultural factors? I look to the workshop to begin to help us find answers to these issues of gender analysis and the social, cultural and geographical underpinnings to plans for poverty eradication.

I notice also that you will address the management aspects of research activities in the country. In this area effective machinery is in my view lacking, and I would hope that the Workshop would have recommendations for the ministry and the Government about how to improve existing machinery or procedures.

I take this opportunity to express the Government's gratitude to the Government of the Netherlands for the offer to fund the Research on Poverty Alleviation in Tanzania. This will go a long way towards facilitating the task of addressing the concerns I have raised.

I shall end by thanking you again for the courtesy of inviting me to be with you this morning; by thanking the organisers of the Workshop for the work they have put into it, and by thanking those of you who have come from outside Tanzania to join us. I hope you have a pleasant and fruitful stay.

It is now my great pleasure to declare the Workshop open. Thank you for your attention.

Keynote Address
by
Mr J.L. Yzermans,
the Netherlands Embassy in Tanzania

Dear Participants to this Workshop,
Your Excellency, the Minister for Science, Technology
and Higher Education,

I thank the organising committee very much for inviting the Netherlands Ambassador to address this important gathering. However, as the Ambassador is at present in the Netherlands, I have the honour to give the Keynote Speech on the Ambassador's behalf.

Tanzania and the Netherlands have had long standing relations in the field of development cooperation dating back to the sixties. Having received about NGL 2.5 billion over the past three decades, Tanzania has by far been the largest recipient of Netherlands' aid in Africa. However if we look at the results of this support, based on a recently completed evaluation of the entire aid programme, the assistance has had a doubtful score in terms of effectiveness and sustainability in several cases. Improper priority setting and insufficient preparation of activities have caused unsatisfactory results in a number of cases. No wonder that research directed at supporting the development process is now receiving increased attention.

History of Dutch Support to Research in Tanzania

Looking at the history of the Netherlands' support to research in Tanzania, we see that since the mid-70s the Dutch have supported several research activities in Tanzania: horticultural research (at Tengeru) Plant Protection research in Zanzibar; fisheries research around Lake Victoria; research in gasification of agricultural waste, soil surveys, and farming systems in Western Tanzania; also AIDS research in that area; in addition to other health related research at Muhimbili. Support has also been given to electrical engineering, botany and chemistry research at the University of Dar es Salaam. Since the mid-1980s support has been given to the Economic Research Bureau. The Tanzanian National Research Master Plan was also co-financed by the Dutch, a clear expression of its interests in this area. Furthermore, during the 1980's about 1000 fellowships were awarded to Tanzanians for further studies in the Netherlands.

New Research Programme

In 1992 a new research policy in the Netherlands' stance on Development Cooperation was introduce expressed in a thorough document called "Research and development". This new policy again stresses the importance of research as an instrument of development cooperation: its importance in improving quality of development assistance provided the research is functional and relevant to development policies, using policy objectives and criteria as a measuring stick.

Therefore, in order to maximise the utility of research an attempt is being made now to integrate research activities into all the relevant policy fields of Dutch development cooperation and to harmonize these as effectively as possible.

In the context of this new policy and also to counteract the high degree of asymmetry in the global research system (most of it being concentrated in the North), new research programmes are to be designed in a number of countries of the South with which the Netherlands have a special relationship. These countries are Vietnam, Bangladesh, Mali, Bolivia and Tanzania. Other countries will be added to the list in due course.

This conference is really the first official manifestation of the creation of such a programme in Tanzania after preliminary consultations for a year. This new programme will be complementary to ongoing research support, not replacing these. The essence of these new research programmes is to place research in a more structural framework and to tackle the reinforcement of local research capacity in relation to development problems over a long period of time using an institutional approach. These will thus be multi-year, broad-based location-specific , and multi-disciplinary research programmes. Their most important and in that sense their *unique* characteristic is probably their demand-orientation! Through these programmes Tanzania should be able to develop its own scientific research capacity and to study its own development problems. Therefore, after agreement on the appropriate institutional framework by the Netherlands and Tanzania, the programme should be completely in the hands of Tanzanian research fellows. The Netherlands will only be concerned to see to it that the programme will in fact be truly multi-disciplinary; long-term oriented;

broad-based location specific; involving a large strata of Tanzanian research fellows and institutions; and of course, using the funds effectively.

This Conference

This conference is an important first step in setting up such a programme in this country. After an orientation phase, in which a representative organisation committee was selected, drawing on important public and private research institutions like the Economic Research Bureau of the University of Dar es Salaam, the Commission for Science and Technology, TADREG and the newly formed Economic and Social Research Foundation, five important topics have been selected for discussion today, all dealing with poverty alleviation, the central theme in the development process. These topics are:

(a) Implications of public policies on poverty alleviation
(b) Social and cultural factors influencing poverty
(c) The use of technology in alleviating poverty
(d) Environmental issues on poverty alleviation
(e) Gender and poverty alleviation

All these topics are placed in the Tanzanian context. The ensuing discussions should assist in formulating a clear research agenda for the programme to be set up afterwards. Once this has been done and an appropriate "intermediary agency" has been created to manage and administer the research and its funds, research proposals by individual researchers from all over Tanzania are expected to be guided and funded through this new channel.

Afterthought

The experience of Dutch support to research in Tanzania has demonstrated that this is not an easy process. Particularly in the early stages, a lot of support was channelled towards supporting the physical infrastructure of existing research institutions and towards training of its respective personnel. In most cases it took quite some time before actual research activities could indeed be supported.

It is therefore hoped that this new set-up will be able to move much more quickly towards supporting actual research. Also, an important aspect of this programme should be its sustainability, a weakness of former efforts in view of very limited funds for research (and remuneration of staff) from the Tanzanian Government itself.

Follow-up

I would like to conclude by praising the coordinators for the subjects they have chosen and the thorough preparation made. It is hoped that this excellent initiative leads to concrete follow up measures and that a few well-defined concrete research themes will be identified.

Your Excellency, ladies and gentlemen, thank you very much for listening to me and I wish you all a very fruitful workshop.

1

Changing Perceptions of Poverty and the Emerging Research Issues

MBOYA S.D. BAGACHWA

BACKGROUND AND CONTEXT

Programme for Research on Poverty Alleviation (REPOA) in Tanzania

Two recent reviews on the state of research and socio-economic policy analysis in Tanzania have lamented on the wide gap that exists between demand and supply for research-oriented policy work and to the high degree to which research and policy agenda are increasingly becoming donor-driven (Doriye *et al*, 1991; Van Arkadie, 1993). In spite of the increasing number of trained and competent professionals, the existing local supply capacity to undertake policy-oriented research still remains inadequate in both quality and quantity. Largely, this is attributed to institutional weaknesses which include: failure to exercise greater local initiative in articulating a coherent and focused research agenda; the emphasis on demand-led consulting which reflects short term donor policy concerns rather than longer term research concerns which reflect national priorities; the individual nature of contracting outside work; and inadequate remuneration and poor work environments.

The inadequacies in the existing local supply of research capacity is coupled with the urgent need to better understand the appropriate policy options by the government, parastatals, the growing private sector, NGOs and the donor community, demonstrating the need to build and strengthen local research capacity. In response to this growing concern and in order to contribute to meeting this need, the establishment of a long term research programme on poverty alleviation (REPOA) in Tanzania has been proposed. The REPOA programme which initially will be sponsored by the Government of the Netherlands, but will be under Tanzanian management, is envisaged to have the following objectives:

(a) building, strengthening, and maintaining local capacity and intellectual culture to develop an independent research agenda and to conduct effectively independent research into problems pertinent to the alleviation of poverty in Tanzania;

(b) building a local capacity with genuine empowerment for administering network affairs within a context of the priorities of local policy and sponsors' agreed objectives;

(c) promoting the sharing of research experiences, problematics and methodologies among scholars, researchers, policy makers etc. from different disciplines and institutions on problems of poverty alleviation in Tanzania;

(d) evolving and articulating coherent and focused, long term network-supported research activities within a multidisciplinary context, so as to build a critical mass of good quality research results that can be readily and effectively used by relevant local and international institutions in designing appropriate policies for alleviating poverty;

(e) improving the links between network researchers and the potential users of research results at the grassroots, national, regional and international levels (i.e., policy makers, NGOs, grassroots organizations, activists, business, academic and donor communities, etc.); and

(f) serving as a knowledge broker by providing information to researchers and putting them in contact with other researchers in the global community at large.

A Workshop for Research Issues

As a first step towards the operationalization of the REPOA programme, a workshop for research on poverty alleviation in Tanzania was held in Dar es Salaam, Tanzania on 11th and 12th of January, 1994. The workshop was jointly organized by four leading research-oriented institutions in the country, namely, the Commission for Science and Technology (COSTECH); the Economic Research Bureau (ERB); the Economic and Social Research Foundation (ESRF); and the Tanzania Development Research Group (TADREG). It was sponsored by the Government of the Netherlands. The intended purpose of the workshop was to discuss and establish a broad-based but coherently focused research agenda with the purpose of articulating further REPOA's research directions.

To this end, papers were commissioned by the Workshop Organizing Committee to provide background for discussion, review previous and current developments, as well as to define specific areas that warrant further research. Earlier on, the choice of the overarching theme and the subsequent sub-thematic variations had been a subject of intense but productive discussion among the members of the Workshop Organizing Committee. After careful consideration of the relevant issues, and bearing in mind the relevance of the theme to Tanzania's development goals and aspirations, it was unanimously agreed that poverty alleviation in Tanzania would be the focus of the selected theme and sub-themes.

In view of the recent global research thrust on poverty (see the next section) five sub-themes were further identified to be the basis for the generation of a much more detailed research agenda as well as to cater for the diversified needs and interests of the potential interdisciplinary researchers. The five sub-themes are:

(i)   the link between poverty and public policies;

(ii)   the poverty-environment linkage;

(iii)   role of technology in poverty alleviation

(iv)   gender issues and poverty and

(v)   the socio-cultural determinants of poverty.

A state of the art paper on each sub-theme was commissioned, along with three other papers - a conceptual framework paper on poverty assessment, a state of the art paper on poverty research in Tanzania and a paper on the institutional framework within which REPOA is to be managed.

The seven papers in this volume are the edited versions of the papers which were presented at the workshop as prompts for further discussion. The institutional framework paper has not been published because the programme is yet to evolve fully. The papers in this collection have incorporated some of the ideas contributed by the workshop participants. To be fair to the authors, while the papers reflect the current views and thoughts of the authors (academic professionals active in the respective fields), none claim to provide the exhaustive and definitive treatment of the subjects they deal with. Indeed in a world where ideas and views are continuously changing, experience rapidly generates new issues that have hitherto been overlooked. By making this collection publicly available the REPOA Secretariat hopes to achieve a broader circulation of the information and ideas contained herein. Most important however, it is hoped that the ideas in this book will initiate and stimulate debate on current poverty issues among policy-makers, development specialists, and academic professionals, who continue to grapple with their efforts to promote development.

Workshop's Major Conclusions

The discussion at the workshop that took place in January 11-12, 1994 was broadly supportive of the chosen theme as deserving high priority in the Tanzanian research agenda and of the relevance of the subthemes chosen. Within the selected themes, the importance of locating analysis of contemporary policy issues in the context of a firm understanding of the historical context was emphasized. In particular the importance of understanding processes of change was underscored.

In considering the possible audience researchers should see themselves as addressing, while there was widespread support for the need for communicate research results to policymakers in government and the donor community, there was also recognition that particularly in light of the evolving political system, there is an equal need for research to be directed to the needs of the community at large, and accordingly to be disseminated widely including to NGO's, the media, community groups, backbench Members of Parliament, etc.

A variety of disciplinary (methodological) approaches were adopted in the papers, and in the discussions alternative approaches were also proposed. There was no general agreement on methodology, but support was expressed for an interdisciplinary approach and the use of a range of approaches.

There seemed to be agreement that for a number of sub-themes, there was both a case for specialized studies, but also the sub-theme should run through many of the separate subjects. That would be true, for example of the gender issue, of the analysis of the impact of liberalization and of environmental issues. Emphasis was also placed on the need to combine approaches (e.g. the need to combine gender and class analysis).

Given the agreement that there were a number of different disciplinary approaches relevant to the study of poverty alleviation and that a wide range of institutions should be involved, there was a consensus that the most appropriate way to organize a research programme was through the agency of a research network.

Throughout the discussions the issue of the relevance of received concepts and methodologies for the measurement and analysis of poverty to the specific Tanzanian environment was questioned, and the need to explore their relevance emphasized.

POVERTY AND THE CHANGING WORLD ENVIRONMENT

Poverty Today

As we cross over the 1980s - the *lost decade* for the developing world - and proceed through the 1990s towards the year 2000, one major global problem, that of poverty, broadly conceived as the "inability to attain a minimum standard of living,"[1] continues to be pervasive in world development. According to the World Bank (1990) and UNDP (1990), poverty and destitution affected about 1.2 billion people in 1985; that was almost one-third of the total population of the developing countries[2]. Today the situation has not improved. A recent report by UNICEF (1994) laments that approximately one-fifth of the world's population live in absolute poverty.

Within developing countries, the burden, breadth and incidence of poverty are spread unevenly within regions and among localities within countries according to the level of development. Nearly half of the world's poor live in South East Asia, a region that hosts about 30% of the world's population. Sub-Saharan Africa's (SSA) share in global poverty is relatively small (16.1%) but it is highly disproportionate because it accounts for 11.1% of the world's population (World Bank, 1990a).

Among localities within countries, especially in Africa and Asia, the poor are often concentrated in rural areas with high population pressure. However, the urban poor, though proportionately small, are increasing much faster than the rural poor. In Latin America, most of the poor are concentrated in urban areas. However, in sub-Saharan Africa, about two-thirds of the population are affected by absolute poverty and there, poverty tends to persist among subsistence farmers, mainly as a result of rapid population growth and low agricultural productivity (SIDA, 1991). In Asia persistent poverty is attributed mainly to high population densities, landlessness and fragmented holdings. In spite of the relatively higher income levels in Latin America, poverty continues to be widespread due to unequal accessibility and distribution of resources especially land and income (UNDP, 1990).

Certain groups within countries appear to be highly disadvantaged. They include women who tend to be less educated and have little access to income generating activities; children especially girls and in some cases certain ethnic groups.

In Tanzania, poverty remains pervasive. The World Bank Development Report 1993 ranked Tanzania (Mailand) as the second poorest country in the world with a GNP per capita of US $100 in 1991. However the per capita expenditure level estimated from the 1991 household survey was put at US dollars 281 (TSh 61,564)[3]. This seem to suggest that official GDP estimates underestimate national income and expenditure. Bagachwa and Maliyamkono (1990) estimated that the national accounts of Tanzania underestimate real GDP by a minimum of 30%. Recent estimates by Sarris and Van den Brink (1983) and Tinios *et al,* (1983), put the extent of underestimation at 60% and 66.4% respectively.

Caution is necessary here because neither the average per capita income nor the per capita expenditure are good measures of welfare. For example, the use of UNDP's Human Development Index (which takes into consideration adjusted real GDP per head, life expectancy, and educational attainment) ranked Tanzania higher than 33 other countries in 1991.

This however, does not imply that the welfare of Tanzanians is high. A number of studies have revealed that the majority of Tanzanians are very poor. According to IFAD, in 1988 nearly 12 million rural Tanzanians or 60% of the rural population were living below the poverty line. About 10% of the population lived in absolute poverty (Jazairy et al, 1992). The 1991 Cornell-ERB survey corroborates this evidence by revealing that over 50% of the population or 44% of the households still live in poverty[4] and that about 12% of the households were severely under-nourished[5] (Tinios et al, 1993). There is a general agreement that poverty is more widespread in rural than in urban areas (Jazairy et al, 1992; Sarris and van den Brink, 1993; Tinios et al, 1993: and World Bank, 1993a).

Most indices of poverty show the rural population to be significantly more disadvantaged than the urban. A recent poverty profile of Tanzania (World Bank, 1993a) finds rural Tanzanians to have bigger families than their urban counterparts. Their dependency burden is greater and their income is less. Average rural per capita income is 63% of income in urban areas and 44% of the average in Dar es Salaam. A typical rural household produces 42% the food it consumes compared to 18% in urban areas and 3% in Dar es Salaam. Almost a quarter of all rural families in Tanzania have to walk to more than 30 minutes to obtain drinking water. Adult literacy rates for the rural is lower (61%) than that in urban areas (79%). Variations in rural incomes are much greater, and much more concentrated (the Gini coefficient is 0.60) than in urban areas (with a Gini coefficient of 0.48).

Poverty in Tanzania is overwhelmingly pervasive in rural areas. Over 59% of rural inhabitants are in households where the adjusted household income is below the poverty line. Over 59% of the farmers are poor and about 85% of all poor people live in rural villages. Within the rural areas, poverty is severe in regions with unreliable rainfall, poor infrastructural development and poor access to markets. Such regions include Dodoma, Lindi, Kigoma, Singida, Rukwa and Ruvuma.

Comprehensive time series data on changes in the extent of poverty in both rural and urban Tanzania are lacking. Even the little information that exist is contentious. Bevan et al (1990) found an increase in rural per capita real incomes between 1969 and 1976/77 and a very substantial drop between 1976/77 and 1979/80 and a very small further drop in 1982/83. Adjustment is said to have stopped the declining real incomes. But nevertheless real incomes at the end of the 1980s, were significantly below those of 1976. This assertion has been questioned by Sarris and van den Brink (1993) on the grounds that much of the economic activity of Tanzania went underground and was not captured in official statistics. What appears to be a decline in real incomes could in fact be simply a decline of official real incomes. Some part of the real official income loss was compensated for by incomes from second economy (or parallel market) activities.

Paradigm Shifts

Growth and its Trickle Down Effects

As correctly observed by Joseph Semboja in this volume, issues of income distribution and poverty recur periodically *albeit* with different levels of emphasis and intensity. This is perhaps not surprising in view of the fact that poverty is intimately linked to the welfare levels of the society and hence to the overall level of development. There is a close but complex linkage between income distribution, welfare levels, and economic growth. In particular, greater equality and less poverty tend to be associated with higher welfare levels and hence higher levels of development.

The differences in emphasis on poverty over time reflect certain developments in societies such as the progression of development thinking, paradigm shifts, changing ideologies, and the lessons from experiences gained in the course of implementing certain policies. During the 1950s and 1960s the major goal of development was to maximize economic growth. The principal assumption underlying the maximum economic growth strategy was that in the long term the benefits of economic growth would *trickle down* and reduce levels of income inequality by raising the share of labour at the expense of the share of capital. Since labour income would be more evenly distributed than property income the result would be lower levels of income inequality and poverty.

In the 1950s and 1960s many saw growth - either through industrialization or agricultural intensification - as the primary means of reducing poverty and improving the quality of life. For example, that was the case with India whose Planning Commission viewed rapid growth as the main instrument for achieving this objective. In Tanzania, too, the overall development policy immediately after independence (1961) was conceived in conventional terms. The two major policy objectives sought were to achieve rapid growth in per capita income and to attain national self-sufficiency in middle- and high-level personnel. In pursuit of these objectives rapid rates of growth in import substituting manufacturing and its increased share in GDP, and the promotion of high value cash crop agriculture were considered essential in maximizing and sustaining overall economic growth.

Redistribution with Growth and Basic Needs Strategies

By the beginning of the 1970s, it had become evident that economic growth alone was not sufficient in guaranteeing full employment and alleviating poverty at an acceptable speed. Actual experiences had shown that poverty persisted even for rapidly growing countries. At the empirical level most of the results on trickle down effects were ambiguous. It was pointed out that there were structural rigidities especially within developing economies which produced results that contradicted conventional predictions. Thus, there were urgent calls for the need to address explicitly the poverty reduction objective.

As a consequence, there was a shift in world opinion away from emphasizing economic growth to first, *redistribution with growth* and then to provision of public welfare services to ensure satisfaction of *basic human needs*. The ILO (1972) Was in particular instrumental in popularizing new approaches to the poverty problem. Attention was given to four major complementary strategies: increasing employment, meeting basic needs, reducing inequalities in income and wealth and raising the productivity of the poor.

In keeping with the new emphasis, the World Bank's World Development Report of 1980 devoted a lot of its coverage to the four above-mentioned strategies to overcome poverty. It also stressed that increasing incomes and reducing poverty would also require investment in human resources. Human development was broadly conceived to encompass education, training, better health and nutrition and fertility reduction (World Bank, 1980).

Crisis and Reform: Structural Adjustment Programmes

The late 1970s were characterized by a global recession. High interest rates, declining commodity prices and internal and external imbalances in the developed countries had created adverse conditions for the developing economies by the beginning of the 1980s. At the same time the developing world was experiencing endemic economic disruptions arising from economic distortions and inefficiencies that had crippled their production, distribution and financial systems. For most of the developing world, the 1980s were a *lost decade*. These problems not only rendered many of the developing economies dysfunctional but created space and opportunity for the emergence of yet another new global development paradigm.

As a consequence of these developments a new turn in economic thinking and policy making took place beginning in the late 1970s. When the world recession began to unfold in the mid-1970s a number of analysts and decision makers spearheaded by the International Monetary Fund (IMF) and a re-aligned World Bank, attributed the recession to the predominance of state intervention in the economies and welfare oriented (basic needs) programmes to the neglect of pure economic concerns. The perception that the government was the driving force of economic growth was giving way to new thinking that advocated an increased role for market forces in the allocation of resources and a much enlarged role for the private sector in production processes and the management of the economy. By the end of the decade, the startling collapse of the Soviet Union and its evident incapacity to reform itself provided *prima facie* evidence of the unworkability and unrealism of the state controlled development model.

In the developed countries, inspired by long periods of conservative governments in the USA, Germany and Britain, Keynesian ideas gave way to neo-liberalism (or the new right) as reflected in the revision of economic policies with more emphasis on supply-side economics (e.g., *Reaganomics* and *Thatcherism*). Consequently, the new model of development which emerged and became popularly known as structural adjustment stressed the efficiency of free market allocation of resources and emphasised deregulation and export orientation so as to achieve international competitiveness based on comparative advantage. The model thus supported the notion of *globalism* or *one world* in which a single market for goods, capital, services, skills and technology prevails. The new focus was on *structural adjustment* as a precondition for growth and, implicitly, poverty reduction.

The Newly Industrialising Countries (NICs) provided the role models. Their *success* was perceived to lie in developing strong manufacturing sectors based on exports. This led to the belief that other developing countries can achieve similar successes provided they were able to *stabilize* and *restructure* their economies. The menu of policies advocated under the SAP model included those that seek to *restrain demand* in the economy by reducing expenditure on imports and releasing resources for exports (e.g., cuts in government spending, reduction in budget deficits, credit squeeze, control over money supply, reducing subsidies, and cuts in real wages). Also included in the menu was *supply switching* measures aimed at providing incentives for shifting resources from non-tradables to tradables (e.g., changes in domestic prices, exchange rate policy and wage controls). Finally, there were also *long-term supply policies* such as trade liberalization, liberalization of interest rates, and financial and credit reforms aimed at raising the long-term efficiency of the economy. By the end of the 1980s, almost all SSA had adopted SAP policy reforms under the aegis of the IMF or the World Bank with many countries having a succession of these reforms (Stewart *et al*, 1992).

Such a global movement, having gained such momentum, may well determine the climate of world opinion for a generation - it may well be that in Tanzania, development policy thinking will take place in the context of staunch support for market forces. For, even the Asian socialist states, which remain resistant to political change, have in fact already carried through more far-reaching economic reforms than have yet been attempted in the erstwhile Soviet Union (Bagachwa and Mbelle, 1993).

The adoption of the Economic Recovery Programme (ERP) in Tanzania in 1986 reflected, to a large extent, this shift in world opinion. Until the mid-1980s, development policies and the system of production and export regime in Tanzania (i.e., overvalued exchange rate, import controls, administrative allocation of foreign exchange and high protective tariffs), tended to discriminate against private sector development, and exports and benefitted chiefly public sector agencies and import substituting firms. A notable feature of the ERP has been the policy emphasis on restructuring the supply side of the economy from an inward-oriented import substitution strategy towards an outward-oriented export-led growth strategy. The new policy advocates the enhanced role of the private sector and the shifting of resources from non-tradables to tradables by changing the structure of incentives, i.e., through an exchange rate adjustment, changes in domestic prices, and relaxation of wage control policies.

According to the proponents of the new paradigm, the emphasis on market forces and outward orientation is known to have a number of theoretical advantages, some of which are alleged to have been demonstrated empirically. Some analysts contend that such policies allow the realization of scale economies; permit exploitation of comparative advantage; foster greater capacity utilization; facilitate employment creation via market expansion; and are a major source of enhanced industrial skills, productivity increase and technological improvement (Bhagwati, 1987; World Bank, 1991). Various studies by the World Bank, relying mainly on conventional measures of growth and efficiency have tended to confirm that countries that have implemented SAPs intensively have had higher economic rates of growth, lower average fiscal deficits as proportions of GDP; and higher manufactured export performance than those that have avoided reform or exited from adjustment programmes (World Bank, 1990b; 1991a; 1992; 1994; Hussain and Faruqee, 1994).

At the theoretical and empirical levels SAPs have been criticized for:

(i)   failing to recognize the untenability of the static equilibrium and the pervasive market failures arising from dynamic and unpredictable externalities;

(ii) lacking strong empirical evidence to justify the link between export performance and productivity increase; and

(iii) failing to recognize other key factors that influence efficiency and productivity especially the role of capabilities in terms of skills and technological endowment (Helleiner, 1992; Lall, 1992).

In practice, critics cite numerous examples of countries who have adjusted intensively for a number of years and yet remain marginal to the world economy and heavily indebted with little prospects for renewed economic vitality (Reed, 1992). Others have questioned the premise that trade liberalization is a necessary component of successful outward oriented strategies. Sachs (1989) has argued that the success of the East Asian countries was mainly due to an active role of a government in promoting exports in an environment where imports have not been fully liberalized. Lance Taylor (1991:119) has argued that there are "no great benefits (plus some loss) in following open trade and capital market strategies". Sebastian Edwards (1993) has strongly questioned the theoretical frameworks used in some of the literature pointing out their simplicity and failure "to address important questions such as the exact mechanism through which exports expansion affects GDP growth, and ignoring important potential determinants of growth such as educational attainment" (p. 1389).

Furthermore, critics point out that the impact of SAPs on growth has been rather weak, creating, in most cases, negative investment effects (Mosley *et al*, 1991). Others, like the ECA accuse the World Bank of selectivity and inconsistency, and hence arriving at misleading conclusions (UNECA 1989). According to the ECA, a major weakness of SAPs is that it uses short-term approaches to solve long-term problems. Such short-term stabilization tends to divert attention from action to attain sustainable longer-term economic growth and development goals (Stewart *et al*, 1992). In some cases it is even contended that the undifferentiated sudden trade liberalization (e.g., reduction in import tariffs) has failed to stimulate efficiency giving rise to a process of deindustrialization in many countries (Lall, 1992, Stewart *et al*, 1992). The World Wide Fund for Nature (WWF-International) has demonstrated through various empirical case studies in Côte d'Ivoire, Mexico and Thailand, that the failure of most governments to incorporate environmental aspects in SAPs has led to serious environmental problems (Reed, 1992).

In some cases reform efforts have failed because of vested interests of certain groups. For example the tradable goods sector opposes devaluation; firms producing import substitutes balk at trade liberalization and farmers object to cutting agricultural subsidies (Haggard and Webb, 1993).

Perhaps one of the major criticism levelled against SAPs is the failure to consider the adjustment's social dimensions; especially the failure to address the issue of poverty alleviation. According to a UNICEF study the burden of economic contraction associated with the failure of adjustment lending to incorporate social objectives fell heavily on vulnerable groups, particularly children and women (Cornia *et al*, 1987).

In Tanzania, the impact of SAPs on the poor remains ambiguous. A recent study reached two tentative conclusions. Economic liberalization by improving the availability of incentive and consumer goods, appears to have brought some benefits for at least certain of the more vulnerable categories of village people e.g., the poor and women. On the other hand, it has failed to lead to economic recovery in areas characterized by production for export (Booth, *et al*, 1993). This supports the view of the World Bank (see Mans, 1994) and corroborates evidence by Sarris and vanden Brink (1993). However, Patricia Mbughuni, in this volume, disagrees with the view.

The New Poverty Agenda

The growing criticism mounted by UNICEF, other NGOs and the UNDP (1990) against the World Bank's sponsored SAPs for failing to address explicitly the issue of poverty alleviation, have been instrumental in facilitating the reemergence of poverty reduction as the primary objective of world development. Poverty alleviation is now back on the international development agenda and may in fact become the forthcoming dominant development paradigm (Lipton and Maxwell, 1992).

Responding to these concerns of the development community, the World Bank has began to reorient its rhetoric towards poverty alleviation. accepting the need for social mitigation programs such as donor-financed Social-Action Programs and Social Dimensions of Adjustment initiatives, to protect the vulnerable groups. The World Bank's World Development Reports for 1990 and 1993 focused on poverty-related issues. The 1990 Report focused on poverty. The 1993 report focused on ways to invest in, and improve health care. According to World Bank President, Lewis T. Preston, ..."sustainable poverty reduction is the World Bank's fundamental objective. It is the benchmark by which our [the Bank's] performance as a development institution should be judged" (World Bank, 1993b: iii). While to some extent the Bank's new interest in poverty is a result of the criticisms levelled against it concerning the skewed distributional impact of SAPs (Gibbon, 1992), the Bank's World Development Report of 1990 helped to bring back the words poverty and poverty reduction onto the donors' development agenda (Ravnborg and Sano, 1994).

The World Development Report of 1990 outlined a three-pronged strategy for reducing poverty. The strategies are

(i)   promoting efficient and less distorted economic opportunities for the poor by making use of the poor man's most abundant asset - labour;

(ii) investing in human capital by providing equitable access to education, health care and other social services and

(iii) provision of well targeted transfers and social safety nets for the most vulnerable groups (World Bank 1990a).

There are two major implications of these strategies. Firstly, given that the majority of the poor live in rural areas and the main productive asset of the poor is their labour, then promotion of economic opportunities translates to raising agricultural productivity and the returns from farm labour. Thus policies that subsidize capital either directly (e.g., budgetary transfers) or indirectly (e.g., currency over-valuation) should be avoided. Policies that focus on labour intensive growth will tend to favour small farmers and micro-entrepreneurs and such policies are consistent with labour surplus economies typical of sub-Saharan Africa. Secondly, in order to prevent living standards of micro-entrepreneurs from falling as they continue to absorb much labour, their labour productivity has to be increased through human and capital investment.

Although the Bank's tripartite poverty strategy has been widely appreciated as providing a useful *new poverty agenda* within a new framework (Lipton and Maxwell, 1992), there are still some issues that are controversial. Two of the major ones are conceptual and one is empirical. Firstly, the impact of liberalizing the market on the poor remains contentious. Secondly, the Bank's call for integrating developing countries into world markets and the perceived benefits on the poor continue to be questioned on grounds of instability of commodity prices, the weak market-power of poorer countries and the hardships of economic recovery imposed by high debt-burdens (Stewart *et al*, 1992; Addison, 1994).

Another issue which raises concern is that the empirical basis of Bank's new agenda was based on the analysis of the experience of ten countries all of which are from being outside sub-Saharan Africa[6]. Could inferences drawn from such analysis be relevant to sub-Saharan Africa? Certainly this is an area that needs further research.

Changing Perceptions of Poverty

Despite the many conceptualizations of poverty (see Mbughuni, Omari and Semboja in this volume), there has been a tendency, especially when it comes to more practical analyses, and particularly where data is limited, to reduce the concept of poverty to a single dimensional issue i.e., as a state of either lack of income or of consumption. Chambers has criticized this conventional view as failing to capture the poor's changing and varied wants and that this perception is meant to suit the professional's whims and needs for numbers (Chambers, 1992).

The UNDP, in its first Human Development Report, criticized the perception of poverty as being lack of either income or consumption. The report cautions that "... there is no automatic link between income growth and human progress" (UNDP, 1990: 10). Subsequently, it defines development not as a *state* but as a *process* where people's choices and the level of their achieved well being are widened. There is, increasingly, a shift in people's perception of poverty away from viewing it as a one-dimensional issue towards seeing it as a multifaceted phenomenon issue. Other aspects of poverty that are increasingly gaining importance include vulnerability and powerlessness (Chambers, 1992); as well as deprivation, isolation, lack of decision making power, lack of assets and insecurity (Chambers, 1992; Jazairy *et al*, 1992).

As for future research, the new changes in perceptions of poverty have helped to generate additional instructive insights in the understanding of poverty. One such insight is the suggestion that future research on poverty should seek to explain poverty as a process and not as a state. That is, the key question should be why the poor lack income and not simply establishing that the poor lack income. Another insight is that the poor people's reality counts in poverty alleviation (Chambers, 1994). Consequently researchers, government officials and development specialists should learn to listen to the poor people's own perceptions about poverty (Booth *et al*, 1993; Chambers 1992, 1994; Ravnborg, 1992). In terms of research methodology the latter implication is consistent with Mbughuni's suggestion (in this volume) that researchers may have to go beyond the conventional macro-level and household budget surveys and include the testing and dissemination of participatory approaches to research and design for poverty studies.

THE EMERGING RESEARCH ISSUES

The Macropolicy-Poverty Linkage

During the early phases of the adjustment era the focus on adjustment highlighted the importance of macroeconomic policies for growth. In the later phases, it has become obvious especially from the mounting criticism of the SAPs and from increasing awareness by the Bank itself that macroeconomic policies also matter for poverty and poverty reduction. In spite of this realization, and despite a decade and half of adjustment experience, the linkage between adjustment policies and poverty remains, empirically, a source of impassioned debate. Against this background the World Development Report of 1990 pursued further the connection between policies and poverty. Using cross-country analysis based on ten countries, it concluded that countries who had been most successful in combatting poverty had adopted a three-pronged strategy: combining policies that promote efficient labour intensive growth, investment in human capital and provision of safety nets.

The macropolicy and poverty linkage is undoubtedly becoming a major item on the global research agenda. While the World Bank is busy assimilating the vulnerable groups analysis in order to deflect criticism of its own lending record (Cooksey, in this volume), the United Nations intends to convene a summit of heads of government in March, 1995 in Copenhagen to discuss ways of alleviating poverty and expanding opportunities for productive employment. At the same time, the UNICEF (1994) report on the state of the world's children continues to draw the world's attention to poverty reduction which it says has continued to affect adversely the development of children.

Concurrently in Tanzania, the macropolicy and poverty linkage was assuming increasing importance. It was being realized that the implementation of the ERP I (1986-89) did not improve the majority's access to basic social services which remained inadequate both in quantity and quality. This was largely because the share of government spending on them was too low. Subsequently, therefore, the Government saw the need to integrate social and poverty considerations in the design of macroeconomic policies and public investment projects. Considerations of this kind were elaborated on the Priority Social Action Programme adopted in 1989 and which became integrated in the second phase of ERP i.e., the Economic and Social Action Programme (ESAP, 1989/90-1991/92). ESAP gave priority to the mitigation of the adverse social impact of adjustment and the rehabilitation of the physical infrastructure (URT, 1990). But a number of questions remain unsettled. For example, are such programmes sustainable given the absence of appropriate institutions for supporting such social funds? Have poor people participated in or benefitted from such programmes? It is hoped REPOA will attempt to throw more light on these issues.

Poverty-Environment Linkage

The environment has emerged as one of the major research issues in the 1990s. Partly, this is because previous development strategies never considered the value of the environment as an essential variable in enhancing human health, increasing productivity, and fostering development in general (World Bank, 1993). One unquestionable shortcoming of the SAPs sponsored by multilateral financial institutions and implemented by individual governments during the 1980s is the failure to address environmental deterioration; especially the potential environmental impacts of policy-based lending (Reed 1992: 3).

It is now widely accepted that the range of economic, social and institutional policies implemented in various countries under the auspices of SAPs have potential environmental impacts. Some of these effects have been negative while others have been positive (Reed, 1992; Crommwell and Winpenny, 1993). For example, in Tanzania, many resource-based commodities are internationally tradeable (e.g., tea, coffee, sisal, cotton, tobacco, minerals, fish, timber logs, etc.). Others like hydropower and coal are substitutes for tradeable commodities. Since the exchange rate is the price linking domestic tradeable goods with foreign goods, devaluation would tend to encourage exports and discourage imports. To the extent that exported commodities use natural resources as inputs, a reduction in the overvalued exchange rate might increase the extraction of primary resources by increasing their price relative to non-tradeable goods, by making exports more attractive than imports, and by encouraging the return of redundant urban workers to land.

Likewise, SAP policies might affect the environment through its influence on farming practices. It could tilt the balance between extensive and intensive modes in favour of the former, by making fertiliser and capital-intensive inputs more expensive. The same effect could be produced by the return of redundant urban workers to the land. It might alter the relative profitability of different crops and this could have an impact on *soil erosive*. There may be incentives for the cultivation of virgin or marginal land. The balance of advantage between large mechanised and smallholder farms might also be affected. The net environmental effects of these factors should be considered. Another possibility is that SAPs might affect the environment through altering patterns of energy use e.g., by making imported commercial fuels more expensive; or, by reducing subsidies on the domestic price of energy, it could encourage the use of wood fuel.

The impact of SAP policies on the environment however, is not easy to predict. It is possible for a given economic reform measure to have variable impact on the environment in two or more different socio-economic settings. This is because of the existence of a complex and differentiated set of structural parameters that may suppress or dilate the impact of a particular economic reform measure. These features are well documented in the literature and include: local physical and geographical circumstances; traditional prevailing practices of cultivation and production; population pressure; poverty; social and gender relations; employment and migration; land tenure, asset distribution and local incentive structure; and the powers and competence of government (Cromwell and Winpenny, 1993).

Partly, however, the recent interest in the environment derives from the often close link between poverty the and environment. The Brundtland Commission stated clearly that:

Poverty is a major cause and effect of global environmental problems. It is therefore futile to attempt to deal with environmental problems without a broader perspective that encompasses international inequality. (WCED, 1987: 3).

Sridath Ramphal and UNICEF (1994) have echoed the same views. Ramphal believes that

Poor people often destroy their own environment - not because they are ignorant, but to survive. They over-exploit thin soils, over graze fragile grasslands and cut down dwindling forest stocks for fire wood. In the context of short term needs of survival each decision is rational; in the longer term and wider context, the effects are disastrous... Poverty is both a cause and an effect of environmental degradation" (Ramphal, 1990: 39).

There is some indicative evidence on the connection between poor countries and resource poor and fragile environments. Countries like Tanzania tend to depend heavily on natural resources for employment and economic growth. In Tanzania, for example, agriculture employed 84% of the total labour force in 1991 and contributed about 62% of GDP in 1992. Agricultural commodities accounted for 55% of Tanzania's foreign exchange earnings in 1992.

Prices for primary commodities have generally been declining and foreign debt has been growing to unsustainable levels in most poor countries. At the same time, most poor countries have been subjected to SAPs in order to raise exports. The combined effects of these developments have placed a heavy strain on the natural resource base of poor countries. Furthermore, within countries the poor typically reside in environmentally sensitive areas e.g., in overcrowded shanty towns near garbage dumps or industrial zones (SIDA, 1991). Their health is constantly being threatened.

However, the causal effects between poverty and the environment appear to be complex and not straightforward. According to the World Bank the "links between environment degradation and poverty are yet poorly understood" and that improved understanding of the links "... remains a priority" (World Bank 1990b: 45, 85). Furthermore, it is not always true, for example, that all the poor resolve their difficulties in meeting today's needs through short term exploitation of the environment. Neither is it always true that they lack knowledge about environmental issues; nor is it always the case that they do not know the longterm consequences of today's actions (Chambers, 1994). These are some of the issues that future research might wish to address particularly when it is borne in mind that some of the most serious environmental problems today originate in rich countries.

Reflecting the growing interest on poverty, environment and development, a United Nations Conference on Environment was held in Rio-de Janeiro in

1992 to deliberate on these issues. The theme was on Development and the Environment. The main message of the subsequent report was "the need to integrate environmental considerations into development policy making" (World Bank, 1993: iii). In 1992, the Tanzanian Government modified the National Conservation Strategy (NCS) initially formulated in 1980, to encompass the goals and priorities set up by the *Earth Summit* in Rio, in 1992 besides the goals of conservation and rational utilization of the environment. Plans are also currently underway to finalize (during the fiscal year 1994/5) the National Land policy which will emphasize land tenure reform, land use planning, common property, land markets and transfer including customary rights, and statutory rights over land particularly of women. There may be a strong case to be made for the creation of new institutions and the strengthening of existing ones if some of these reforms are to be effectively implemented. But even if they are to be efficiently implemented, will they benefit the poor?

Role of Technology in Poverty Alleviation

The role of technology in poverty alleviation has been a subject of intense debate. At the conceptual level some skeptics point to the difficulties associated with the transfer of technological solutions developed in one socioeconomic context (usually in a developed country) to another (i.e., a developing country). According to this view technological determinism is bound to prevail in developing countries.

The pessimists draw much of their support from the observation that almost all major technological innovations take place in developed, high-wage and high-income countries. In such countries the direction of technological change is towards labour-saving innovations. The technology transfer process in the developing countries is bound to exhibit this labour-saving bias. As a result developing countries do not have technological alternatives other than those with high capital-labour ratios found in developed countries. If adopted in a poor country such capital intensive technologies would tend to aggravate unemployment, thereby exacerbating poverty.

The optimists argue that there is considerable scope for selecting technologies that are consistent with different socio-economic settings. The new technologies, in particular, have increased the range of technological options available for production (Stewart 1987; Tiffin *et al*, 1992). Some analysts have tended to link technological advancement with increased productivity and the raising of living standards. It is sometimes argued that recent advances in agricultural biotechnology could potentially play a crucial role in assisting poverty alleviation and reducing poor farmers' costs by eliminating dependence on petro-chemical inputs through the development of pest-resistant plant varieties or by increasing use of biological control systems (IDRC, 1992; ILO, 1992). Others, however, have challenged this view by pointing out the vast disparities in income and wealth within developed countries and between rich and poor countries. Additionally IDRC has pointed out the disastrous environmental impacts of past industrial development in the industrialized and technologically advanced countries, claiming that such a development pattern is unsustainable (IDRC, 1992).

In spite of these controversies, it is now widely recognized that any strategy to promote more sustainable patterns of development must draw upon technology. The view taken by Chungu and Mandara in this volume, is that technology, broadly defined as a mix of knowledge, organizations, procedures, machinery, equipment and human skills to produce socially desirable appropriate products, could be a major factor in combatting economic backwardness or poverty. Thus new technologies and potential future technologies hold out the prospects for providing a wide range of solutions to the problem faced by the poor communities of Tanzania. Such appropriate technologies ought to, be researched into, identified and popularized. The REPOA programme could assist Tanzanian policy makers in studying and forecasting the implications of the existing, new, and emerging technology for the poor.

Beyond Macroeconomics: Role of Gender and Other Socio-Cultural Factors in Poverty Alleviation

As suggested earlier, even the World Bank is increasingly becoming aware that while stabilization policies are essential for achieving internal and external balances which are prerequisites for sustainable long term growth and poverty reduction, causes and solutions to poverty go beyond macroeconomics and efficiency pricing. Other socio-cultural factors matter.

Within the poor the burden of adjustment has been uneven. Those who have suffered most have been women and children. The major explanation for this lies in the degree of relative accessibility to, and control over assets, social services, and other economic resources by different social groups; and the traditional or patriarchal division of labour, power and responsibility by gender. It has been reported that while women in sub-Saharan Africa generally work 11-14 hours daily, men work for 8-10 hours daily. And yet, in spite of the fact that women are involved in everyday household maintenance, non-farm income generating activities as well working in agriculture, it is men who generally have greater access to the cash economy and public life (Cecelski, 1987). Form level survey data in Tanzania indicates that women were putting in a significantly longer workday: about 10.4 hours compared to 7.8 hours for men (World Bank, 1991b).

Women in general are disadvantaged. They not only bear more of the workload than men but are generally less educated and are under represented in the labour market. Today, one out of three households in the world has a woman as a sole bread winner; and yet two-thirds of the illiterate population are women (UNIFEM, 1989). According to the 1988 Census, women in Tanzania constituted 51% of the total (23.2 million) population but accounted for only 32% of the total employees in Government.

Issues of gender are consequently relevant in explaining the incidence and breadth of poverty. In terms of analysis this suggests that we have to look beyond macro-level measures of poverty such as GNP and household level surveys of income and access to resources because these do not always make the particular situation of women's poverty visible. As Patricia Mbughuni puts it in this volume, intra-household dynamics are such that poor women are *more impoverished* than poor men.

Moreover, any meaningful analytical framework for analysing poverty must incorporate the behavioural context in which poverty persists in a particular society. More specifically it is essential to understand the causes, motivations and constraints of poor men and women. Not all of the motivations and constraints are economic in nature; others are culturally or socially determined. For example, why are certain ethnic communities in Tanzania more enterprising than others? What are the effects of witchcraft, traditional patterns of conspicuous consumption, etc. on development? How can we explain the *laissez faire* (*Uswahili?*) type of approach to life among certain communities in Tanzania? Such and other related questions need carefully designed research methodologies if they are to generate meaningful answers.

THE FUTURE CHALLENGE: THE RESEARCH AGENDA

Since poverty remains a problem of staggering dimensions as we prepare to enter the 21st Century, it is crucial to understand its incidence, breadth and causes in order to devise sound and effective policies for its sustainable reduction. This suggests the need for poverty assessment which in its simplest form addresses three principal questions:

First and foremost is the question of *who is poor*? Answering this question boils down to defining the poor, and identifying their characteristics in terms of spatial concentration, socio-economic, cultural, demographic and gender characteristics, living standards and accessibility to assets.

Once the poor (and, implicitly, the non-poor) are known then a logical extension of the analysis would be to turn to the question *why are they poor*?

Having characterized and identified the poor and the reasons for being poor, then the next step should be to understand *what are the policies or strategies* that can facilitate sustainable poverty reduction?

Chapters Two through Eight attempt to elaborate more on these research questions in the context of Tanzania. The main thrust in these chapters is to review the existing studies on poverty in Tanzania with a view to identifying research gaps and issues that need further investigation.

In *Chapter Two*, Joseph Semboja presents an ambitious survey of economists' approaches to the concept of poverty and its measurement. The chapter also discusses the merits and demerits of various indicators of poverty; the criteria for selecting particular poverty indicators; identification of units of analyses and the determinants of poverty. The characteristics of the poor are neatly summarized using Fields's (1980) poverty profile. Finally the chapter ends up with a suggestion that proper assessment of the impact of policy reform measures on poverty, ought to take into consideration an appropriate counterfactual situation.

Workshop participants emphasized the need to distinguish absolute poverty from relative poverty. Absolute poverty is the inability to attain a specified (minimum) standard of living. It reflects the absolute economic well-being of the relevant part of a given society (i.e., the poor) in isolation from the welfare distribution of the entire society. Relative poverty reflects the relative living standards of the poor in relation to the entire society.

But as the discussion that ensued suggested, it would be difficult to have a single widely acceptable definition of poverty when it comes to practical research. In view of the emerging perception of poverty as a multi-faceted issue, the concept of poverty is likely to remain fluid. Some of the differences in interpretation could be minimized, however, by undertaking research on a multi-disciplinary basis. Such integrated or team research efforts could also facilitate the generation of data on a wider scale from a diverse set of circumstances using both qualitative and quantitative analytical techniques. To be meaningful and relevant, moreover, such analyses should not only take into consideration the processes which determine policy priorities (e.g., changing priority given to the poverty agenda by government, donor community, NGOs and other sponsoring agencies) but also the changing needs of the poor.

In terms of the analytical framework, a possible starting point in poverty assessment would be to delineate a poverty line (i.e., the level of income associated with a minimum acceptable level of nutrition and other necessities of life). A count of people whose income fall below this line would constitute the poor. It should then be possible, depending on data availability, to categorize the poor by their spatial, nutritional, ownership of assets, socio-economic, cultural demographic and other desirable characteristics using relevant socio-economic or nutritional indicators.

In Chapter Three, Brian Cooksey, drawing mainly on patchy and fragmentary pieces of information available on Tanzania, carefully constructs an absolute poverty line which defines the income required to meet a minimum calorific consumption level. Although he finds little empirical information about the nature, causes, incidence and trajectory of poverty in Tanzania, it has been possible to draw useful indicative insights on the poor in Tanzania from the limited evidence available.

One such insight is the revelation that the majority of Tanzanians are very poor. According to some estimates, about 60% of the rural population and 10% of the urban population lived in absolute poverty in 1988. Typically, income or expenditure comparisons between rural and urban areas show a greater incidence and depth of poverty in rural than in urban areas, with Dar es Salaam showing the least.

Apart from a general agreement on the broad spatial rural-urban patterns, evidence on the intensity of poverty for those below the poverty line is partial and ambiguous. Cooksey concludes his survey in a rather pessimistic mood. He notes that our knowledge of poverty in Tanzania is very limited in all important respects. The limited information that exists suffer from serious methodological and quality problems. Furthermore, most of the studies covered by his survey come to diametrically opposed conclusions on major issues such the depth and spatial distribution of poverty, its inter- or intra community nature and the impact of economic crisis and adjustment policies on various income and occupational groups.

But a more optimistic interpretation of Cooksey's conclusion is that the huge gaps in existing knowledge justifies the urgent need for undertaking more systematic and scientific research on the nature, spatial distribution, causes of, the direction and rate of change in poverty in Tanzania. Other potential research areas identified by the author include: trends in informalisation; emergence of non-statist political activism; social dimensions of natural disasters; nature of donor support programmes; impact of macropolicies on population growth; the social and environmental consequences of competition over land for different uses and the impact of organic and chemical fertilizers on agricultural farming systems, soil fertility and the environment in general.

A question was raised and would probably continue to be raised as to whether the delineation of a poverty line would be an appropriate approach. Some workshop participants noted that one criteria in research design should be whether the method empowers the poor or not. Perhaps the potential feasibility of participatory research strategies (as suggested by Mbughuni in this volume) should be explored. Others suggested that it would be instructive to bear in mind the political dimension of poverty especially the access to power and to stress the role of other factors that may influence poverty such as factors influencing food availability, land productivity and the role of educational policies.

In response to the call made by Cooksey on the need for further research on poverty, in *Chapter Four* of this volume, Fidelis Mtatifikolo lays the basis for future research on the macropolicy-poverty linkage in Tanzania. The chapter brings to light some of the salient implications of public policies on poverty and poverty alleviation in Tanzania. It is clear from the discussion that in principle poverty was one of the three *enemies* besides ignorance and disease which the Tanzanian government vowed to get rid of immediately after independence.

But was this vow accompanied by appropriate policies and programmes seeking to alleviate poverty? The good news is that, in principle, some attempts were made and various reports, commissions and strategies on how to alleviate poverty were prepared and/or formed. The bad news is that most policies were ill-conceived and were not properly coordinated and implemented. Many policies considered pro-poor were not so in practice. Price controls, for example, created artificial scarcities resulting in high parallel market prices. Both could not benefit the poor. Wage controls amidst high inflationary conditions reduced the incentive to work resulting in lower productivity levels. Poverty alleviation through perfect targeting of public spending programmes to those below the poverty line is bound to be administratively costly and could be associated with corruption. It also presupposes *surplus* funds which do not exist in poor countries like Tanzania. Projects targeting the poor have tended to exclude participation by the poor and could not be sustained after donors have pulled out (Omari, in this volume). Social action programmes to mitigate poverty by using aid to ease the hardships of adjustment programmes or by encouraging the poor to participate in the project cycle have featured high in recent ERP policy documents. However, effective implementation has not been possible mainly due to lack of appropriate institutions, adequate funds and/or operational strategies (Mascarenhas, in this volume).

Is there a way out for the poor in Tanzania? Certainly appropriate policies have to be researched into and worked out. Perhaps, it is suggested, such research could start with the preparation of an inventory of the various studies and programmes on poverty. Other researchable issues would include: the possible impact of recent policies which seek to mitigate the negative social effects of adjustment to specific groups and those seeking to increase greater participation in project and decision making by the poor; the role of pressure groups in poverty alleviation; and the efficacy of new market-based policy reforms in alleviating poverty.

In addition, some workshop participants suggested that we should learn from past experience. The importance of understanding past policies was emphasized, including a proper understanding of the causes of past failures. It would also be necessary to explore the reasons for the absence and the timing of the appearance of various policies (e.g., land policy). Furthermore, it was suggested that research on policies should consider the importance of a number of aspects of government performance including government capacity/ weaknesses and the roles, of NGO's, parliament (*Bunge*), and local government in implementing poverty focused programmes. Others emphasized the need to study the inter-relationship between democracy, human rights and poverty; and that the poor should be defined broadly to include the disabled. Overall the efficacy of the *trickle down* effect was strongly questioned; and a call was made to explore the effectiveness of *trickle up* effect measures in alleviating poverty.

In *Chapter Five*, Adolpho Mascarenhas argues that one logical starting point for the research on poverty in Tanzania is the recognition of the linkage between poverty, environment and development. There is some connection between poverty and resource poor and fragile environments. Efforts by Tanzanians and the world community at large to tackle current environmental threats must therefore face the stark realities of poverty and the skewed distribution of resources and opportunities within and among districts and regions. However, while this linkage is well established it is not yet clear as to whether it is poverty that is the major cause and effect of global environmental problems or the *vice versa*.

While different perceptions of the poverty-environment linkage are likely to assume importance in academic debates, when it comes to research, it is worth paying more attention to more practical issues such as the parameters that have a strong bearing on the environment. Some of these parameters include population growth and mobility and the relationship between poverty and resource poor environments, etc. One important research area mentioned by Mascarenhas is conflict resolution, especially as it relates to the rights of the pastoralists and the impoverishment of the peasants. Other areas for future research include the dynamics of integrating traditional and modern agro-ecological practices; institutional aspects of poverty and the environment especially the role of the relevant ministries and institutions related to environment; the role of local governments and NGOs; the impact of biotechnology on the environment and agricultural output; and the environmental impacts of liberalization and privatization.

In addition, some workshop participants pointed to the need for a study on environmentally friendly technologies. Others suggested that it would be instructive to carry out a long-term historical study of the impact of public policy on the environment, including coverage of the colonial policy.

One possible cause of poverty in Tanzania could be the rudimentary level of technological development. In *Chapter Six* of this volume, two development engineers Chungu and Mandara, develop this hypothesis further and suggest what they consider to be a future research agenda in this area. Their main contention is that technological development is not only a major determinant of the level and pattern of national economic development but also a major determinant of international competitiveness. As such, it is erroneous for planners to continue treating it as an exogenous variable or, simply, a *black box*.

To this end, the authors recommend that if Tanzania is to manage a technological revolution it should not follow the conventional evolutionary path followed by the industrially advanced countries, but a strategy of *leapfrogging* in strategically selected sectors and industries. Such a strategy presupposes, however, a number of prerequisites including articulation of a *vision*; formulation of a long term perspective plan; and acceptance of technology as an important strategic variable in the development process.

The author's menu of the relevant research agenda includes ways of cultivating a science and technology-oriented culture; identification of industries in which Tanzania has a competitive advantage; search for a relevant techno-economic development policy and building of institutions that would constitute an enabling technological environment; as well as a study of the whole question of indigenous intellectual property rights in Tanzania.

During the discussion that ensued, the need and value of understanding the South-East Asian experience was emphasized. It would be useful for example, to understand how societies which, starting from Tanzania's current level of development thirty years ago achieved a technological revolution. The need for studying the national science and technology climate was emphasized. The importance of the need to study cultural attitudes to technical change and ways that had been used to overcome resistance to change elsewhere in the world was noted. Why has there been resistance to innovation in Tanzania?

Some participants in the workshop pointed out the need to have a clearer view of grass-roots implications and to understand indigenous technology, particularly local knowledge and adaptations of technology in grass-root problem solving. Local people tend to understand better local conditions. Other participants aired a number of specific concerns including technology for sustainable energy use, the implications of modern bio-technology, and modern information technologies. It was particularly felt that the implications of trade and foreign investment liberalization for the development of national technological capacity should be studied.

In *Chapter Seven* Patricia Mbughuni extends the analysis of poverty beyond macroeconomic variables by introducing gender issues. After surveying the existing literature on gender issues in Tanzania, the author identifies and discusses at length a number of areas of research critical to facilitating a strategy for poverty alleviation which will also benefit women. A prerequisite to such research would be a gender conceptualization and analysis which creates space to explore the interrelationship of productive and reproductive roles and allegiances of women, their range of resources, and their strategies.

Analytically and in terms of research methodology her main contribution is in highlighting the importance of using gender-sensitive concepts, and urging the need to go beyond macro-level and household-level surveys, and complement, and where possible, to substitute participatory research within the empowerment framework for conventional research methodologies. The list of areas for research which she proposes is long. But the major focus is on differentiation among women, especially the intersection of gender and class with special attention to poor women; changing patriarchal ideologies, forms of control; and forms of cultural expression as well as women's resistance.

Additionally other workshop participants suggested that emphasis ought to be placed on the importance of studies which take account of the historical perspective emphasizing the process of change, in a multi-disciplinary framework, and which address issues of power as well as income. Changing attitudes towards the status of women, in a long-term perspective, merited a study too. Other issues raised by the participants included the importance of laws related to property rights, the effects of rural/urban migration on rural women, the changing position of old women and the impact of liberalization on the work-load of rural women. The impact of AIDS and of structural adjustment on commercial sex was proposed as a possible future research area.

It was further pointed out that gender studies were about the relationship between men and women, and therefore included the study of men. In addition it was also considered necessary to study the relationship between rich and successful women and the poor, and the relationship between urban and rural women. The importance of the socialization process and the educational system in determining attitudes was emphasized. The need to study performance in schools and gender stereotyping in schools was also suggested.

And finally, in *Chapter Eight* Cuthbert Omari broadens the analysis of poverty in Tanzania by introducing certain crucial socio-cultural factors. Perhaps one ought to look into the investment patterns of the poor in order to explain the prevalence of what is termed *uswahili* culture among poor Tanzanians, i.e., the tendency to be easily satisfied with very little money or assets. Other important socio-cultural factors that could explain the incidence and breadth of poverty in Tanzanian society include ethnicity, religion, family networks, social claims on wealth, gender, informality, and traditional patterns of consumption, accumulation, and beliefs.

According to Omari, future research areas should not only be confined to the testing of hypotheses and generation of new information but should also involve the testing of certain concepts. The author mentions as a potential research area, the testing of the relevance of received concepts and methodologies for the measurement and analysis of poverty to the specific Tanzanian environment. Other research areas being suggested by the author, include adult mortality, the new poor, the relationship between poverty, informal sector and the state; investment patterns among the poor; the extent to which the poor participate in targeted development projects; and the extent to which religion influences poverty.

Some participants felt the need to study the specific nature of Tanzanian poverty to be timely. There was a lively discussion on the *new poor* - was it just the retrenched, or was there a much larger group of *new poor*? Were retrenched public servants really poor, as they were well used to generating supplementary income? By concentrating on this group was there not a danger of neglecting the truly deprived? A number of manifestations of social change were addressed and the need for better understanding of the process of change emphasized (e.g. the appearance of beggars and street children changing attitudes to family size; the changing role of the extended family, etc). Furthermore, the issue of the deterioration in national culture was raised, including the decline in self-reliance (dependence on government), and decline in national commitment (increases in stealing and embezzlement).

NOTES

1. World Bank (1990a: 26)
2. These were people living on less than US $370 per capita a year (World Bank 1990a)
3. World Bank (1993a)
4. These were persons below a poverty line expenditure level of TSh. 46,173 (US $211). The expenditure level reflects what is necessary for a basic but adequate diet for an adult and includes minimum levels of expenditure.
5. These were households consuming less than 1500 Kcal per equivalent adult
6. Countries covered included Brazil, Colombia, Costa Rica, India, Indonesia, Malaysia, Morocco, Pakistan, Sri Lanka and Thailand.

REFERENCES

Addison, T. (1994). "Poverty Reduction in Development Corporation: The Story So Far" Paper presented at conference on Poverty Reduction and Development Corporation, Copenhagen, Denmark (February 23-24).

Bagachwa, M.S.D. and A.V.Y. Mbelle eds. (1993). *Economic Policy Under a Multiparty System in Tanzania*, Dar-es-Salaam: DUP.

Bhagwati, J. (1987). "Outward Orientation; Trade Issues". In V. Corbo; M. Goldstein and M. Khan (eds). *Growth-Oriented Adjustment Programs*. Washington D.C.: IMF/World Bank, pp. 257-90.

Booth, D; F. Lugangira; P. Masanja; A. Mvungi; R. Mwaipopo; J. Mwami and A. Redmayne (1993). "Social, Economic and Cultural Change in Contemporary Tanzania: A People Oriented Focus", Report to SIDA. Stockholm: Swedish International Development Authority.

Cecelski, E. (1987). "Energy and Rural Women's Work: Crisis, Response and Policy Alternatives". *International Labour Review*, Vol. 126 No. 1, (January-February).

Chambers, R. (1992). "Poverty in India: Concepts, Research and Reality", in B. Harriss, S. Guhan and R.H. Cassen (eds) *Poverty in India: Research and Policy*. Delhi, Calcutta, Madras: Oxford University Press, pp. 301-332.

___, (1994). "The Poor and the Environment: Whose Reality Counts?", Paper presented at the Conference on Poverty Reduction and Development Cooperation, Copenhagen (23-24 February).

Cornia, G.A.; R. Jolly and F. Stewart (eds) (1987). *Adjustment with a Human Face*, Vol. 1 and 2 Oxford: Oxford University Press.

Cromwell, E. and J. Winpenny (1993). "Does Economic Reform Harm Environment? A Review of Structural Adjustment in Malawi". *Journal of International Development*, Vol. 5 No. 6, pp. 623-649.

Doriye, J.; S. Odunga; and B. Van Arkadie and S.M. Wangwe (1991). "Review of Economic Analysis and Management in Tanzania", Dar es Salaam.

Edwards, S. (1993). "Openness, Trade Liberalization and Growth in Developing Countries". *Journal of Economic Literature* Vol.XXXI (Sept.), 1358-1393.

Fields, G.S. (1980). *Poverty Inequality and Development*. Cambridge: Cambridge University Press.

Gibbon, P. (1992). "The World Bank and African Poverty 1973-91". *Journal of Modern African Studies* Vol. 30 No. 1, (June), pp. 135-162.

Haggard, S. and S.B. Webb (1993). "What Do We Know About the Political Economy of Economic Policy Reform?" *The World Bank Research Observer*, Vol. 8, No. 2, (July) pp. 143-68.

Helleiner, G.K. (1992). "Structural Adjustment and Long-Term Development in Sub-Saharan Africa". In F. Stewart *et al*, eds (1992), pp. 48-78.

Hussain, I and R. Faruqee, eds. (1994). *Adjustment in Africa* Washington D.C: The World Bank.

International Development Research Centre - IDRC (1992). *Technology and the International Environmental Agenda: Lessons for UNCED and Beyond.* Ottawa: IDRC.

ILO (1972). *Employment Incomes and Equality: A Strategy for Increasing Productive Employment in Kenya.* Geneva: ILO.

___, (1992). *Strengthening Technological Capabilities: A Challenge for the Nineties.* Geneva: ILO.

Jazairy, I; M. Alamgir and T. Panuccio (1992). *The State of the World Rural Poverty: An Inquiry into Its Causes and Consequences.* London: International Fund for Agricultural Development IFAD.

Lall, S. (1992). "Structural Problems of African Industry". In F. Stewart *et al* (1992), pp. 103-144.

Lipton, M. and S. Maxwell in association with J. Edström and H. Hatashima (1992). "The New Poverty Agenda: An Overview". Discussion Paper 306, Sussex: Institute of Development Studies.

Mosley, P.; J. Harrigan and J. Tage (1991). *Aid and Power: The World Bank and Policy-Based Lending.* London: Routledge.

Ravnborg, H.M. (1992). "Sensing Sustainability Farmers as Resource Managers". CDR Working Paper 92.6. Copenhagen: Centre for Development Research.

Ravnborg, H.M. and Sano, H. (1994). "Operationalization of the Poverty Objective in Development Assistance". Paper presented at Conference on Poverty Reduction and Development Corporation, Copenhagen, Denmark (February 23-24).

Reed, D. ed. (1992). "Diverging Views on the Adjustment Decade". In D. Reed ed. (1992). *Structural Adjustment and the Environment.* London: Earthscan Publications, pp. 21-47.

Sachs, J.F. (1989). "The Debt Overhung of Developing Countries", in G.A. Caluo *et al*, (eds) *Debt Stabilization and Development: Essays in Memory of Carlos Diaz-Alejandro* Oxford: Blackwell, pp. 80-102.

Sarris, A.H. R. Paruqee, eds. (1994). *Adjustment in Africa* Washington D.C. The World Bank.

Swedish International Development Authority - SIDA, (1991). "Poverty, Environment and Development" Paper prepared for the Secretariat of the 1992 United Nations Conference on Environment and Development.

Stewart, F. (ed.) (1987). *Macro-policies for Appropriate Technology in Developing Countries.* Boulder and London: Westview Press.

Stewart, F., S. Lall and S.M. Wangwe (eds) (1992). *Alternative Development Strategies in Sub-Saharan Africa.* London: Macmillan.

Taylor, L. (1991). "Economic Openness: Problems to the Century's End", in T. Bunuri (ed.) *Economic Liberalization: No. Panacea*, Oxford and NY: Oxford University Press, Clarendon Press, pp. 99-147.

Tiffin, S.; F. Ostimehin and R. Saunders (1992). *New Technologies and Enterprise Development in Africa*, Paris: OECD.

Tinios, P; A.H. Sarris; H.K.R. Amani and W. Maro (1993). "Household Consumption and Poverty in Tanzania: Results from the 1991 National Cornell-ERB Survey". Paper prepared. Under the auspices of the CFNPP, Africa Economic Policies Project supported by USAID.

UNICEF (1994). *The Stae of the World's Children*, New York: OUP.

United Nations Development Fund for Women - UNIFEM, (1989). *Strength in Adversity: Women in the Developing World*. New York: UNIFEM.

United Nations Development Programme - UNDP (1990). *Human Development Report 1990*. New York: UNDP.

United Republic of Tanzania (1990). *Economic Recovery Programme II (Economic and Social Action Programme) 1989/90-1991/92*. Dar es Salaam Government Printer.

Van Arkadie, B. (1993). "Note on Work on Economic Research Bureau (ERB): A Discussion Document", Dar es Salaam (mimeo).

World Bank, (1980). *World Development Report 1980* Washington D.C.: The World Bank.

___, (1990a). *World Development Report 1990* Washington D.C.: The World Bank.

___, 1990b). *Adjustment Lending Practices for Sustainable Growth*. Washington D.C.: The World Bank.

___, (1990c). *The World Bank and Environment*. First Annual Report, Fiscal 1990. Washington D.C.: The World Bank.

___, (1991a). *Restructuring Economies in Distress*. Washington D.C.: The World Bank.

___, (1991b). "Tanzania: Women and Development", World Bank Report No. T. 9108 TA (June. Washington D.C.: The World Bank.

___, (1992). *World Development Report 1992*. Oxford: OUP.

___, (1992). *The Third Report on Adjustment Lending: Private and Public Resources for Growth*. Washington D.C.: The World Bank.

___, (1993a). "Tanzania - A Poverty Profile", draft of August, Population and Human Resources Division, East Africa Department, Washington D.C.

___, (1993b). *World Development Report 1993*. Oxford: OUP.

___, (1994). *Adjustment in Africa: Reforms, Results and the Roads Ahead*. Washington D.C: The World Bank.

World Commission on Environment and Development - WCED, (1987). *Our Common Future*. Oxford: Oxford University Press.

2

Poverty Assessment in Tanzania: Theoretical, Conceptual and Methodological Issues

J. SEMBOJA

INTRODUCTION

What is poverty? How is it measured? What are its causes? How can it be alleviated? These questions are common in academic and policy making circles. Various approaches to the understanding of poverty and strategies for its elimination have been adopted. Yet poverty has persisted and, in some areas, risen. This suggests that the subject is more complex than can be handled by a single discipline.

This chapter deals with poverty mainly in economic terms and theory. However, it is expected to provide an important input into the research on poverty alleviation in Tanzania undertaken from the stand point of a variety of disciplines.

Until recently poverty did not feature as a separate study in mainstream economic theory. Economists were, of course, concerned about poverty and already in the nineteenth century there were pathbreaking studies by social scientists on poverty but for economic theory it largely appeared as an addendum to analyses of income distribution. This was true both for functional and size approaches to income distribution.

The theory of poverty can be derived from ideas of the classical school, which focused on the laws that govern the distribution of factor incomes, and were later incorporated into the labour surplus model. According to this approach, development is defined in terms of the growth of the modern sector, which expands at the expense of the traditional sector. The theory predicts an increase in inequality and (especially relative) poverty in the initial stages of development and a reduction in inequality and poverty at a later stage. (Lewis, 1954 and Fei and Ranis, 1964).

As an extension of the marginalist theory of value, the neoclassical school which became dominant in the second half of the nineteenth century (and retains that dominance) postulates that in a perfect market, prices of factors and goods are simultaneously determined competitively and, depending on their scarcity and productivity, factors are paid according to the value of their marginal product. In spite of the limitations arising from the assumption of perfect competition a theory of poverty can be derived from such an approach, as household incomes will be determined by the factor incomes received by the household, that is, the earnings from household labour and property.

Alongside the mainstream neoclassical school, there were other attempts to explain income distribution in a more macroeconomic, neo-Marxian and Keynesian framework (Kalecki, 1950, Kaldor, 1955/56 and 1966). However, these were not based on the assumption of perfect competition and, they may therefore be more relevant to studies of income distribution and poverty alleviation in developing economies.

The economic theory of the *size distribution of income* is not as developed as that explaining *functional distribution,* although the latter has implication for the former. However, the link is not precise and attempts to develop alternative theories for the analysis of size distribution have not been very successful. Yet size distribution is a more direct measure of welfare and, therefore, poverty levels. Within the neo-classical tradition, the most important attempt to explain skewness has come from the "human capital" theory, which has explored the implications of the heterogeneity of labour resulting from differences in acquired skills. The human capital school has argued that, based on the calculations of the present value of the discounted future income streams of alternative occupations, individuals choose where and how much to invest in education in order to optimize earnings; individuals with longer periods in school are compensated with higher annual earnings. Lifetime inequality is therefore not as current as is suggested by inequality in annual incomes. Thus, according to the school, observed levels of inequality and poverty are justified.

The human capital school has been criticized for, among other things, focusing too much on the supply side of the labour market. Factor payments are determined by supply and demand in a compartmentalized market. (Tinbergen, 1970). Furthermore, inequality and poverty levels are also explained by differentials in access to education and training, and these can be improved by equalizing that access. But schooling is important not only as an investment in human capital but is also a screening device which identifies people with attributes that are demanded by employers so that greater educational equality may not ensure equal opportunity for employment, productivity, payment and promotions. The actual situation depends on the market structure, custom, status, on-the-job training, and many other aspects of the labour market. Under these conditions equal earnings are unlikely.

Some attempts to develop theories of poverty aimed at defining, measuring and explaining the concept in the context of developing economies were made in the early stages of the development of modern development economics. Already in the early 1960s Indian economists were working on issues of poverty. (Pant, 1962 quoted from Fields, 1980). In the newly independent developing countries poverty was increasingly recognized as a serious social problem and countries had to do something about it. At the international level, the ILO World Employment Programme, which made its impact two decades ago, redefined the employment problem as one of poverty, and much of its vast output was concerned with poverty issues; an implicit, rather eclectic, theory of poverty could be extracted from its voluminous reports. The outcome of that body of work was the development of the "basic needs" approach to development, which had become influential in the donor community by the end of the 1970's. Also in the early 1970s the World Bank pursued a "redistribution with growth" approach which stressed increases in the productivity and purchasing power of the poor.[1]

The "redistribution with growth" approach did not last long. The shift from poverty concerns to market oriented policies of the structural adjustment was motivated by falling economic growth rates in many countries after mid-1970s. Declining output was considered to be the main cause of increased poverty and, thus, growth (not inequality) became the pressing problem.

More recently poverty issues have once again moved to the top of the development agenda, reflecting the concern that economic reforms undertaken by many countries in the 1980's may have raised income inequality and poverty levels (cf. World Bank, 1990, and 1993, Squire, 1991 and Morrisson, 1992). These concerns are globalized because the same multilateral institutions have sponsored and directed these reforms. The response of the World Bank reflects concerns within the organization no doubt, but must also have been influenced by robust criticisms the World Bank and the IMF were subject to by those seeking "adjustment with a human face" (e.g. Cornia, Jolly and Stewart, 1987). Such an approach to adjustment has been seen by others to be an adaptation of the "basic needs" and "redistribution with growth" ideas to fit the circumstances of the 1980s, especially in Sub-Saharan Africa. (Gillis, et al, 1992: 99).

The new efforts to address poverty and income distribution have focused on size distribution of income and poverty and extend into topical issues of gender, environment and technology.

The main objectives of the chapter are to review and define the concept of poverty and, to highlight the various analytical and empirical approaches to studying poverty. The remaining part of the chapter is divided into four sections. Section Two attempts to explain the recent global concerns on issues of equity and poverty. It is suggested that these issues have long featured in the social, political and economic discussions because of their linkage with social welfare and economic growth. Section Three defines the concept of poverty and discusses the various measures and the related conceptual issues. Section Four attempts to explain the incidence of poverty. Various issues are discussed. These are the relationship between economic performance and poverty, the poverty profile and the effect of policy reforms on the incidence of poverty. Concluding remarks are provided in Section Five.

RENEWED EFFORTS TO ISSUES OF EQUITY AND POVERTY

As noted in the introduction income distribution and poverty are issues which recur periodically, *albeit* with different levels of intensity. In some sense, development policy is necessarily about poverty alleviation, but there has been a fluctuation between periods in which the view predominates that the main focus of policy should be on promoting growth and periods when it is argued that the poverty dimension should be the explicit concern of policy. And the recent global concerns on issues of equity and poverty are based on the suggested linkage between these variables and the current economic reforms. In this section I shall attempt to describe these linkages with the objective being to explain the recent global concerns.

Social Welfare

One approach to income distribution and poverty policy is via welfare economics, which in general attempts to systematically explore the bases on which one outcome of policy can be judged better than another, and in so doing attempt to address the ways in which equality can be treated as a policy goal.

The relationship between equality and poverty and the level of welfare has featured in the economics discussions since the old school of welfare economics, the utilitarian school. According to the school, if societies have equal incomes, the level of social welfare will be higher for those with lower levels of income inequality, other things being equal. This conclusion was based on the assumptions of additive individual economic welfare, diminishing marginal utility of income and similar utility function among individuals, which allowed for inter-personal comparable cardinal welfare functions and implied that maximization of individual utilities through income redistribution requires income equality.

The utilitarian thesis was unsustainable because of its restrictive assumptions and failure to consider the distribution of welfare as an aspect of inequality.

The new school of welfare economics considered utility in a purely ordinal perspective, incomparable among individuals and not additive into a group utility. Instead, it adopted the concept of Pareto efficiency by which a feasible allocation is efficient if, given the distribution of resources, no individual can be made better off without making the other(s) worse off. This rendered the issue of equity both irrelevant and unnecessary. Economic efficiency was considered separate from distributional issues, the former dealing with positive economics and the latter with value judgements.

Yet it is known that not all Pareto - efficient points can generate maximum social welfare for the society. Only by introducing equity considerations can a point which is both Pareto - efficient and can generate maximum social welfare for the society be identified.

Based on additive social welfare function and inter-personal comparability, Atkinson (1970) has shown that, if societies have equal incomes, irrespective of the form of the social welfare function, U(y), social welfare is higher in those with lower levels of income inequality. The reverse is also true, that is, irrespective of the form of U(y), societies with higher levels of social welfare experience lower levels of income inequality. Dasgupta (1973) has shown that the Atkinson thesis can be generalized to include a class of non-additive social welfare functions and any symmetric social welfare function which is quasi-concave and increasing in individual utilities.

The assumption of inter-personal comparability is defensible if we consider a social welfare function with individual income and non-income as exogenenous variables, i.e. $W = W(y_1, ... y_n; v_1, ... v_n)$, so that W may be a decreasing function of some non-income variables. As long as non-incomes are not equally distributed, even individuals with similar incomes will experience different levels of welfare. A preference relation, R, can then be defined to come up with a structure of inter-personal comparisons (Sen, 1973). Thus the relationship between income distribution and social welfare is defensible, and that greater equality imply higher welfare levels. This also leads to the conclusion that lower levels of poverty imply higher levels of welfare, based on the proposition that greater equality (among the poor) leads to lower levels of absolute poverty (Fields, 1980:26).

Economic Growth

Issues of equity and poverty have also been linked to economic growth in two directions. The first relates to the effect of growth on equity and poverty and the second focuses on the effect of equity and poverty on economic growth.

The Effect of Growth on Equity and Poverty

Various theories have been used to analyse the effect of growth on equity an poverty. Only a selected few will be reviewed.

The first group belongs to the neo-classical school. According to this scho the long term effect of economic growth is to lower levels of income inequalit and poverty. This is because economic growth increases the capital-labour rati and, consequently, raises the share of labour at the expense of the share capital, provided that the elasticity of substitution is less than unity. Sinc labour income is more evenly distributed than property income, the result lower levels of income inequality and poverty as national income increases. Th policy implication of the neo-classical argument is that growth oriented polici will also generate more equal income distribution. This line of argument foun support among policy makers who argued for rapid industrialization in poc countries for sustained growth and employment generation, as the basis for more equal distribution of income and reduced poverty levels.

A number of empirical studies lent support to this approach. Kuznets (1955 weighing the historical evidence, agreed with the neo-classical conclusion abor the long-term effect of growth, but noted that income inequality and poverty wi rise in the initial stages of growth before declining in the later periods. The ris in the levels of inequality and poverty is explained by three factors, namely, th concentration of savings in the upper income brackets, the increase in the shar of incomes from the non-agricultural sector at the expense of the moi egalitarian incomes from the agricultural sector, and the widening productivi differences between agriculture and non-agriculture arising from an increasin technological gap. Morgan (1953) emphasized factor and commodity immobilit as characterized by monopolies, high interest rates, concentration of lan ownership and inadequate educational facilities for the poor in tradition: societies as causes of initial inequality. The decline in the levels of inequalit and poverty during the later stages of development is attributed to political an legislative measures aimed at limiting accumulation of property and transferrin incomes to the lower brackets.

Kuznets thesis was further supported by empirical findings (Kuznets, 196: in spite of its theoretical weaknesses (Cline, 1974 and Todaro, 1969). Th Lewis (1954) model is consistent with the Kuznets thesis, attributing th declining inequality and poverty at a later stage to the growing demand fc labour for the expanding non-agricultural sector.

Ahluwalia (1976), using cross-section information performed two tests of th absolute impoverishment thesis and came to the conclusion that incomes of th poor rise systematically with the level of economic development. However, th elasticities of absolute income with respect to per capita income for poc ountries were less than unity implying that the poor gain absolutely but lose elatively.

Galenson (1977) selected non-randomly a sample of high economic growth ountries and observed that growth was accompanied by increased consumption f basic goods and services -foods, housing, medical care, education and other ocial indicators - reflecting rising standard of living. This is in agreement with he neo-classical view that what matters are policies that promote growth.

Fields (1980) using a representatively chosen sample of thirteen poor ountries found that: firstly, absolute poverty declined in ten and rose in three nd, secondly, in general the evidence supported the "trickle-down theory" - ine countries experienced rapid/moderate growth with declining poverty levels, hree experienced rapid/moderate growth with increasing poverty and one xperienced slow growth with declining poverty.

In spite of the support for the neo-classical conclusion from various studies, levelopment analysts have pointed out that the relationship between interest and vage rates is based on the unrealistic assumption that there exists a wide range f choice of techniques of production (Sutcliffe, 1971), developing countries can leliberately choose capital-intensive technologies to maximize long-term bjectives (Sen, 1972) and structural conditions may produce results which ontradict the neo-classical predictions (Stewart and Weeks, 1969, Todaro, 1969 nd Harris and Todaro, 1970).

The main source of domestic financing of the industrialization process is the gricultural sector. This is done through pricing, taxation, subsidized credits, ubsidized imports and protection of "infant" industries. The transfer of esources from agriculture raises the inter-sectoral income gap and the level of overty in the agricultural sector.

Some trade theorists have argued that persistent declining terms of trade gainst developing countries results in a transfer of income from developing to leveloped countries. Since the largest share of exports from developing ountries is agricultural, most of the income transferred originates from this ector. This increases the agricultural - non-agricultural income gap and poverty evels of the agricultural population. Trade policies may also raise income nequality and poverty, depending on the elasticities of demand and supply and he administration of the policy tools (e.g. devaluation).

Furthermore, some empirical findings have not supported the neo-classical heory. Based on cross-section information Adelman and Morris (1973) have rgued that development, measured by GNP per capita, is accompanied by a elative decline of average income of poor countries; recent experiences from Asia (eg Taiwan and S. Korea) do not support the neo-classical thesis; using the Ahluwalia-Chenery (1974) index which is the weighted index of income growth see Section 3.2.4) research results from thirteen poor countries were mixed:

four countries did poorly, four did better and five were largely unaffected by the index than would be indicated by their GNP growth experiences and; based on a non-random sample of the relevant countries, Griffin (1977) provided evidence to show that poverty persisted even for rapidly growing countries.

In the 1970s and early 1980s the ILO argued that growth alone would not reduce absolute poverty to acceptable levels. It, therefore, advocated strategies that would increase employment, meet basic needs, reduce income and wealth inequalities and raise productivity of the poor (cf. ILO (1972) and ILO/JASPA (1982)). The World Bank supported this proposition after observing that although "there is a strong correlation between the extent of poverty in a country and its GNP per person...." the proposition that the solution to poverty is economic growth "needs to be carefully qualified".(World Bank, 1980:35). More recent World Bank studies have argued that rapid and politically sustainable progress on poverty alleviation can be achieved by pursuing policies which promote both economic growth (World Bank, 1990 and World Bank, 1993) and provision of basic social services. (World Bank, 1990). And, as stated earlier, in the late 1980s the "adjustment with a human face" approach was advocated (Cornia, et al, 1987) to incorporate ideas on "redistribution with growth" by the World Bank and "basic needs" by the ILO.

From the above discussion it appears that the question whether or not economic growth reduces income inequality and poverty is complex and that when considering medium term prospects for a given country (e.g. Tanzania), the practical context in which policy is made, appeals either to general theory or the broad historical record are likely to be inconclusive.

The Effect of Income Inequality and Poverty on Growth

The effect of income inequality and poverty on growth can be looked at from the demand and supply sides. It can be argued that a transfer of income from the high to low income brackets will lower savings and therefore, negatively affect investment and growth. However, for many developing countries with mainly subsisting populations, increased consumption is a pre-requisite for growth. Figueroa (1975) has argued that the production profile of an economy reflects its demand profile. Consumption raises demand for the expanded output and the effective supply of labour and productivity. As correctly pointed out in the *World Development Report 1980*, "Development Strategies that bypass large numbers of people may not be the most effective way for developing countries to raise their long-run growth rates".(World Bank, 1980:36).

Current Global Concerns

During the 1980s the focus of adjustment was on growth oriented policies. The idea of "adjustment with equity and poverty alleviation" was abandoned. (Killick, 1989). This was partly a reaction to poor growth experienced during the second half of 1970s and early 1980s which was attributed partly to overemphasis on basic needs/equity oriented policies at the expense of macroeconomic efficiency policies of the 1970s.[2]

Was adjustment in the 1980s linked to rising levels of inequality and poverty? (cf. World Bank, 1990, Morrison, 1992, Squire, 1991 and World Bank, 1993). In some cases the linkage is supported by empirical evidence, in others it is not. The results of adjustment programmes on equality and poverty depend on, other things being equal, baseline situations. Thus, generalization can not be justified. (Morrison, 1992). This calls for further research to determine the linkage between adjustment and poverty and the type of policies that promote growth with equity and poverty alleviation.

A quick perusal of current research reveals a global thrust in research in this area. The focus is on countries which are implementing IMF and World Bank sponsored stabilization and structural adjustment programmes. And many of the research projects are funded by the donor community, including the multilaterals.

Globalization of research in this area is partly linked to donor funding of these programmes. This is because it raises questions on the appropriateness of these programmes in raising standards of living of people and alleviating poverty. It also challenges the leadership of multinational institutions, especially the IMF and WB in directing and supervising global development policy.

There are also other reasons behind the globalization of research in this area. The effects of increasing misery in developing countries is no longer confined to residents from the region. Job seekers flooding from poor to developed countries cause concern to the latter's population with regard to their security of employment and the productivity of the aid they have given to the poor countries[3]

Recently, environmental issues have also been linked to growing income inequality and poverty. The poor live in regions where arable land is scarce, agricultural productivity is low and drought, floods and environmental degradation are common. Many live in semi-arid zones or steep hill-slope areas that are ecologically vulnerable. The areas are isolated, lacking opportunities for non-farm employment and access to basic social services and infrastructure. (World Bank, 1990). In these areas, social, economic and demographic factors interact to push the poor into low-productivity marginal lands. Thus, pressure for wood gathering, inappropriate farming techniques, overgrazing, population growth, etc, lead to further soil erosion and desertification that lead to increased poverty.

The linkage between the environment and poverty is complex but has not been researched fully. And since environmental issues are considered to be global, pressure has mounted from the donor community to undertake studies in this area.

Other issues which have influenced the focus of research on poverty are the fashionable gender and the recurring technology issues. Indirect evidence suggests that women are more severely disadvantaged than men. They face higher illiteracy rates; cultural, social, legal and economic obstacles, and work longer hours for lower pay compared to men. There are also indications that female headed families face higher rates of poverty (World Bank, 1990 and ILO, 1972), but this may not be a global phenomenon (Cooksy, 1994). The linkage between gender and poverty has not been thoroughly researched. A study in this area should assist in formulating policies that would allow full utilization of the women's potentials.

Technology policy is also closely linked with income inequality and poverty concerns. It is generally agreed that capital intensive technologies are inconsistent with policies that lower inequality and poverty levels. Therefore, employment strategies have to address the questions of what and how to produce. And, in this context, there are four issues to resolve: the product mix and its adaptation to income levels and expenditures, the change of factor proportions to favour cost effective labour intensive technologies, change in the direction and speed of technical innovations in favour of domestic factor endowments and, research and development to advance appropriate technology consistent with policies that lower inequality and poverty levels. (ILO, 1972). These issues are complex, requiring detailed studies of relevance both to the urban and the rural economies.

THE CONCEPT OF POVERTY AND ITS MEASUREMENT

The Concept of Poverty

Various definitions of poverty have been given. They can be grouped into two categories, the "absolute" and "relative" poverty approach definitions. Some definitions are too broad to be of much practical relevance to studies on poverty. (cf McNamara in World Bank, 1975:v and World Bank, 1980). They will not be discussed in this chapter.

A practical and commonly used definition of absolute poverty is the inability to attain a specified (minimum) standard of living (cf World Bank, 1990, Atkinson, 1991, World Bank, 1993, Fields, 1980 and Bigsten, 1983). The definition focuses on the absolute economic well-being of the poor, in isolation from the welfare distribution of the entire society. It implies knowledge of the minimum standard of living, commonly referred to as the poverty line. The poverty line, commonly expressed in real terms, is normally held constant in the short run, but is adjusted in the medium to long term to reflect changes in a country's priorities and level of development. (Atkinson, 1991). It can be specified following the basic needs approach in which the minimum standard of nutrition and other non-food basic necessities are included. (cf ILO/JASPA, 1982). The various methods used to determine the poverty line will be discussed shortly.

The advantage of using the absolute poverty approach is that changes in the welfare position of the poor can be traced and the extent of poverty eradication can be measured. Thus, many studies on poverty, have adopted this approach.

The relative poverty approach focuses on the economic well-being of the poorest x% of the population. It takes into account the welfare distribution of the entire society. The population share of the poor is held constant, as the average level of welfare changes. This approach is appealing, both socially and politically, because individuals relate to others at all levels of economic well-being, implying that poverty is a dynamic concept which changes with time and space as well as the level of education and communication. Improved education and communication expand the poor's reference group by raising awareness of the standard of living in other societies. And the poor may refuse to live on the basic minimum necessary for physical survival. However, the concept of relative poverty suffers from two obvious weaknesses. Firstly, it determines *a priori* the extent of poverty and makes its elimination impossible. Secondly, it ignores mobility into and out of poverty. Thus, many studies, including this one have not adopted this approach.

Measures of Poverty

Various measures of absolute poverty exist. Below we describe briefly some commonly used ones.

The Headcount Index

The headcount index is defined as the proportion (percentage-wise) of the population below the poverty line. Computation of this index, therefore, requires determination of the poverty line. (To be discussed shortly).

The Poverty Gap

A major problem with the headcount index is that it fails to gauge the extent of poverty, i.e. the extent to which the poor fall below the poverty line. The poverty gap solves this problem by providing information on the amount needed to raise the incomes of the poor to the poverty line, thereby eliminating poverty.

The computed aggregate income shortfall as a percentage of aggregate income provides a poverty gap measure, showing the extent of poverty in the country.

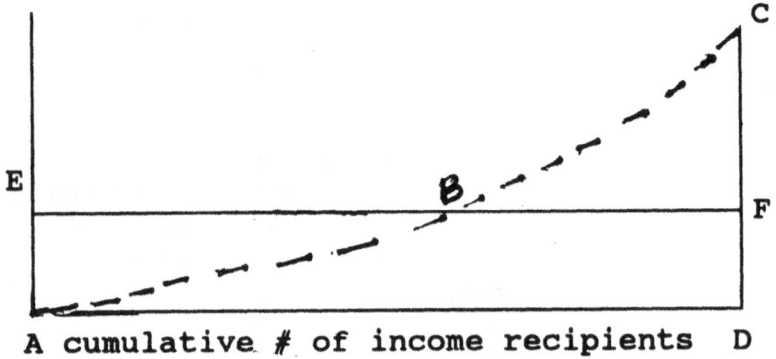

Figure 1: The Poverty Gap

Several policy relevant measures can be derived from the poverty gap concept, as shown in Figure One. (See Bigsten, 1982:59) for the original reference). EF is the poverty line. The first policy measure is the redistribution potential obtained by dividing the area   BCF by ABE, the second is the marginal taxation to alleviate poverty obtained by dividing the area ABE by BCF, the third is the reallocation of government expenditure potential obtained by dividing government expenditures by the area ABE and, the fourth is the percentage of government expenditures necessary to alleviate poverty obtained by dividing the area ABE by government expenditures.

The Sen Index

Proponents of the absolute poverty approach have suggested that the extent of poverty falls when: the proportion of income recipients with incomes below the poverty line falls; average income of those below the poverty line rises and; for the same number below the poverty line and the same average income among them, intra income inequality declines (Fields, 1980:26). The headcount index takes into account only the first proposition and the poverty gap considers only the second. However, Sen (1976) has developed an index of poverty which considers all the three propositions.

The Sen's poverty index which is derived from the social welfare concept and assumes that the welfare of a person is proportional to his rank in income distribution is given by:

$$P = H (I + (1-I) G)$$

where

P is the poverty index

H is the proportion of the population in poverty

I is the proportionate average income gap,

i.e. $(p^*-y)/p^*$

p^* is poverty line and

y is the average income of the poor.

G is the Gini coefficient of income inequality among the poor.

The Ahluwalia-Chenery Index

In an attempt to integrate welfare considerations into analyses of development Ahluwalia and Chenery (1974) developed a weighted index of income growth, Y_g, which can be taken to be a measure of growth of social welfare for particular groups/sectors:

$$Y_g = w_1g_1 + w_2g_2 + \ldots\ldots w_ng_n$$

where

g_i is the rate of growth of income of group *i*

w_i is the welfare weight assigned to the growth of group *i*th income.

Ahluwalia and Chenery (1974) proposed three weighting schemes. Firstly, is *the GNP weights* which uses the groups' shares in total income. The problem with this scheme is that it gives more weight to the rich than the poor, for the same percentage increase in income. Secondly, is the *population weights* or the *equal percentage weights* which assigns each group the same welfare weight, ie. $w_1=w_2=\ldots\ldots=w_n=1/n$. Thirdly, is *the poverty weights* which gives greater weight to income gains of poorer groups, ie. $w_1 > w_2 > \ldots\ldots > w_n$.

According to this measure, the extent and direction of divergence between the weighted index of income growth and the growth rate of income indicates the extent and direction to which growth is distributionally biased. And, in spite of its inherent subjectivity in the choice of weights, it has the advantage of allowing policy makers to set development targets and monitor development performance not only in terms of GNP growth but also in terms of the distribution pattern of income growth.

Social Indicators

The above mentioned indicators of poverty utilize household incomes and/or expenditures. Although incomes/expenditures provide a good indication of the standard of living of the poor, they do not adequately capture some important dimensions of welfare such as health, education, clean water, access to public goods or common property resources, etc. Thus, social indicators have often been used to complement the income/consumption based indicators of poverty. The various social indicators which have been used include the under five mortality (per thousand), the life expectancy (years), net primary school enrolment rate (percent), etc. (World Bank, 1990). Some indirect measures have also been used, for example, the number of physicians, teachers, hospital beds, schools, etc. Care has to be exercised in using infrastructural facilities since they do not necessarily correspond to quantity and quality of service produced. Cases of capacity underutilization and lack of operating inputs are common in developing countries. Nevertheless many social indicators are measurable and are being used.

However, social indicators are difficult to combine into a single measure of social development. Earlier, the Overseas Development Council (ODC) developed the physical quality of life index (PQLI) based on an unweighted average of scale values (ranging from 0 to 100) for life expectancy, infant mortality rate and literacy rate (Morris, 1979, quoted from Gillis, et al, 1992). Recently the UNDP has for its part developed a human development index (HDI) by combining indicators of real purchasing power, education and health. The HDI is the unweighted average of the relative distances (deprivations) measured in longevity (life expectancy), education (literacy and mean years in schooling) and resources (modified income per capita to measure utility). The HDI can be adjusted to incorporate aspects of gender and income distribution. It can also be disaggregated for application in sectors, subregions, urban -rural, etc. (UNDP, 1993).

Both the PQLI and the HDI are interpreted to suggest that the rich (poor) do not always enjoy higher (lower) quality of life. However, Gillis, et al (1992: 80-81) have observed that in general, if oil exporting countries are excluded, the indices produce country rankings which are highly correlated with GNP/capita. The same conclusion was reached for the individual social indicators. It is likely that if the exercise was performed for different income groups within the country, the conclusion by Gillis, et al would hold.

It is however important to note that the various measures of poverty may produce conflicting results. (cf Fields, 1980:177-178). So that sometimes conclusions on the changes in the incidence of poverty may have to take into account non-quantitative evidence, eg. casual observations.

Some Conceptual Issues

In measuring poverty a number of conceptual issues have to be addressed. These include the determination of poverty line, the choice of poverty indicator, the unit of analysis, the choice of equivalence scale and information gathering.

The Determination of Poverty Line

Various methods are used to determine the poverty line. The poverty line can be obtained by ascertaining the income needed to purchase a nutritionally adequate diet consistent with the food preferences of the poor, and then multiplying this figure by a factor of, for example, 1.4 for the case of Tanzania where the poor spend about 71% of their incomes on food[4]. This statement can be formalized using a slightly modified Atkinson (1991) measure as follows:

$$P^* = (1 + (h - 1)) \, px$$

where

P* is the poverty line,
x is the vector of food requirements,
p is the corresponding price vector, and
h is the reciprocal of the share of expenditure in food.

This method has been used in the United States and has the advantage of using household information which is considered to reflect more accurately the characteristics and preferences of the poor[5]. Its variant was also used by the ILO in Tanzania. (ILO/JASPA, 1982).

Other less demanding poverty lines are based on income level at which more than a specified (usually high - e.g. 70%) percentage is spent on food, clothing and shelter (e.g. in Canada); a specified percentage of the average national income (e.g. as proposed by the European Commission); a specified dollar figure (e.g. as used in the *World Development Report 1990)*; the minimum wage in the poor regions (e.g. in Brazil); etc. (See details and references in Atkinson, 1991, World Bank, 1990 and Fields, 1980). Sometimes very general poverty lines are specified, e.g. Sahn and Sarris (1991) focus on the low-income rural smallholder households, without specifying income levels and, sometimes the concept is abandoned altogether, e.g. Collier, et al (1990:24-25) have argued that it is irrelevant when the majority are poor.

As already mentioned the poverty line is expressed in real values and is, in many cases, held constant in the short run. This means that adjustments for price changes have to be made using appropriate price deflators. If the poverty line is expressed in foreign currency or comparison across countries is to be made, the use of purchasing power parity (PPP) rather than the official exchange rate is recommended. This method is adopted in the *World Development Report 1990*. This is because the extent of absolute poverty has been found to be sensitive to the choice of exchange rate. Fields (1980:138) reports results obtained in other studies to confirm this.

Apart from adjustments needed to maintain the real value of the poverty line, there are socio-economic and political justifications to review the real value of the poverty line. The real value may rise in a step pattern or in a continuous fashion. The former is more common although studies leading to implementation of the latter are also available. (Atkinson, 1991). It is important that consistency between the real value of the poverty line and the economic and social objectives is maintained. For example it is expected that in determining the poverty line, the level of entitlement to social assistance is considered.

Choice of Poverty Indicator

Various indicators have been used to measure the standard of living. When poverty is defined in terms of a single broad indicator of economic resources two indicators can be used. The standard of living can be measured by using total consumption/expenditure (including home produced goods and services). Alternatively total income can be used. There are justifications for preferring income over consumption in measuring living standards. Firstly, current consumption and income may not necessarily be the same. This may arise if individuals decide to dissave, borrow or share in consumption with others to avoid a decline in consumption or; if the structure of the market forces individuals to reduce consumption through rationing. The use of permanent income to avoid seasonal fluctuations may minimize problems associated with the former difficulty[6]. The second justification for using income rather than consumption is based on the appropriateness of the former as an indicator of resources. In dealing with measurements of poverty, it is more appropriate to focus on the budget constraints and opportunities open to individuals rather than consumption choices. Furthermore, there are arguments of rights to resources which support the use of income as a measure of standard of living. (Atkinson, 1991).

Poverty can also be defined following the basic needs approach. (ILO/JASPA, 1982). Here the focus is on individual items of consumption and poverty is measured multidimesionally rather than in terms of a single indicator. As noted by ILO/JASPA (1982) the difficulty of determining the basic needs and apportioning weights to determine the poverty line is not insignificant.

As already mentioned poverty can also be defined in terms of social or demographic indicators such as life expectancy and literacy. (WB,1990).

Following this approach, the physical quality of life index (PQLI) and the human developed index (HDI) which incorporate social indicators have been developed. (Morris, 1979 and UNDP, 1993).

A subjective indicator of poverty referred to as apparent prosperity index (API) has also been attempted (Lanjouw and Stern, 1991). The apparent prosperity concept is based on the proposition that prosperity is associated with consumption or lifestyle - quality of housing, food, clothing, possession of durable and luxurious goods, etc. Furthermore, in the localities, affluence is common knowledge, widely understood and easily identified[7]. Thus households/individuals can easily be classified into groups such as very poor, poor, modest,......., very rich. There are, however, problems of inability to distinguish between lifestyle or consumption and income as well as those arising from intra-household inequalities of lifestyle which complicate the classification exercise. But the other indicators of poverty are not free from these problems either.

Unit of Analysis

In this chapter, a unit of analysis refers to individuals who are assumed to combine resources when poverty assessments are made on them. The unit may be a common residence where individuals may share housekeeping facilities, a household where spending decisions may be jointly made, a family and an individual. (cf Atkinson, 1991, for elaboration). There are advantages and disadvantages of choosing any of these and the choice should be guided by the purpose or objective of the study.

Focus on the family and, to some extent,the household has justification given the widespread income sharing among the members (including dependents); joint decision making among members regarding allocation of goods and services; the difficulty of attributing incomes (from joint activities) to specific members and; the joint commitment of members to supplement incomes of disadvantaged members, even if it implies working overtime (Fields, 1980:139). The basic needs approach may favour the use of family and household rather than the individual since concern is on total rather than individual income. The use of residence is also acceptable. The problem with these choices is that some items (e.g. food) in the expenditure bundle are more individualistic (private) while others (e.g. housing) are essentially public. And there may be considerable inequality, among members, in the distribution of the former. However, since inequality within the unit of analysis can not easily be observed, it is assumed that members share the same standard of living.

The focus on the individual as a unit of analysis has several strengths. Families may distribute resources inequitably, e.g. in favour of the head of the household or family; the labour market employs individuals with specific characteristics and rewards them accordingly and; some key indicators of economic development, e.g. infant mortality rates and school achievements, pertain exclusively to individuals. The minimum rights approach to poverty, by focusing on minimum entitlements or rights to individuals would favour the individual as a unit of analysis. Studies on the gender dimension of poverty may also belong here.

Equivalence Scales

Equivalence scales are applied for units of analysis other than the individual or to make allowance for age, sex, disability, etc. on an individual. Various methods have been used by different countries and studies. They produce different results.

Buhmann, et all (1988) have proposed the formula for computing equivalence scales as:

equivalent income = total income/n^e

where

n is the number of members in the unit, and
e is the elasticity of unit "need" with respect to size.

The value of e varies from zero, when no adjustments for size are made, to one, which is the same as computing per capita income.

Estimation of e may be based on subjective estimation of what the needs are; observed consumption patterns; policy makers estimates as derived from benefit scales and; statistical studies. The value of e has tended to rise monotonically from the first to the fourth-method. And as Bahmann, *et al* (1988) have shown the choice of scale has a significant effect on the extent and composition of the poor.

Data Collection

Appropriate policy measures to alleviate poverty can be adopted if the right variables are chosen and accurate data are obtained to answer these questions: what is poverty? who is poor? What is the extent of poverty? what are the causes of poverty? how can poverty be alleviated?

There is an ongoing debate about the appropriate method for undertaking research aimed at answering these questions[8]. There are those who believe that these questions can not be answered by anyone other than the poor himself or herself. These advocate participatory methodology in undertaking research on poverty. (See, for example, Chambers, 1994). The strength of participatory methodology is based on its ability to identify non-economic variables, not so easily captured by conventional methods, eg household surveys. Furthermore, perhaps more importantly, in the participatory research, the direction and content of research are determined by the respondent, the poor; in the conventional methods the direction and content are pre-determined by the researcher. For these reasons, it is argued, the participatory approach is superior to the conventional approach.

The question is, can the two approaches be considered to be substitutes or complementaries? My personal view is that they are complementaries for the following reasons. Firstly, the participatory approach requires more time and resources per unit of area/respondent than the conventional approach. For the conventional approach the methodology for research and the technology for storage and analysis of the data are sufficiently developed and the experience has accumulated overtime. Moreover for many of the variables, the data base on which additional information can be added exists - an essential element for time series analysis. Secondly, it can be argued that there is, in general, a positive correlation between income and non-income variables. This implies that, by and large, conventional methods will be able to identify the poor and its characteristics.

It seems more cost effective to apply the participatory approach when the basic data is available or for cross-checking or when there are doubts about the available data.

The extent of use of each of the two approaches will vary by project depending on focus (eg gender) and context (rural-urban based, level of education, etc.).

EXPLAINING POVERTY

Economic Growth vs Poverty

To what extent do incomes of the poor rise with economic growth? This issue has already been covered in an earlier section. No repetitions will be made in this section. It only suffices to mention that no conclusive evidence is available to support the proposition that growth is a *sufficient condition* for poverty alleviation. However, sufficient evidence exists to support the proposition that growth is a *necessary* condition for *sustained* poverty alleviation and that poverty alleviation without growth will be unsustainable, as experiences from Tanzania and Sri Lanka have shown.

Ravallion and Huppi (1991) have found that intra-sectoral rural effects and growth effects are more important in the explaining aggregate poverty change in Indonesia.

Poverty Profile

Fields (1980:44) defines poverty profile as the socio-economic make-up of the poor. In the literature on poverty the following features are predominant: land ownership, sex, age, family size, occupation, education etc.

Table 1 presents a summary of the main conclusions based on a study of the poverty profiles of six poor countries.

Table 1: A Summary of Poverty Profiles in Six Poor Countries

	Poverty Predominant in	Brazil	Malaysia	Taiwan	Thailand	Pakistan	India
1.	Female headed families	Yes	Yes	Yes	No	-	-
2.	Families headed by old aged	No	No	Yes	No	-	-
3.	Very low level of basic education	·Yes	Yes	Yes	Yes	Yes	Yes
4.	Agricultural or rural sector	Yes	Yes	Yes	Yes	Yes	Yes
5.	Specific regions	Yes	-	-	Yes	-	Yes
6.	Large families with young children	Yes	Yes	-	Yes	-	-
7.	Families with few regular non-farm workers	Yes	Yes	-	-	Yes	-
8.	Self-employment	-	Yes	-	-	Yes	-
9.	Landless families	-	-	-	-	-	Yes

Notes: - means no information given. *Source:* Fields (1980:145-161)

Many of these determinants of poverty have been analysed, sometimes econometrically tested, and found to be important in other countries, including Tanzania (cf. Lanjouw and Stern, 1991 and Collier, et all, 1990). Collier et all (1990) have also found ownership of livestock to be an important explanation of poverty incidence in Tanzania. Decision to include specific variables in a study of poverty is determined by the objective, nature and context of the study. For instance, a study on the impact of technology on poverty would not find general poverty profiles to be very useful.

Assessing the Impact of Policy Reforms on Poverty

There has been growing concern over the impact of adjustment on poverty. There is a general feeling that adjustment policies have intensified poverty. This conclusion is often reached by following the evolution of various indicators and attributing the changes to adjustment. This is incorrect since a number of factors are at play and their impacts on poverty have to be separated. These factors include the adjustment measures, the preceding crisis and long-term factors such as population growth. This difficulty has been correctly pointed out by Sahn and Sarris (1991).

Like any other policy, the correct approach to the analysis of the impact of adjustment policy is to assess what would have happened without adjustment. This entails developing an appropriate counter-factual situation. It provides allowance for choice among economic policy alternatives. Various methods to develop an appropriate counter-factual situation have been proposed (cf Bourguignon, 1991 and Bourguignon, 1991 and Newman, 1991). Ongoing attempts by researchers such as Sarris (1993) to develop a (Computable General Equilibrium) CGE model for Tanzania will enhance our understanding of this issue. In the mean while, other less ambitious models, such as use of demand systems, may be used to develop counter-factual situations.

CONCLUDING REMARKS

Issues of income distribution and poverty have featured periodically in the development debates since the classical period. Various theories have been developed to explain changes in the levels of income inequality and poverty. A good number of them have been reviewed in the chapter. The various methods for measuring and evaluating poverty have also been reviewed.

At the level of policy, the degree of intensity and the components of focus have varied by period among the institutions such as the World Bank and the ILO and countries. There have been periods of "adjustment for growth with equity and poverty alleviation" when it was felt that equity and poverty alleviation did not automatically result from growth. There have also been periods of "adjustment for growth" when it was felt that over-emphasis on "basic needs" at the expense of growth has slowed down growth and, consequently, reduced the size of the cake for distribution and poverty alleviation.

Four questions can be raised from the chapter.

Firstly, which of the theories is more relevant in explaining changes in income inequality and poverty in Tanzania? Can this be decided *a priori* or is it an empirical question?

Secondly, it is increasingly being accepted that growth is a necessary condition for poverty alleviation in poor countries. Tanzania is just coming out of a prolonged period of economic decline and stagnation. Is this the right time to talk about poverty and "basic needs"? What are the resource implications of such a concern?

Thirdly, are there only two mutually exclusive alternative policies-"growth with increasing inequality and poverty levels" and "declining inequality and poverty levels without growth"? Can't one kill two birds with one stone? This seems to have been the ILO's idea in the 1970s with a focus on labour intensive technologies and the development of smallholder agriculture. What went wrong with the idea?

Fourthly, Tanzania is now a market economy. Therefore, poverty has to be seen to be a consequence of lack of access to market income, that is, assets and labour power. Since the aim is poverty alleviation, could a study on access/non-access to market income be the appropriate starting point for a study on poverty? This might imply a study of the process whereby some become rich, in order to understand how others are excluded.

NOTES

1. This approach is distinguished from the "basic needs" approach which emphasized the provision of public services, along with entitlements to the poor to ensure accessibility.

2. Obviously other factors, such as bad governance, contributed to the poor economic performance.

3. The flow is not entirely one way. Much of the technical assistance tied to aid has marginalised job seekers in recipient countries.

4. 71% refers to the rural population which can conveniently be classified as poor. (See Sahn and Sarris, 1991).

5. Proponents of participatory research would not agree entirely about the quality of household surveys. (See, for example, Chambers, 1994 and Ravnborg and Sanc, 1994).

6. This deals with what other analysts refer to as the *vulnerability* aspect of poverty. (See, for instance, Ravnborg and Sano, 1994).

7. Although Lanjouw and Stern (1991) do not refer to participatory research, this seems to be what was done.

8. This came out clearly in a conference on *Poverty and Development Cooperation* held at Copenhagen, Denmark, 23-24 February, 1994.

REFERENCES

Adelman, I and Morris, C.T. (1973) *Economic Growth and Social Equity in Developing Countries*, Stanford: Stanford University Press.

Ahluwalia, M. and Chenery, H. (1974). "The Economic Framework" in Chenery, H. et all (eds) *Redistribution with Growth, New York:* Oxford University Press.

Atkinson, A.B. (1991) "Comparing Poverty Rates Internationally:Lessons from Recent Studies in Developed Countries", *The World Bank Economic Review* Vol. 5 No. 1. pp. 3-21.

Atkinson, A.B. (1970). "On the Measurement of Inequality", *Journal of Economic Theory*, September. Vol. 2, pp 244-263.

Bahman, *et al.* (1988). "Equivalence Scales, Well-Being, Inequality and Poverty" *Review of Income and Wealth*, 34.

Bigsten, A. (1983). *Income Distribution and Development: Theory, Evidence and Policy*, London: Heinemann.

Bourguignon, F. (1991). "Optimal Poverty Reduction, Adjustment and Growth". *The World Bank Economic Review,* Vol. 5, No. 2. pp.315-338.

Bourguignon, F. *et al.* 1991. "Distributional Effects of Adjustment Policies: Simulations for Archetype Economies in Africa and Latin America", *The World Bank Economic Review,* Vol. 5, No. 1. pp. 339-366.

Chambers, R. (1994). "The Poor and the Environment: Whose Reality Counts?", Paper presented at a conference on *Poverty and Development Cooperation* held at Copenhagen, Denmark, 23-24 February.

Cline, W. (1974). "Distribution and Development: A Survey of Literature", *Journal of Development Economics.* Vol 1, No.4, pp. 359-400.

Collier, P. et al, (1986) *Labour and Poverty in Rural Tanzania.* Oxford: Clarendon Press Oxford.

Cornia, G.A., Jolly, R. and Stewart, F. (eds.) 1987, *Adjustment with a Human Face,* 2 Vol. New York: Oxford University Press.

Cooksey, B.(1994). Who is Poor in Tanzania? A Review of Recent Poverty Research. Paper presented at a seminar on *Research on Poverty Alleviation in Tanzania,* Dar es Salaam, 11-12 January.

Dasgupta P. et al.(1973). "Notes on the Measurement of Inequality", *Journal of Economic Theory,* No. 6.

Fei, J.C. and Ranis, G. (1964). *Development of Labour Surplus Economy,* Homewood, III.: Richard Irwin.

Fields, G.S. (1980). *Poverty, Inequality and Development.* Cambridge: Cambridge University Press.

Figueroa, A. (1975). "Income Distribution, Demand Structure and Employment: The Case of Peru", *Journal of Development Studies* Vol. II, No. 2, pp. 20-31.

Galenson, W. (1977). "Economic Growth, Income and Employment", Paper presented at a *Conference on Poverty and Development in Latin America*, Yale University, April.

Griffin, K. (1977). "Increasing Poverty and Changing Ideas about Developing Strategies". Paper presented at the *Conference on Distribution, Poverty and Development*, Bogota, June.

Gillis, M., Perkins, D.H., Roemer, M. and Snodgrass, D.R. 1992, *Economics of Development*. London: W.W. Wprdpm & Company.

Harris, J. and Todaro, M. (1970). "Migration, Unemployment and Development: A Two-Sector Analysis", *American Economic Review*, March.

ILO, (1972). *Employment, Incomes and Equality: A Strategy for Increasing Productive Employment in Kenya*, Geneva, ILO.

ILO/JASPA. (1982). *Basic Needs in Danger: A Basic Needs Oriented Development Strategy for Tanzania, Addis Ababa* United Printers.

Kaldo, N. (1966). "Marginal Productivity and Macroeconomic Theories of Distribution", *Review of Economic Studies*, Vol. 33, pp. 309-319.

Kaldor, W. (1955/56). "Alternative Theories of Distribution", *Review of Economic Studies*.

Kalecki, M. (1950). "The Distribution of the National Income", in American Economic Association, *Readings in the Theory of Income Distribution*, London: Alien & Unwin

Killick, T. (1989). "Some Unsettled Questions", *Tanzania Journal of Economics*, Vol. 1, No. 1. pp. 3-18.

Kuznets, S. (1963). "Quantitative Aspects of the Economic Growth of Nations: VIII, Distributions of Income by Size", *Economic Development and Cultural Change*, XI. pp 1-80.

Kuznets, S. (1955). "Economic Growth and Income Inequality", *American Economic Review*, Vol. 45, No. I. pp. 1-28.

Lanjouw, P. and Stern, N. (1991). "Poverty in Palanpur", *The World Bank Economic Review*, Vol. 5, No. 1. pp. 23-55.

Lewis, W.A. (1954). "Economic Development with unlimited Supplies of Labour". *Manchester School of Economic and Social Studies*, Vol. 20.

Morgan, T. (1953). "Distribution of Income in Ceylon, Puerto Rico, The United States and The United Kingdom", *Economic Journal*, December. Vol. LXIII pp 821-834.

Morrison, C. (1992). "Adjustment and Equity". *OECD Development Centre Policy Brief*, No. 1.

Morris, D.M. (1979), *Measuring the Condition of the World's Poor: The Physical Quality of Life Index*, New York: Pergamon Press.

Newman, J. et all. "How Did workers Benefit from Bolivia's Emergency Social Fund?" *The World Bank Economic Review,* Vol. 5, No. 1.

Pant, P. (1962). "Perspectives of Development, India, 1960/61 - 1975/76: Implications of Planning for a Minimum Level of Living" reprinted in Srinivasan, T.N. and Bardhan, P.K. (eds). 1974. *Poverty and Income Distribution in India,* Society, Calcutta: Statistical Publishing Society.

Pareto, V. (1897). *Cours d'Economic Politique,* Lansanne. Pigou, A.C. (1932). *The Economics of Welfare,* 4th ed., London: Macmillan.

Ravallion, M. and Huppi, M. (1991). "Measuring Changes in Poverty: A Methodological Case Study of Indonesia During an Adjustment Period", *The World Bank Economic Review,* Vol. 5, No. 1. pp. 57-82.

Ravnborg, H.M. and Sano, H.O. (1994). Operationalization of the Poverty Objective in Development Assistance", Paper presented at a conference on *Poverty and Development Cooperation* held at Copenhagen, Denmark, 23-24 February, 1994.

Sahn, D.E. and Sarris, A. (1991). "Structural Adjustment and the Welfare of Rural Smallholders: A Comparative analysis from Sub-Saharan Africa", *The World Bank Economic Review.* Vol. 5 No. 2. pp. 259-289.

Sarris, A. (1993). "Macroeconomic Policies and Household Incomes: A Dynamic Computable General Equilibrium Analysis for Tanzania", mimeo.

Sen, A. (1976). "Poverty: an Ordinal Approach to Measurement", *Econometrica,* Vol. 44. No. 2 pp. 219-231.

Sen, A.K. (1973). *On Economic Inequality,* Oxford: Clarendon Press.

Sen, A.K. (1972). *Choice of Techniques: An Aspect of the Theory of Planned Economic Development,* Oxford Basil Blackwell.

Squire, L. (1991). "Introduction: Poverty and Adjustment in the 1980s", *The World Bank Economic Review,* Vol. 5 No. 2. pp. 177-185.

Stewart, F. and Weeks, J. 1969. "The Employment Effects of Wage Changes in Poor Countries", *Journal of Development Studies.* July.

Sutcliffe 1971. *Industry and Development* London: Addison- Wesley Publ. Co.

Tinbergen, J. (1970). "A Positive and Normative Theory of Income Distribution", *Review of Income and Wealth,* Vol. 16. No. 3, pp. 221-234.

Todaro, M. (1969). "A Theoretical Note on Labour as an 'Inferior' Factor in Less Developed Economies, *Journal of Development Studies,* July.

World Bank. (1993). "Poverty and Structural Change in Côte d'Ivoire", *Development Brief,* No. 20.

World Bank. (1990. *World Development Report 1990,* Oxford: OUP New York, UNDP.

UNDP (1993). *Human Development report, 1993.*

3

Who's Poor in Tanzania?
A Review of Recent Poverty Research

BRIAN COOKSEY

INTRODUCTION

According to IFAD, in 1988 nearly 12 million rural Tanzanians, or 60 percent of the rural population, were living below the poverty line. For the rural population of Sub-Saharan Africa as a whole, the figure was over 200 million people (also 60 percent). Of the 66 developing countries with the highest levels of poverty, over half are in Africa (IFAD 1992). Since by most definitions, a large proportion of Tanzanians are "poor", it makes some sense to focus the discussion in this chapter on absolute rather than relative poverty. However, relative (meaning subjectively experienced) poverty is a potentially crucial determinant of social behaviour, including political identity, organisation and action. Dividing people into categories of "poor" and "non-poor" according to some "objective" measure may tell us more about the measure than the people being measured.[1]

Much research takes the absolute poverty line as the income required to meet a minimum calorific consumption level. The definition includes a basic basket of consumer goods which is larger for urban than rural areas. Individuals and households falling below this minimum level are considered to have chronically or acutely inadequate diets, and are defined as absolutely poor. At the extreme, insufficient food leads to ill-health, indigence, starvation and death. In the modern period, Tanzania has fortunately not had to deal with this extreme of poverty on a significant level. However, poor harvests led to the importation of over 150,000 tonnes of maize in 1978-80, and there are recent examples of localised food shortages caused by crop failure, flooding, and the influx of refugees. The government recently warned that widespread famine may result from the recent drought. The difficulties with the nutrition-based definition of poverty will become evident in due course.

Poverty *as experienced from the actors' point of view* has not been a subject of social science research in Tanzania, which severely limits the discussion of relative poverty. In what follows, relative poverty is taken to mean the incidence of absolute poverty between different population groups.

LOCATING THE POOR: GEOGRAPHICAL AND DEMOGRAPHIC CHARACTERISTICS

Although Tanzanian policy makers have been concerned with poverty and its eradication for many years, remarkably little is known about the nature, causes, incidence, and trajectory of poverty in the country. Far too much of the poverty literature consists of policy-oriented reviews and summaries of previous research, far too little consists of original empirical (especially micro level) studies. Moreover, a substantial amount of primary data, for example, the 1988 population census, which could be used with relative confidence to chart certain aspects of national patterns of poverty, has not been analysed within a poverty perspective.

There is no recent research directly concerned with the geographical distribution of poverty in Tanzania. The census is a valuable but apparently untapped source. Broad intercensal comparisons could be made on the basis of data from the previous (1978) national census (TADREG [1992a] does this for primary education). Household budget surveys and other surveys of income, expenditure, health or other poverty relevant characteristics of the population are based on relatively small samples, of which regional sub-samples typically consist of less than 100 households. Moreover, purposive sampling techniques may require that, say, "rich" farmers are sampled predominantly in one or two regions irrespective of their actual prevalence in those regions. Thus, regional or lower level poverty profiles cannot be simply read off disaggregated national sample data.

For this reason, none of the major recent national studies attempt to locate poor people by region or district. An exception is the World Bank's Poverty Profile (1993), which ignores the above limitation imposed by sampling techniques. Moreover, the reliability of the data used in this Profile has been seriously questioned by those who undertook the original survey (Tinios et.al. 1993). Although the "cleaned" data from this survey are the basis for some of the following discussion, there are still serious doubts about their reliability, as the authors are at pains to point out.

There is general agreement that poverty is more widespread in rural than in urban areas. Typically, income or expenditure comparisons between rural areas, Dar es Salaam and other urban area show a greater incidence and depth of poverty in rural areas, with Dar es Salaam showing the least. This pattern obtains even though the poverty line for Dar es Salaam is much higher in money terms than elsewhere. Different poverty lines are defined to reflect price levels, consumption patterns, and different necessities of life (such as housing and transport).

Table 1 compares the income required to purchase a minimum food (and other basic essentials) basket in the different localities. This translates into the ability to secure an adequate calorific intake and minimum standard of living. The table gives a range of minimum daily (adult equivalent) calorific requirements.

Table 1: Calorifically Defined Poverty Lines
for Tanzania Mainland (TShs/capita) (1991)

Daily energy requirements:	Income (Tshs) All	Rural	Urban non-DSM	DSM
1900 calories	25 13	28969	50866	
% of households	50.5	55.6	28.9	23.0
% of population	43.6	50.1	21.2	16.2
2000 calories	27721	33186	54950	
% of households	54.4	59.3	34.6	26.5
% of population	47.6	54.1	26.4	18.3
2100 calories	29831	37777	59138	
% of households	58.1	63.2	37.1	29.7
% of population	51.4	58.2	29.2	20.4

Source: Tinios et.al. (1993) (Table 6.1.3)

The table shows the proportion of poor households or of poor people who fall below the income level required to meet different daily levels of calorific intake in urban and rural areas. (The differences between "households" and "population" poverty figures reflect differences in household size and dependency ratios between different income groups).

Taking 2000 calories per day as the minimum requirement puts well over half the rural households below the poverty line. An annual income of Shs 27721 per annum per adult equivalent defines this limit in monetary terms. Likewise, just over a quarter of the population of Dar es Salaam falls below the annual income limit of Shs 54950 required to secure the same level of calorific intake in the city, and about a third of the population in other cities. In income terms the poverty line in Dar es Salaam is twice that of the rural areas.

Overall, the poor consume only 1654 calories per adult equivalent a day, compared with an impressive 4500 calories for the "non-poor" (enough one imagines to guarantee life-threatening levels of obesity). "About 12 percent of households were consuming less than 1500 kcal per equivalent adult. Those can be considered as severely undernourished." (Tinios op.cit., p43) Below these are referred to as the "very poor".

The study does not go very deeply into the important questions of the intensity of poverty or the range of inequality for those below the poverty line. One interesting finding is that "inequality appears to be primarily inter- rather than intra-regional." (p.33). Previous research (Collier et.al. 1990, analysing much earlier data) concluded the opposite, that inequality is largely intra- rather than inter-village, indeed "only 16 percent of overall inequality could be explained by inter-village differences. ... 84 per cent of inequality resulted from intra-village differences." (Collier p.129). This author did not find that intra-village inequalities led to the domination of village politics by economic elites, which earlier observers, concerned to neutralise the kulak class enemy of Ujamma socialism, had identified.

A "targeted" strategy designed to alleviate poverty will vary according to whether poverty is found to be widely scattered throughout the country or concentrated in particular, resource-poor, economically backward, environmentally degraded, or isolated places. Major intra-village inequalities in income, land or cattle ownership would normally be expected to influence village politics. Projects aimed at improving the lives of the poor (or women, or the young) are often highjacked by local elites (or men, or the old). This is only one of many problems associated with the concept of "targeting" the poor (World Bank 1990).

A very general idea of the range of inequality as measured by household expenditure is shown in Table 2 as provided by Tinios (op.cit.).

Table 2: Share of Expenditure of the top
and botto 5%-25% of the Population

		Rural	Non-DSM
Bottom 5%	0.9	.1	.1
Top 5%	15.8	6.9	12.
Bottom 10%	2.3	.5	2.
Top 10%	26.3	7.3	23.5
Bottom 25%	8.7	.1	10.5
Top 25%	50.	2.3	44.7

Source: Tinios et.al.,op.cit., Table 5 3.1

The table shows that income inequalities nation lly are extremely large, and greater in rural than in urban areas, especiall Dar es Salaam. The top 5 percent of the population in rural areas consumes 17 ti es as much as the bottom 5 percent; in Dar es Salaam it is 11 times as muc . Such measures, however, must be open to a wide range of error, especially at the top of the urban income ladder. The unofficial economy is estimated conservatively at between 40 and 60 percent of the official economy, and it is likely that much of this activity takes place at the higher income levels (Bagachwa 1993). The income and spending patterns of the rich, including savings and investment, would be so unique as to make any comparisons with other groups on a single income scale rather uninformative. The above table challenges the idea that "poverty is rather evenly spread", discussed further below.

At the village level, income inequalities are a function of such factors as differences in land and cattle ownership, the use of hired as opposed to family labour, the quality of agricultural technology employed (hand hoe, oxen, tractor), access to credit and farm inputs, marketing and off-farm income earning opportunities. Low levels of social differentiation may be conceptualised within the well-known Chayanovian view of peasant society, in which the welfare of peasant families varies according to the stage in the cyclical development of the peasant household, which determines the number of old and young dependents and thus the availability of labour. The gender composition and health and strength of family members will also affect peasant family fortunes and misfortunes (Chayanov 1966).

The Chayanovian view of inequality is that it tends to even out between peasant households since only the amount of production will take place which meets the collective needs of individual households, and beyond which boredom and drudgery make further productive effort irrational. The key feature distinguishing peasant from capitalist economy is that in the former labour is not costed as an input to production. The same argument has been used in reverse to explain the persistence of peasant economies in Europe well into the modern age: self-exploitation within a basically capitalist agricultural sector, goes beyond an "economically rational" level in peasant households for whom land ownership is a traditional cultural norm.

If land is relatively freely available, correlating household welfare with labour availability seems a sensible procedure. According to Tinios et. al., there is a significant inverse relationship between family size, number of dependent children and poverty in both urban and rural households. Considering just the rural data, very poor, poor, and non-poor households have respectively 7.22, 6.98, and 5.64 members, and 2.98, 2.94, and 2.11 children under the age of thirteen (op.cit., Table 6.2.1). But many under 13s are not enroled in school or take time off during the peak agricultural season (TADREG 1992a, 1993). Girls and boys farm, look after young children, and tend livestock. Are they workers or dependents? Secondary analysis of census data (not performed to date to our knowledge) could shed more light on the important question of family size and poverty. The "availability" of labour is a concept which needs to be handled carefully. Since income from labour is generally not shared equally between household members its availability is likely to be a terrain of negotiation and struggle.[2]

Those who maintain that poverty is relatively evenly spread in rural Tanzania argue that, unlike in Asia and Latin America, land is not generally in short supply, whereas labour and technology generally are (Sarris and van den Brink 1993). Thus "... most people can ensure their food needs through subsistence production, and it is that circumstance that probably accounts for the low degree of inequality." (p.188) The authors' conclusion that inequality is generally low contrasts with the findings of Tinios et.al. reported above. Also, the idea that "land" is not in short supply does not hold in Kilimanjaro, Bukoba, Upare, Lushoto, and parts of Mwanza, Morogoro, Mbeya, Iringa, and other densely populated and highly commercialised parts of the country, however true it may be "in general". Perhaps the conclusion should be that the availability of good quality arable land and other resources is highly variable and, in a context of population growth and environmental deterioration, a subject of much future research interest. The question of inter- and intra-"village" inequality is clearly relevant and important to study in this context. For the moment, there is no consensus in the literature on the issue.

The well-watered highland, banana/coffee/livestock farming system is inherently more productive than the semi-arid, pastoral, agro-pastoralist or coastal cashew/cassava systems, and has higher potential for intensification, improving yields and maintaining environmental balance (FSG/Sokoine 1992). The degree of market involvement and mean household income in the different systems will vary accordingly. There are inequalities in household income both within and between different locations and farming systems, with a large share of inequality being inter-"regional".

Potential surpluses are not realised in any of the above farming systems as a result of inefficient marketing, credit, farm inputs supply, pricing, extension services and other factors. The low functional efficiency of the state bureaucracy and the continued politico-bureaucratic control of much of the agricultural economy, despite a decade of "liberalisation", further inhibit economic growth and help perpetuate widespread poverty. Whereas from 1976 to 1986 Kenya coffee smallholders received between 77 and 98 percent of world market prices, Tanzanian smallholders received between 23 and 37 percent (Lele 1989:9). Post-liberalisation devaluations which should have allowed sustained increases in farm gate prices tended to benefit the unreformed cooperative unions and marketing boards (Booth 1991).

Is there a demonstrable relationship between cattle ownership and household income, expenditure and poverty? Collier et.al. (1990:54-5) claim that "livestock ownership is ... a decisive factor in explaining income inequality. '...in a sense, livestockness' is the Tanzanian equivalent of landlessness in rural Asia, ... and it is this which differentiates the rural population into two sizeable groups ... among those who own livestock it is likely to be a substantial source of income." (Quoted partially in World Bank 1993:48). Likewise, a 1980 study found that "Differences in living standards were largely attributable to differences in human capital and in ownership of non-labor resources such as livestock." (World Bank 1993, citing World Bank Development Report 1990. [The 1980 study is not identified]). Tinios et.al. found that among the rural very poor 8.6 percent of household annual expenditure consisted of livestock products, compared to 14.6 percent for the non-poor (op.cit. Table 6.2.2).

Though significant, these figures hardly support the idea of livestock ownership as being *the* vital differentiating factor in rural poverty. Trying to prove that owning cattle is or is not an index of relative wealth on the basis of survey results does not seem a very fruitful activity. A better approach might be to consider pastoralism in relation to state policy, land law, and competition over natural resources between farmers, game parks/hunting, and pastoralists. The Lands Commission Report (Shivji forthcoming) documented a rapid commercialisation of farm, range, and peri-urban land following the liberalisation policies of the World Bank and the government. As the Lands Commission report was presented to the President, the government was pushing legislation through parliament abolishing traditional land tenure rights. The incidence of local and foreign purchasing of land titles for tourism, hunting, cattle ranching and commercial farming (or simple speculation) is so high that landlessness may become a major political issue in coming years. The question of the impact of government policy on pastoralists (it is said to stimulate landlessness and the growth of a cattle owning "petty bourgeoisie") is discussed in Mustapha (1990).

GENDER AND POVERTY

As this is the theme of a separate chapter by Mbughuni (in this volume), only a summary treatment of the gender dimension of poverty is presented here. According to the Tinios study, in Tanzania as a whole, female headed households are less common among the poor than the non-poor. This finding is surprising and contradicts the popular view that single-parent female-headed households constitute one of the most "vulnerable groups" (Mbilinyi, Sender and Smith). However, dividing the variable into its urban and rural components reveals a divergent pattern: whereas in Dar es Salaam female headed households constitute 12.4 and 14.5 percent of very poor and non-poor households respectively, in rural areas the figures are 11.7 percent female headed households among the very poor and only 5.7 percent for the non-poor (Tinios op.cit Table 6.2.1). FSG/Sokoine University found significant differences in a composite score of household and personal possessions between more and less highly-endowed zones (Mbozi, Hai versus Dodoma, Newala, Urambo). (1992 Volume 1:174-5). Female headed households were disproportionately poor in terms of possessions in Newala, Kwimba and Mbozi, above average in the richest area (Hai, Urambo) and about equal in the poorest zone (Dodoma). We would agree with FSG/Sokoine University's sensible conclusion that researchers should try to avoid:

> the danger of making general statements about the relative wealth or poverty of rural households. Local factors seem to predominate in determining who is poor and why. (1992, Vol.1:175).

Not enough is known about the impact of economic crisis and adjustment policy on women farmers and workers. One interpretation is that both "the crisis" and adjustment policy "augment the processes of impoverishment, proletarianisation and peripheralisation of labouring women." (Mbilinyi 1991:ix). On the other hand, if in towns and some rural areas female-headed households more than hold their own in income terms, it would seem that some women are also capable of taking advantage of income generating opportunities. There is evidence that the most significant income generating opportunities for women have been in the parallel economy (ibid). Off-farm income opportunities, including farm labour, petty trade and plantation work, lead to both an intensification of women's workload (they still have domestic, including farming, responsibilities) but to the possible loosening up of gender relations, to the extent that it is less feasible for the male head of household to appropriate the value of female labour than under a mixed subsistence-cashcrop household economy (Tripp 1989). These examples alert us to the issue of income distribution within the household and changes in distribution under different economic regimes (Sender and Smith 1990).

SOURCES OF INCOME

A common division of source of income is own consumption, sale of crops, off-farm income, and transfers. Not surprisingly, the poor have a higher proportion of own consumption in their total income than the non-poor, of which cereals and other staples are the major component. According to Tinios (op.cit: Table 6.2.2) total purchases for the rural very poor were just over half of total household consumption compared with two-thirds for the non-poor. Own production of food accounted for 43 percent of consumption of the rural very poor, and 32 percent of the non-poor.

Off farm income as a percentage of total income is probably higher for the less poor rural households than for the poor or very poor, reflecting different education levels and consequent income earning opportunities (Collier et.al. 1990). The post liberalisation period has seen a rapid increase in off-farm income opportunities, an especially significant trend given the relative stagnation in agriculture under "adjustment" policies. Highly labour-intensive gold and gemstone mining is estimated to employ at least as many workers as the government sector (Chachage 1992). According to Booth et.al. (1993:73) this trend could lead to "a decline in the relative position of the poor."

However, in a study of six farm production systems on mainland Tanzania the Food Studies Group/Sokoine University found that less than five percent of respondents reported employment or self-employment outside agriculture as their main occupation (1992, Vol.1:171). A significant minority of agro-pastoralists gave off farm income as their major source of livelihood. Food produced by the household lasted from between 9 months (Hai) and 11.5 months (Mbozi) with very little variation over a three year period (1988-90). Pre-harvest purchases varied from 34 percent of household consumption (Hai) to 12 percent (Newala, Mbozi) (Vol.3:12). Most households reduce food insecurity by combining cash crop and subsistence production. It is possible that the poorest of the poor are increasingly surviving on casual labour on others' (including smallholders and plantation) land, with payment in kind (food) or through access to land for subsistence, but longitudinal data are not available to identify trends.

An important type of poverty is that related to temporal shortages of food, for example, pre-harvest lean months. Poor people often sell food crops when they have a surplus and buy at higher prices during the lean months. Food shortages during these months may be reflected in levels of malnutrition, disease, epidemics, even infant mortality. However, a village case study by Bantje (1980) found that low birth weight was more closely correlated to demands for female labour than to short-term food availability or other factors.

In many semi-arid areas, more serious food shortages, even famine, occur every few years as the rains invariably fail from time to time. Such crop failures can wipe out food reserves, both local and national, and could conceivably push the most vulnerable groups into the "extremely poor" category for longer or shorter periods. The very poor are by definition the least likely to be able to go into the market to earn money and/or buy food when subsistence crops fail. Thus the importance of early warning systems for poor harvests and the efficient mobilisation of national surpluses and food aid, all of which depend on a well-functioning state bureaucracy.

PUBLIC GOODS

Access to public goods such as education and health facilities is ignored in much of the poverty literature. Education levels are usually strongly related to income and consumption levels, and to indices of malnutrition, discussed below. As a result of earlier policies, primary schools and health facilities are much more equally spread throughout rural Tanzania than in many other poor African countries. But using measures such as primary school enrolment ratios and distance from nearest water source or health clinic as indices of welfare ignores the question of the functioning and quality of the services available. Going to school is not much use if it fails to inculcate literacy. There are indications that an incomplete primary education is as good as no education at all when it comes to behaviourial change (e.g. family size, child nutritional practices and mortality). Thus gains from increased availability of services may be vitiated by the poor quality of the service provided. Donor-funded water projects are often not properly maintained on completion, indicating the use of inappropriate technology or failure to involve the local community, especially women, in project implementation (Therkilsden 1989).

TADREG found there was no correlation between immunization status and distance from nearest immunization facility in two poor districts in Singida Region (TADREG 1992b). Mother's education level (none vs primary) did not affect immunization status either.

An analysis of primary enrolment ratios showed significant variations between districts, from a low of around 30 percent of 7-13 year olds to a high of around 70 percent (TADREG 1992a). Examination performance also varied significantly between districts and between boys and girls. The best performing districts were almost all urban. There is a relatively high concentration of Grade A teachers in the urban areas, although schools are overcrowded compared to many rural areas. Overall, enrolment ratios are falling nationally, and "the entire sector is seriously underperforming and in many cases no longer appears to provide a service which parents are prepared or able to make good use of." (TADREG op.cit.p24).

This conclusion was strongly corroborated by a follow up study of parental attitudes towards primary education in rural areas (TADREG 1993). The present policy of "cost sharing" at all levels and the rapid expansion of private secondary education is likely to increase inequalities based on locality, ethnicity, class and religion. Fewer girls may obtain government boarding school places if and when the district quota is abandoned. Half the places in government day schools are "reserved" for girls.

NUTRITIONAL

Since inadequate nutrition has been chosen as the basic criterion for defining poverty, it is important to examine the recent literature on food availability and trends in nutritional status. As with the income and consumption issues discussed above, we find the available data rather inconclusive.

Table 3 summarises regional data on three measures of malnutrition for children under five years of age.

Table 3: Indices of Malnutrition for under 5s by Region, Tanzania Mainland 1991/92

Height for age	Weight for height	Weight for age
Dar es Salaam 28	Dodoma 2.6	Mara 18.9
Shinyanga 35	Iringa 3.1	Shinyanga 19.7
Mara 37	Rukwa 4.1	Dar es Salaam 19.
Arusha 39	Ruvuma 4.5	Mwanza 20.7
Mwanza 39	Mwanza 4.5	Tabora 24.1
Kilimanjaro 40	Mara 4.5	Mbeya 24.4
Singida 40	Tabora 4.8	Rukwa 25.2
Tanga 44	Kagera 5.0	Kilimanjaro 26.0
Kagera 44	Kilimanjaro 5.2	Kagera 26.8
Tabora 45	Morogoro 5.4	Lindi 28.5
Rukwa 48	Kigoma 5.5	Arusha 29.4
Mbeya 50	Shinyanga 5.5	Tanga 30.5
Kigoma 52	Mbeya 5.6	Ruvuma 32.9
Coast 55	Lindi 5.8	Singida 33.5
Ruvuma 57	Arusha 5.9	Morogoro 34.0
Lindi 58	Coast 6.0	Kigoma 34.1
Dodoma 59	Dar es Salaam 6.8	Coast 36.7
Morogoro 61	Mtwara 6.8	Dodoma 37.0
Iringa 61	Singida 6.8	Iringa 37.1
Mtwara 65	Tanga 14.7	Mtwara 48.7

Source: Adapted from Bureau of Statistics, Demographic and Health Survey 1991/92 p. 109. Note: Figures represent percentage of children below -2 standard deviations of the median of the reference population. (N=6095)

By the definitions used, nearly half the mainland sample was found to be stunted (46.6 percent, Zanzibar 47.9), and 19.7 percent were classified as severely stunted (-3 SD or more from the median). In numerical terms, more than 2 million children are moderately malnourished (under 80 percent standard weight for age) and nearly 300,000 are severely malnourished (under 60 percent standard weight for age) (UNICEF 1990). Stunting is an index of long-term malnutrition: in terms of weight for height, the figures are much lower, indicating that although many of the children surveyed were short for their age they were not underweight for their height (an index of short-term malnutrition). Only in Mtwara, Lindi and Coast do children appear to be both stunted and underweight for their height. These three regions also appear at the bottom of the weight for age index, which does not   distinguish between long-term malnutrition (stunting) or more immediate malnutrition (wasting). Iringa and Dodoma appear   near the bottom of the first and third anthropomorphic measures of malnutrition and at the top of the second,   indicating a high degree of adjustment to chronic long-term malnutrition. It is doubtful whether much meaningful analysis can be performed at such an aggregate level as the region. One suspects that variations in the incidence of malnutrition are high within regional sub-populations. There are no district level data available, although many village case studies have been undertaken over the years (Kavishe 1990, Unicef 1990).

There appears to be no significant difference in malnutrition between children whose mothers have not gone to school and those who have incomplete primary education. Children whose mothers completed primary and secondary/higher education are significantly less malnourished on both height for age and weight for age measures (Bureau of Statistics, op.cit. p.109). There are no significant differences between boys and girls on any of the three indices.

Measures of mothers' body mass show Mtwara, Arusha, and Coast to have the most underweight mothers and Shinyanga, Dar es Salaam and Iringa to have the fewest (ibid. p.112).

FOOD, HEALTH, DISEASE, MORTALITY

Measures of national food production and availability usually show a positive balance, while nutritional surveys indicate insufficient calorific consumption and widespread malnutrition. TFNC figures for 1987/88 indicate a national food production level of 122 percent of calorific requirements accompanied by a moderate protein energy malnutrition level of 28 percent (affecting 6.2 million people) and severe PEM of 3 percent (0.7 million) nationally (cited in Kavishe op.cit.).

This apparent contradiction between food production and consumption has been explained in terms of socio-cultural norms concerning feeding and weaning, rural women's workload which prevents regular feeding, and unequal consumption at the household level. Other possible explanations are the practice of selling post-harvest surpluses and then buying (at higher prices) during pre-harvest shortages, the tendency for food production statistics to be exaggerated, and the coexistence of food surplus and food deficit areas in the country. (The 1988 regional figures show Lindi, Coast and Dodoma to be all food deficit regions, satisfying respectively only 78, 71, and 64 percent of food requirements). But in general "the rates of malnutrition in different areas of the country are not correlated with agricultural production." (Sarris and van den Brink 1993:136).

There are no major large-scale attempts to study the interrelationship between nutritional status, morbidity, and mortality, although it is widely accepted that malnutrition contributes to both illness and death, particularly among young children. Severely malnourished children in Tanzania are 11 times more likely to die from disease than adequately nourished children (UNICEF 1990). For moderately and mildly malnourished children the corresponding figures are three times and twice as likely to die than adequately nourished children.

The following table shows that life expectancy has risen and infant and child mortality fallen steadily over the years.

Table 4: Trends in Life Expectancy
and Child Mortality in Tanzania

Year	Life expectancy	IMR	CMR	U5MR
1957	35	190	110	300
1967	41	160	101	261
1978	51	137	100	231
1988	54	107	72	179

Key: IMR: death 0-12 months
CMR: deaths 13-60 months
U5MR: deaths 0-60 months
Source: Kavishe (1990)

Another source quotes current life expectancy of 49 for men and 50 for women, and IMR and U5MR of 115 and 192 respectively (TGNP 1993:98). If reliable, these figures indicate a disturbing reversal of the secular trend in life expectancy and child mortality. HIV/AIDS has been systematically decimating certain social, economic and ethnic groups, and may be a contributory cause to such a trend among both children and adults. By 1990, nearly half a million women of child bearing age (7 percent of the adult female population) were estimated to be infected with HIV on Tanzania mainland (URT 1993:17). Cuddington (1993:186) estimates that as a result of AIDS by the year 2010 the Tanzanian economy will be between 15 and 25 percent smaller than it would have been without AIDS. The author claims that this is a conservative estimate. The poverty implications of the continued spread of HIV/AIDS are obvious and dramatic, and will be the subject of considerable future research initiatives.

National maternal mortality rates of between 200 and 400 per 100,000 births are cited in the literature, or between 2,000 and 4,000 deaths a year. It is extremely difficult to establish national or local trends in maternal mortality, given the large margin of error involved in measurement. Causes of maternal mortality are discussed in TGNP (1993:99-100).

District rankings of infant and under five mortality for Tanzania mainland are available for 1985 (Unicef). The lowest levels reported are in cattle-herding districts in Arusha Region (Ngorongoro, Monduli, Arumeru). In Table 3 Arusha was above average for height for age, but below average on the other two indices of malnutrition. One wonders whether a common measure of height for age is appropriate when, for instance, Maasai are quite clearly genetically taller than the Bantu tribes further south. There is no reason to assume that infant and child mortality is below average among pastoralists. Kilimanjaro's six districts are all in the lowest ten in terms of infant mortality, although this would not be predicted from the rather average ranking of Kilimanjaro Region in Table 3.

Maternal education is closely related to child mortality rates, varying from an U5MR of 162 among children of uneducated mothers to 101 for those with post primary education (Bureau of Statistics 1993:73). This source comes up with the rather unlikely finding that there is no difference in mortality rates between urban and rural areas (ibid.).

A serious problem with using calorific consumption levels as a proxy for poverty and risk of ill-health/mortality is that it is hazardous to assume that chronic undernutrition automatically means high morbidity or risk of death. According to Pacey and Payne (1985:56), even the 1500 Kcal per day limit, which we have taken as separating the poor from the very poor, "refers to people who are likely to be experiencing hunger, often painfully and for long periods, but whose essential body functions are not impaired." The technical issue is that "we do not know the efficiency with which energy in food is converted and used by the body." (ibid.). Thus:

Malnutrition can be detected only by biochemical, anthropometric or physiological tests. It cannot be deduced from an individual's level of food intake, nor can it be estimated from the average intake of the population. (p.39)

People have different calorific requirements in different climatic zones (cool highlands, hot lowlands), but this does not seem to be taken into account in studies of nutrition. Generally:

whether or not a person suffers from malnutrition depends on factors such as the ecological setting, the season, the incidence of disease, the domestic environment, the work being done, control over production, the wages received, and the market price for food. The aim would be to understand the epidemiology of malnutrition in terms of its distribution among various ecological regions and socio-economic classes." (p.121).

This is a substantial critique of the rationale for using *imputed* aggregate calorie consumption as a proxy for poverty. It seems extremely improbable that research could ever establish valid and reliable causal relations between nutrition, health status and mortality on any other than an extremely limited (micro) level. However, there is a clear and well established correlation between levels of malnutrition and vulnerability to disease and death in infants and young children.

TRENDS IN THE INCIDENCE OF POVERTY

We have found throughout this literature survey that there is little or no agreement among researchers, even in broad terms, as to who have been the income and welfare winners and losers in the pre- and post adjustment periods. Two main interpretations of the crisis period can be identified. One school maintains that the poor in both urban and rural areas did not suffer unduly during the crisis years as a result of their high degree of auto-consumption and opportunities to operate in the parallel economy. Since the urban middle class are more dependent on the market, they are more vulnerable to external economic shocks. "... some of the households earlier classified as middle class must have fallen below the poverty line by the mid-to-late 1980s." The crisis even *benefited* medium and large farmers who increased food and cash crop production for the parallel market. (Sarris and van den Brink 1993:189). After adjustment began in 1984, to 1989, these same medium and large farmers suffered a real income decline, as did the upper income urban households. We can only speculate on what has happened to income in the post-1989 period. The involvement of the urban middle class in second economy activities on a vast scale, particularly in the adjustment period, is not mentioned.

Other similar conclusions come from Collier (1986), who claims that rural incomes rose by 25 percent between 1976 and 1980, and Bevan (1990) who identifies a 50 percent improvement between 1976 and 1982. Sarris and Tinios (1993) find a 50 percent increase in per capita expenditure between 1976 and 1991, and a substantial fall in inequality of income distribution during the same period. Malyamkono and Bagachwa (1990) explain apparent falls in economic activity by the rise of the informal economy during the "crisis" period.

A contrasting school of thought finds significant declines in income for the majority of the population during the "crisis" period (1978/9-1983/4), with adjustment bringing significant income gains in recent years. According to Wagao and Kigoda (1993:16) rural incomes fell by no less than 50 percent between 1976 and 1982, and urban incomes by 50 percent between 1976 and 1984. The World Bank (1993:14-15) claims that incomes have risen in the period of adjustment (especially after 1984/86); one source claims that average rural incomes increased by *367 percent* between 1982 and 1992! Another controversial assessment is that under adjustment "in rural areas, while food consumption has increased substantially, non-food consumption has been broadly constant per capita." (World Bank 1991:35).

An intermediary position is that "the majority of rural people are not rich and their incomes fell rapidly during the crisis and adjustment processes." (Mtatifikolo 1992:65). According to FSG/Sokoine University: "... it is the relatively larger and richer farmers that have shown themselves more capable of responding to incentives" by being able to take risks and obtain scarce inputs (1992,Vol.1:182). In recent years, maize and rice markets have expanded, tobacco, cotton and cashew production increased, but coffee production has stagnated or fallen as farmers turn to dairy and vegetables. Improved producer prices do not explain more than a part of the increases, however (ibid p.182/3).

It is part of the folk memory of those who lived through the crisis years that the extreme shortages of consumer goods in both urban and rural areas was the major negative influence on consumption during the late seventies and early eighties. Local industries were operating at a small fraction of capacity, and imports were largely limited to cross-border smuggling. CDP et al (1987) found that in the majority of 65 sample villages in Tanga and Mwanza Regions items such as sugar, cooking oil, soap, kerosene, cigarettes, basic clothing and footwear were rarely or never available (1986 data). Shortages were so widespread that both the better and worse off income groups had similar consumption preferences. Two years later the situation had changed dramatically, as "own-funds" imports of consumer goods flooded into the country, financed largely by parallel economy activities (Cooksey 1989). The argument that only the urban middle class suffered as a result of "the crisis" is counter-intuitive to say the least, even when we include second economy activities of all kinds.

Although as Wagao and Kigoda state "The statistical base for providing judgement on the ... level and trend of income inequality ... is exceedingly weak" (1993:12-13) this has not prevented different observers from presenting their conclusions with a high degree of confidence and conviction.   I n summary, there is general agreement that poverty is widespread in Tanzania, particularly in rural areas. But there the agreement ends. The main studies of the incidence of and trends in poverty mentioned above come to diametrically opposed conclusions on major issues, including the depth and spatial distribution of poverty, its inter- or intra-community nature, and the impact of economic crisis and adjustment policies on various income and occupational groups. Explanations for these conflicting views must lie in the theories, research methodologies, data collection techniques and analytical approaches which are implicit or explicit in the different studies. The studies reviewed are largely descriptive rather than analytical and quantitative rather than qualitative. Much depends, therefore, on the reliability of the survey data and the indices of poverty employed.

Although it is beyond the scope of the present chapter to look more deeply into these intriguing and vitally important issues, they should be incorporated into any future research strategy. In particular, the *structural relations* of poverty need to be theorised in advance of data collection. These relations can be identified from the face to face to the global level. An approach which sees poverty essentially in terms of inadequate income, consumption, or employment opportunities is a poor basis for explaining poverty in terms of socio-economic relations. This theme is discussed further in the final section below.

ADJUSTMENT AND POVERTY

In some respects the new interest in poverty is a result of the criticisms levelled against the World Bank concerning the distributional impact of SAPs (Gibbon 1992). According to the original World Bank strategy, a successful SAP in a country like Tanzania is supposed to benefit the mass of smallholder families by improving the rural-urban terms of trade. Thus SAPs benefit the poor. This holds for both food grain and export crop producers. Although this is clearly a sound basis for questioning the rationale of the "adjustment with a human face" school of thought, the World Bank seems to have assimilated the "vulnerable groups" analysis in order to deflect criticism of its own lending record.

There are nevertheless sound reasons for not making too quick a leap from adjustment to improved income or welfare. Short-term reasons are discussed here, longer-term issues are discussed in a later section.

First, liberalisation to date seems to have increased the price of farm inputs and the marketing margins of marketing board and cooperative unions but not improved farm gate prices for export crops in real terms for more than a short period in the mid eighties (World Bank 1990:114). Supply responses on the part of export crop producers have therefore been weak, and some argue more related to increased supply of consumer goods and less inefficient marketing than to improved prices. Grain liberalisation has not improved farm gate prices but has improved the efficiency of marketing by ending the monopoly of the National Milling Corporation. However, private traders are less willing than NMC and cooperative unions to haul grain uneconomically from remote areas for the Dar es Salaam market, which could have the effect of increasing regional income inequalities.

Another set of problems relates to the patriarchal nature of much village society. There is a school of thought which sees no necessary relationship between rising real income from agriculture, trade, or off-farm income and improvements in household nutritional status. Apparent increases in malnutrition in a context of increased commoditisation may reflect oppressive gender relations. For example, there may be an intensification of women's labour requirements not rewarded with income from crop sales, which may end up as discretionary consumption of the head of household (Mbilinyi 1990). On the other hand, levels of infant and child mortality in most of rural Kilimanjaro Region, where commoditisation is far advanced by national standards, are lower than in most urban areas of the country.

The partial nature of economic liberalisation is reflected in the apparent increase in off-farm income generation through trade, casual employment, and mining. According to Booth et.al. (1993:71) "further diversification of household efforts into commercial activities and casual wage-earning places greater weight on locational advantages, and less on land resources, than would a more agricultural based recovery."

CAUSES OF POVERTY

> Poverty is not simply a matter of physical and material deprivation but a much more complex social phenomenon with economic, cultural and socio-political dimensions. (Wagao and Kigoda 1993:4)

The causes of poverty are multiple and highly complex in their interrelationships. The preceding text has relatively little to say about causality. Like the studies which it cites, it is mainly concerned with describing rather than explaining the incidence of poverty. The descriptive approach has severe limitations: there is little understanding of the incidence or trajectory of poverty in Tanzania, even ignoring the definitional problems mentioned in the text. *A more holistic approach to poverty research is called for, an approach which is sensitive to the influences of ecological and environmental, social, cultural and economic forces, and to their interrelations.* To date, there has been no attempt to link global, national and local causes of poverty into a general theory. Such an undertaking would be very ambitious. Some of the major issues are discussed below.

The global context

Some observers see the radical liberalisation of trade following the recent NAFTA and GATT agreements as likely to cause further polarisation between rich and poor both within and between developed and underdeveloped regions and countries. The following quotation illustrates an extreme version of this point of view:

> The globalisation of market forces has already undermined local and regional ways of life in many parts of the world. For the Third World, global free trade means the destruction of agrarian communities and peasant traditions, as local farming practices are undercut by mechanised western agribusiness. This in turn means the accelerated migration of impoverished agricultural workers to swollen mega-cities. ... In both Third and First Worlds the Gatt proposals are a recipe for social upheaval and political instability on a vast scale. (John Gray, *Guardian Weekly* 21 November, 1993, p.12).

According to a recent World Bank/OECD report, two-thirds of the benefits of the new GATT agreement will accrue to the OECD countries themselves. "In Indonesia, sub-Saharan Africa, North Africa and the Mediterranean countries ... real incomes are expected to decline - together they will lose some $7 billion a year in earnings. The GDP of African countries is expected to decline by between 0.2 and 0.5 percent." (Goldin I, Knudsen O and van der Mensbrugghe D, (1993), cited in The Ecologist Vol 23, No 6 Nov/Dec 1993, p220).

It is difficult to imagine an economic recovery strategy for Tanzania or other primary produce exporters which does not include a heavy dose of export promotion; yet the above gloomy prognosis seems to imply that increased trade (and competition between producing nations) hold out little hope of economic salvation. The "external" backdrop for poverty research in Tanzania must be the growing challenge posed by competition for international markets.

The Local Context

The internal liberalisation of agricultural markets under SAPs mirrors the global policies of the IFIs, the multinational corporations, the USA and its major trading partners. Analysis of the distributional consequences of economic growth often assumes a national frame of reference. Recent studies conclude that rapid economic growth from a relatively low base is not incompatible with poverty reduction (World Bank 1990). But Tanzania is not South Korea or Taiwan. The negative aggregate impact of export promotion on the terms of trade for tropical products is often cited as a major weakness of the IFI's prescription for economic recovery in sub-Saharan Africa.

Other poverty-relevant elements of the liberalisation strategy are the recent abolition of traditional land rights, which is leading to land grabbing for agriculture, ranching, hunting, tourism, mining or speculative purposes. Similarly, increasing export incentives may have serious environmental consequences, tobacco growing being one obvious example. Since market liberalisation has so far largely failed to improve export incentives for traditional crops (coffee, tea, cotton, tobacco, [partially] cashews), the environmental impact of the policy is yet to be fully appreciated. Some environmentalists argue that present forms of economic development may be fundamentally incompatible with environmental conservation. This issue should be a major focus of future "poverty" research, including sustainable agricultural practices and technology, forestry, and water management (Kikula and Mwalyosi 1993:14,19). Which sections of the poor stand to lose (or gain?) most under a more market-oriented economic regime should also be a subject for future research.

Anecdotal evidence and press reports indicate a huge misuse of donor import support funds and widespread tax evasion by both the private and the parastatal sectors. The accumulated losses of state industries, marketing boards, and cooperative unions represent an enormous drain on national resources and continue to compromise reform efforts. Donor agencies are becoming increasingly impatient with the Tanzanian government's inability to implement the institutional reforms (parastatal closure/privatisation, civil service retrenchment, liberalisation of agricultural marketing) contained in past Economic Recovery Programmes. Without the current US$1.2 billion annual injection of donor funding (three times the value of exports) it is hard to imagine how the Tanzanian economy could survive.

There are few major published works which attempt to analyse the linkages between the politics and economics of the liberalisation period, although Booth et. al. (1993) have made a useful start in this direction. In their study of 12 villages throughout the country, the authors found little evidence that economic liberalisation was having a beneficial impact on smallholder agriculture. There was a widespread feeling, especially among women, that "multipartism" could put an end to Tanzania's enviable post-independence record of "peace and tranquillity". Recent unpublished survey results from eight mainland regions reveal a widespread feeling among villagers that the ruling CCM party has abandoned its traditional concern for the welfare of farmers and the poor to the advantage of businessmen, traders and foreign commercial interests (Sivalon forthcoming). Although CCM is widely seen to have failed to bring development to the rural areas, there is little or no faith that the opposition parties and leaders could do any better. In the first multi-party by-election to be held in the country (Ileje, January 1994), the CCM candidate received about three-quarters of votes cast. Less than 20 percent of Sivalon's sample said they would vote for an opposition party presidential candidate running against any of the top possible CCM candidates.

Who Cares About Poverty?

Who is concerned with poverty issues, and why? At the level of policy and research, the two main candidates are the government and the donor community. The poverty concern, which was once a major theme of local policy-making, has become very much a donor theme in recent years, first through the initiative of Unicef and then the World Bank and a range of bilateral donors. The local research and policy interest is largely, though not entirely, donor-driven. Since liberalisation, poverty issues have not been a major preoccupation of the government, as pointed out elsewhere in this report.

Donor agency activities regarding poverty issues need not correspond to their formal policy positions, of course. Many examples could be cited demonstrating the possible deleterious effects of both trade and aid on different population groups. The GATT/OECD projections of the benefits of trade liberalisation foresee both winners and losers, with SSA as the main loser. Aid flows could increasingly come to mean balance of payments support to compensate for worsening terms of trade and loss of market share.

The European Community was recently shown to be dumping subsidised beef in West Africa at the expense of Sahelian cattle owners (Eurostep 1993). Large-scale waste and misuse of EC development assistance has recently been revealed (Guardian Weekly November 28/11/93). Poor performance in the use of development assistance over the years has brought the donor-recipient relationship under increasing scrutiny (NGDO-EC News November 1993:2). This source indicates that "Less than 1.8% of the funds from the 6th EDF had been allocated to health at the end of 1992, and only 3% to education and training." International pressure to increase aid flows ignores the fact that these are often counterproductive from the point of view of poor people. *The proposition that current "aid" increases poverty is highly provocative, not to be dismissed lightly, and should be included in any poverty research agenda.*

Many local examples could be cited concerning project assistance with a poverty rationale (small-scale credit for women, support for NGOs, education, health and water projects, job creation in the informal sector) where non-intended beneficiaries more or less predominate. World Bank projects in Tanzania and elsewhere, especially in Africa, consistently show negative rates of return. Despite constant critical internal assessments on its own performance and the poor "absorptive capacity" of borrowing countries, and growing international condemnation of its record in project aid, the World Bank continues to launch large projects in countries like Tanzania (Msemakweli, November 1993).

The World Bank's 1990 *Making Adjustment Work for the Poor* does not explore the idea that governments and donor agencies may not have the political or managerial capacities to target vulnerable groups as in the examples cited above. The World Bank's conversion to the "poverty with a human face" school of thought and its relation to the SDA programme is discussed in Gibbon (1993:46).

It has been argued that structural adjustment policies privileging "market forces" inevitably generate classes of winners and losers. The threshold beyond which investment in mitigating the effects of adjustment becomes counterproductive from the point of view of enhancing economic growth (and growth is the main objective of adjustment) has been defined by the Bank as extremely low; thus its modest anti-poverty programmes (Gibbon op.cit). Is it possible that the future of Tanzania's farmers and cattle-owners will be increasingly threatened by the agribusiness multinationals which control the grain trade and the protectionist/dumping practices of the surplus producing nations? This is not incompatible with the logic of GATT and the traditional SAP free trade strategy. If this is the case, it is difficult to imagine what could be done to mitigate the long-term impact of trade liberalisation on poverty, short of the implausible "delinking" or "autarky" of dependency theory.

POVERTY AND POLICY

Which Audience, Who's Demand?

Researchers may undertake research for multiple purposes and audiences. Some of the major motivations are:

(a) to earn the respect of fellow researchers;

(b) to gain promotion and advance one's career;
(c) to inform policy makers and opinion leaders;
(d) to lobby politicians;
(e) to provide a service to the private sector;
(f) to help churches, NGOs and CBOs fight poverty and injustice;
(g) to contribute to national development;
(h) to support donor agency projects and programmes;
(i) to inform the general public;
(j) to find out what's going on (intellectual curiosity);
(k) to supplement official income;
(i) to obtain rents.

Is there a critical mass of capable researchers with specific motives for 'doing "poverty" research': a disinterested interest in "finding out", a strong desire to influence national policy and the course of events, a commitment to a locality, community or other secondary group, a concern with professionalism and group solidarity? There is a considerable pool of experienced researchers, but of late it has shrunk somewhat for a number of reasons. Those with pressing pecuniary needs are more likely to be tempted to do better paid short-term consultancies than in depth, time consuming and poorly remunerated research. This problem has become so acute at the University of Dar es Salaam that an office has been opened in an attempt to coordinate and formalise individual consultancy work undertaken by staff members. For understandable reasons, some potential researchers are tempted to work for donor agencies and NGOs, which may prevent them from doing research. Many senior researchers also have onerous administrative responsibilities and other commitments.

The upshot of all this is that senior researchers willing and able to work on poverty issues may be in relatively short supply, at least in the short-run. Solutions to this problem could include the following:

(a) training middle-level academics and others to upgrade their research skills;
(b) increasing remuneration for research to make it more competitive with consultancy work;
(c) undertaking joint projects with Northern research centres and universities;
(d) collaboration with research oriented NGOs and private foundations and companies;
(e) lobbying with donor agencies to sponsor researchers to do more research and less consultancy work.

AID AND THE RESEARCH MILIEU

Support for research in Tanzania is often one of numerous components of a bilateral or multilateral aid programmes, with no guarantee of temporal continuity. Ad hoc or more institutional support for research comes from the Rockefeller and Ford Foundations, IDRC, SAREC, and other sources. Budgeted expenditure for research in sectoral institutes and research centres is generally inadequate to do any serious research, so that donors often support the local research body with training opportunities, consultancies, vehicles and equipment, as part of a package of assistance.

Major research funding is usually associated with a donor backed programme or sectoral project. The largest recent example is the Social Dimensions of Adjustment programme (part of the second Economic Recovery Programme) which had an important research component funded by the World Bank and UNDP. This support was coordinated by the Planning Commission. Currently, the Planning Commission is also coordinating the National Plan of Action for women and children, as follow up to the 1991 Children's Summit. Various targeted support for vulnerable groups, including research, figure in the activities of this proposed multi-billion US$ programme. Other donor supported programmes with a poverty focus and research components include the current World Bank Social Sector Strategy and Unicef's Child Survival and Development programme. Coordination of these activities with government ministries, including the research components, remains a problem. Although its future is uncertain, the Planning Commission works closely with the Treasury in developing a social sector policy and securing donor support.

The Social Dimensions of Adjustment project did little primary research and has led to no new poverty initiatives to date. According to Wagao and Kigoda:

> the SDA project has not adequately addressed the framework within which the poor can be assisted ... there seems to be no action-oriented measures which could link analysis and programmes of action." (op.cit.p.62)

According to Mtatifikolo (1992:66) there was no clear link between the SDA programme and the government's macro policies. There seems to be no formal linkage between the Unicef-inspired NPA and the SDA or its successor programme, even though they share a number of similar components.

The current education 8th IDA (US$35m) has a large research component, but to date very little research has been commissioned by the Ministry of Education and Culture. The Ministry does not seem to have a research agenda to complement its policy making and planning responsibilities. This is regrettable, given the enormity of the recovery efforts required to restore popular confidence in education.

In the past, some donors have supported the national research coordination body, previously UTAFITI now the Commission of Science and Technology. The major problem with this arrangement is that the relationship between the government body, the government (for policy purposes) and the potential researchers is generally tenuous. A number of donors abandoned this arrangement when they found that their support was being used for general budgetary support or was simply not being used because of the cumbersome procedures involved in commissioning research.

Giving research funds to sectoral ministries can lead to sub-standard work being produced. Another pitfall is that the Ministry may not have a solid research agenda, or indeed, have any interest in looking too closely at what is going on. Insufficient research capacity and self-interest make much Ministry-based research an unpromising option.

The genesis of projects is important. This project originated in the Netherlands and not in Tanzania. There is therefore a typical project problem concerning "ownership". The above discussion suggests that the likelihood of generating practical outcomes from a poverty-oriented research programme has to be demonstrated rather than assumed. Research does not have to have practical relevance, of course, but it is difficult to justify funding a long-term poverty programme which does not attempt to have an impact on the course of events.

The originality of the proposed DGIS research support is that it is long-term, meaning that there will be adequate opportunities to monitor and evaluate its effectiveness, and modify it accordingly. The DGIS programme will have to confront a number of problems in implementation stemming from the points discussed above. At the risk of straying from the themes of this chapter, a number of possible solutions to the problems mentioned above may be suggested.

(a) The programme should be overseen by a small group of experienced researchers drawn from different social science disciplines and diverse institutional settings (university, government, NGO, private sector) and managed by a small full-time secretariat;

(b) Benchmarks for routine monitoring and evaluation of programme performance and impact should be established and respected;

(c) Fees for commissioned studies should be adequate to attract top researchers into participating in a long-term, multiple component research programme;

(d) Formal channels for liaising with and reporting findings to the government, the funding agency, and other interested parties should be spelled out;

(e) The programme should include the publication of a regular research bulletin and hosting regular workshops and conferences;

(f) Studies which relate to academic course work and which can give research exposure to groups of students and junior researchers should be encouraged;

(g) basic research collaboration with Northern universities and research centres should be strongly encouraged.

ELEMENTS OF A RESEARCH STRATEGY
Knowledge Gaps

Surprisingly little is known about the nature and causes of and trends in poverty in Tanzania, as described above. The conceptual and methodological difficulties with household budget surveys and cross-sectional household income/ expenditure surveys have become increasingly evident in this review. It would require great boldness to propose a policy designed to attack the problem of poverty with targeted or other interventions on the basis of available knowledge of its nature, spatial distribution, incidence, and rate of change.

Poverty has been defined *ab extra* as if the personal or collective experience of poverty was of a secondary order of importance. Yet, as is well known, the experience of both absolute and (more crucially) relative poverty has been a powerful source of political action, revolt and revolution throughout recorded history. One hypothesis is that present trends in international and local-level accumulation are preparing the ground for growing political unrest and violence. Whilst this may not be an easily researchable topic, it does suggest that the state could sponsor poverty research not with a view to reducing it but rather to controlling its political consequences. This view is in line with the following gloomy prognosis of future trends in poverty and inequality in Tanzania:

> In the coming years the main dynamics of income distribution will be between the few emerging rich and the majority poor within both the urban and rural sectors and between sectors. Economic differentiation in rural areas is likely to create a growing portion of the rural population which can no longer maintain itself on the land. (Wagao and Kigoda 1993:34)

This review has found that our knowledge of poverty in Tanzania is very limited in all important respects. Where data or research findings exist, serious questions of methodology and the quality of field data arise. Different researchers on all basic issues -incidence, depth, distribution, causes of and trends in poverty - have reached diametrically opposed conclusions. To all intents and purposes, any new poverty research agenda is in certain respects virtually starting from scratch.

Guidelines for Future Poverty Research

A future major poverty research programme should:

(a) Put more emphasis on the subjective experiences of poor people;
(b) Use a mix of methodologies;
(c) Sponsor a mix of in-depth analysis and more strategic research;
(d) Be concerned with multiple causality and micro-meso-macro linkages;
(e) Use existing (eg census) data more thoroughly;
(f) Be more self-critical regarding research methodologies and techniques;
(g) Review research findings and reports in critical fora;
(h) Be more objective and critical in relation to government and donor agencies;
(i) Make research-policy linkages explicit;
(j) Use research as an opportunity for training researchers, and informing the public on trends in poverty;
(k) Aim to be collegial, intersectoral, collaborative, and transparent;
(l) Publish accounts and be cost-conscious and -effective.

Research Themes

Given the huge gaps in existing knowledge, it is rather difficult if not presumptuous to claim to know where a research agenda on poverty issues should start. The present review is more of a partial overview, privileging a particular body of research, and many issues have received little or no attention (e.g. farm systems research, rural and community development, the social sectors, gender analysis, ecological/environmental causes of poverty, the history and anthropology of poverty). More work needs to be done and more researchers and institutions need to be consulted before a meaningful research agenda can be put together.

A number of chapters in the present volume refer to common sectors, themes, and poverty issues, and a few of these can be highlighted. The main thrust of the research proposed in different chapters is towards the identification, measurement, and explanation of poverty, particularly among the rural population. The causal factors figuring in research proposals include ecological/environmental conditions, patriarchal gender relations and other conditioning socio-cultural factors such as family structure and religion. The relationship between politics, government and poverty is another important theme mentioned by a number of authors.

Mbughuni, Omari and Mascarenhas see gender as an important vector of poverty research. Mascarenhas mentions the general relationship between gender, resource management, and conservation as an important research focus.

The multiple demands on the labour of women make it difficult for them to get out of the poverty trap. The growing involvement of women and children in the urban and rural informal economy in response to the economic crisis is mentioned by Omari. Mbughuni also refers frequently to issues of household economy, production, and the informal sector. Thus, *gender and the informalisation process* constitute two major areas for future research.

There is a predominantly *rural* focus in the research proposals, reflecting the rural concentration of the population of Tanzania and the incidence of poverty. But should urban poverty be ignored? Omari and Mbughuni mention some urban research themes. The disproportionate importance of urban poverty (and wealth) as a focus of political action mentioned above and continued rapid urbanisation underline the importance of studying urban poverty.

Chungu and Mandara, Semboja, Mascarenhas and Omari mention the issue of technology. Some of the socio-cultural issues discussed by Omari are also reflected in Mbughuni's chapter. Little or no mention is made of environmental factors except in Mascarenhas' chapter.

Research methodology and relations to policy are discussed in a number of chapters. The need to undertake more intersectoral or holistic research has been stressed above. It is surely vital that future poverty research should contribute to theoretical and methodological debates on the relationship between economic growth and poverty creation/alleviation. Mascarenhas calls for more dialogue between economists and ecologists on the appropriate costing of natural resources and proposes that research should be used to assist in conflict resolution, for example, in relation to the rights of pastoralists. He and Mtatifikolo propose research on the policy process itself, while Omari suggests research on government and donor agency projects and programmes concerned with targeted poverty alleviation. In other "adjusting" countries, resources for alleviating the impact of adjustment have been used primarily to compensate or provide credit for "retrenched" civil servants. Will the same happen in Tanzania? Mtatifikolo mentions the need to coordinate poverty initiatives and suggests an inventory of ongoing poverty research and projects.

A number of chapters discuss the use to which research findings are put. It is clear that informing government and donor policy will be a major goal of the proposed research agenda. A number of chapters carry the message that poverty issues are likely to become more acute in coming years, which is a good reason for studying them. Yet none of the authors distinguish between basic and more strategic or project/ programme related research. Although there is no hard and fast distinction to be drawn between policy and basic research, it is important to be clear on the audiences for whom one undertakes research. The research audience will affect the methodology employed and the means of dissemination of research findings. Although government and funding agencies are the *de facto* primary audiences of most research, other audiences are important too, not least the poor themselves, the general public and local and external non-government development organisations.

Mbughuni sees gender and poverty research as helping to formulate strategies to strengthen the position of poor women to meet their own goals and make a livelihood. Other uses of research mentioned are to develop theoretical and conceptual frameworks in dialogue with field research, and to develop participatory and empowering research methodologies.

Research proposals identify different levels and units of analysis. Mascarenhas mentions the need to situate research on national and community level poverty within a global perspective. The primary focus of Chungu and Mandara is the national economy, in particular the industrial sector. Mascarenhas favours location specific research and a loose district focus for environmental studies in general. There are no proposals in the accompanying chapters for national coverage poverty surveys, but many case studies of one kind or another are proposed. A number of potentially important research themes are mentioned below.

Perennial poverty themes which need to be addressed include the following:

(a) The definition and causes of poverty, starting from a critical appraisal of the methodology, thematic content, and empirical conclusions of past research, and a better use of existing secondary sources and "grey" materials.

(b) Mapping and monitoring the geographical and social incidence of poverty in relation to natural resource endowments, the availability of land, socio-cultural and economic conditions and power relations at different levels. This would include undertaking strategic base-line studies for establishing trends.

Certain themes will emerge with the course of events. For example, any of the following could have important poverty implications meriting research and analysis:

(c) trends in informalisation (growth of informal modes of urban and rural accumulation);

(d) the emergence of non-statist types of political activity including the possible mobilisation of (sections of) the "poor" e.g. to protect the commons and political rights (empowerment);

(e) "natural" disasters: the social dimensions of flooding, drought, pest invasions, epidemics, population movements;

(f)   trends in the quantity and nature of donor support to the government and other local actors; "targeting" aid on the poor; support for the social sectors (health, education, water);

(g)   the impact of sectoral and macro-economic adjustment policies on various population groups;

(h)   the social and environmental consequences of competition over land;

(i)   the potential impact of using different (traditional, alternative, appropriate, labour saving) technologies in agriculture, including organic rather than chemical fertilisers and integrated rather than monocrop agriculture for "sustainable development".

NOTES

1. Bourgeois society is ruled by equivalence. It makes the dissimilar comparable by reducing it to abstract qualities. Such abstraction must wilfully disregard the specificity of the material objects under its consideration." (Adorno and Horkheimer [1944:7], quoted by Docherty [1993:9]). This wilful disregard of specificity is a functional prerequisite of much of the poverty literature reviewed below, and of the totality of international agency comparisons of social and economic "indices" of wealth/poverty and social conditions in different countries.

2. Marjorie Mbilinyi, personal communication.

REFERENCES

Bagachwa, M. and Naho, A. (1993). "A Review of Recent Developments in the Second Economy in Tanzania." Paper Presented At the ATERB/USAID Seminar on Policy and Poverty in Tanzania (November 9-10). Dar es Salaam.

Bantje, H. (1990). "Seasonal Variations in Birthweight Distribution in Ikwiriri Village." BRALUP Research Papers (New Series), No. 43, pp. 23.

Bevan, D.L. et. al. (1988). "Incomes in the United Republic of Tanzania during the Nyerere Experiment". *Employment and Labour Incomes*, pp.61-83.

Booth, D. F. Lugangira, P. Masanja; A. Mvungi;, R. Mwanipopo; J. Mwami and A. Redmayne (1993). *Social, Economic and Cultural Change in Contemporary Tanzania.* Stockholm: SIDA.

Booth, D. (1991). "Timing and Sequencing in Agricultural Policy Reforms: Tanzania." *Development Policy Review*, Vol. 9, pp.353-379.

Bureau of Statistics (1988). *1988 Population Census: Preliminary Report and regional breakdowns.* Dar es Salaam.

Bureau of Statistics (1993). *Demographic and Health Survey* (June). Dar es Salaam.

CDP, AfroAid and BUMACO (1987). "A Survey of Demand Priorities among Villagers in Tanga and Mwanza Regions and Implications for Policy". DGIS, Dar es Salaam (mimeo).

Chachage, S. (1992). "New Forms of Accumulation in Tanzania: The Case of Gold Mining." Paper presented at the Workshop on Structural Adjustment and Social Change, Maseru (November).

Chayanov, A.V. (1925). *Organization Krest'yanskogo Khozyaistva.* translated as *The Theory of Peasant Economy,* D. Thorner, R. Smith and B.Kerblay (eds), Irwin, California, 1966.

Chayanov, A.V. (1966). *The Theory of Peasants Economy.* California: Irwin.

Collier P., Radwan S., and Wangwe S. (1990) *Labour and Poverty in Rural Tanzania.* Oxford: Clarendon.

Cooksey, B. (1989). Incentive Goods in Rural Tanzania 1986-89. A Summary of Research Findings. World Bank.

Cuddington, J.T. (1993). "Modelling the Macroeconomic Effects of Aids with an Application to Tanzania." *The World Bank Economic Review*, Vol. 7, No. 2 (May), pp. 173-189.

Docherty, T. (1993). *Postmodernism, A Reader.* Hemel Hempstead, Harvester/Wheatsheef.

Food Studies Group/Sokoine University (1992). Agricultural Diversification and Intensification Study. International Development Centre, Oxford (3 volumes).

Gibbon, P. (1992). "The World Bank and African Poverty 1973- 91." *Journal of Modern African Studies*, Vol. 30, No. 1., pp.30-49.

Gibbon, P. (1993). "The World Bank and the New Politics of Aid." *European Journal of Development Research*, Vol. 5, No. 1 (June), pp. 135-162.

Goldin, I., Knudsen, O. and van der Mensbrugghe, D. (1993). "Trade Liberalisation: Global Economic Implications." OECD/World Bank, Paris.

IFAD (1992). *"The State of World Poverty: An Inquiry into its Causes and Consequences."* London: IFAD.

Kavishe, F.P. (1990) Malnutrition in Tanzania: A Situation Analysis. Dar es Salaam, TFNC Report No.1251.

Kikula, I. and Mwalyosi R. (1990). "Environmental Management in Tanzania: Challenges and Strategies for Tanzania." International Conference on Development Challenges and Strategies for Tanzania (October). Dar es Salaam.

Lele, U. (1989). *Sources of Growth in East African Agriculture.* Washington: MAIDA (World Bank).

Maliyamkono, T.L. and Bagachwa, M.S. (1990). *The Second Economy in Tanzania.* London: James Curry.

Mbilinyi, M. (1990). *Big Slavery.* Dar es Salaam: DUP.

Msemakwili, J. (1993). "Does Tanzania Need More World Bank Projects?" *Express,* October 21st. p. 13.

Mtatifikolo, F.P. (1992). "The Social Context of Reforms: Poverty and Poverty Alleviation in Tanzania." in M.S.D. Bagachwa, A.V.Y. Mbelle Brian Van Arkadie eds. *Market Reforms and Parastatal Restructuring in Tanzania.* Dar es Salaam: 57-71. Economics Department and Economic Research Bureau, UDSM, pp.

Mtatifikolo, F. (1991). "Poverty and Poverty Alleviation under Adjustment Process: Framework, Experience and Lessons for Tanzania." 7th National Economic Workshop, Dar es Salaam.

Mustafa K. "The Pastoralist Question", in O'Neill, N. and K. Mustafa. (Eds) (1990). *Capitalism, Socialism and the Development Crisis in Tanzania.* Avebury: Aldershot. pp.101- 124

Pacey, A. and Payne, P (Eds) (1985) *Agricultural Development and Nutrition,* FAO and UNICEF

Sarris, A. and van Den Brink R. (1993). *Economic Policy and Household Welfare during Crisis and Adjustment in Tanzania.* Cornell University Food and Nutrition Policy Program. New York: University Press.

Sarris, A. and Tinios, P. (1993) *Consumption and Poverty in Tanzania before and after Adjustment*, Ithaca, Cornell University Food and Nutrition Policy Program.

Sender, J. and Smith, S. (1990). *Poverty Class and Gender in Rural Africa.* London and New York: Routledge.

Shivji, I. (1994) *Report of the Presidential Lands' Commission*, Scandinavian Institute of African Studies, Uppsala, Sweden (forthcoming).

Sivalon, J. (1994) "Political Transition in Tanzania: A Preliminary Investigation into the Political Attitudes of Rural Tanzanians", Dar es Salaam, *TADREG Working Papers* (forthcoming).

Tanzania Development Research Group (1992a). "Poverty-Focused Primary Education Project: An Analysis of Key Data and Documentation". ODA, Dar es Salaam. (mimeo).

Tanzania Development Research Group (1992b). "The Provision and Acceptability of Child Immunization Services in Tanzania." *TADREG Research Report*, No. 4.

Tanzania Development Research Group (1993). "Parental Attitudes Towards Education in Rural Tanzania." *TADREG Research Report*, No.5.

Tanzania Gender Networking Programme (1993). *Gender Profile of Tanzania.* Dar es Salaam.

Therkilsden, O. (1989). *Watering White Elephants.* Centre for Development Research, Research Publication 7 Copenhagen: Scandinavian Institute of African Studies.

Tinios, P., Sarris, A., Amani H., Maro W. (1993) "Households, Consumption, and Poverty in Tanzania: Results from the 1991 National Cornell-ERB Survey". Seminar on Policy and Poverty in Tanzania, Dar es Salaam.

Tripp, A.M. (1989). "Women and the Changing Urban Household Economy in Tanzania." *Journal of Modern African Studies*, Vol. 27, No. 4, pp. 145-59

UNICEF (1989). *The Situation of Women and Children in Tanzania.* Dar es Salaam.

UNICEF (1990). "Monitoring the Situation of the Poor." ESAR Network on the Adjustment and Financing of Services Meeting. Nairobi.

United Republic of Tanzania (1993). *Achieving the Goals of Tanzania Children by the Year 2000.* Dar es Salaam

Wagao, J. and Kigoda, M.A. (1993). "Poverty Alleviation in Tanzania". UNDP, Dar es Salaam.

World Bank (1990). *Poverty: World Development Report.* Washington DC.

World Bank (1990). *Making Adjustment Work for the Poor in Sub- Saharan Africa.* Washington DC.

World Bank (1991). *Tanzania Economic Report: Towards Sustainable Development in the 1990s.* Report No. 9352-TA (two volumes). Washington DC.

World Bank (1993). *Tanzania: A Poverty Profile.* Report No 12298-TA. Washington DC.

4

Implications of Public Policies on Poverty and Poverty Alleviation: The Case of Tanzania

FIDELIS P. MTATIFIKOLO

INTRODUCTION

Nature of Public Policies in Relation to Primary Incomes

This chapter is about public policies and their links to poverty and its alleviation generally, with the special context of Tanzania being taken as a case study. Public policies refer to statements of intent by government authorities that have the effect of influencing or explicitly directing the course of action in the socio-economic system. A normal blueprint may take the form of a three to five year Plan, a Perspective Plan, a Declaration, etc., as generally guided by the Constitution. This blueprint may be operationalized through an annual plan which is made explicit in the annual budget. The Fiscal, Monetary and other "policies" translate plans into operations. It is these actions on the part of government that have a direct bearing on primary and secondary incomes, the main indicators of well being (and ultimately the key concepts in measurement of poverty).

Primary incomes derive from "primary claims on resources which arise directly out of the productive process of work and accumulation" and secondary incomes are a result of the transfer of primary claims" (Stewart, 1983). Some of the typical primary incomes are a result of the labour process (employment), rental property, and returns from investments or productive assets; whereas secondary incomes may involve subsidies on consumables, direct transfers and social actions that empower the recipients to actively engage in productive work.

It is generally accepted that from a policy perspective basic interest is in the well being of the most disadvantaged. Most social dimension interventions are concerned with the plight of these groups (the disadvantaged or, specifically, the poor) and the main focus, consistent with long term objectives of development, is to increase their primary incomes while it may be necessary also, in the interim, to, augment them with secondary incomes. In as far as the disadvantaged groups are economically active a potential exists for raising their primary incomes. Four approaches to such a policy have been singled out. Firstly one can increase their access to productive assets such as affordable credit, grants, commodity aid and natural resources. Secondly, one can raise returns on assets that these groups have access to. In most cases the single most important resource available to the disadvantaged is their labour power; thus raising their skills and employment opportunities will help to enhance their primary incomes. Thirdly, one can promote employment opportunities. Fourthly, one can invest in human capital, especially in the standard areas of education, health, nutrition and food security.

In Tanzania, public policies that have had a great bearing on primary incomes and therefore on poverty and its alleviation revolve around concepts like the Incomes Policy and Salaries/Wages policies, policies on the production and trade regimes (especially on producer and consumer prices) and fiscal/monetary policies (especially taxation and the monetary phenomena in the inflationary process). All these are traceable to some distant years. However, it is also known that in the recent decade the economy has been undergoing change through the structural adjustment processes (especially, SAP, ERPI and ERPII) and the current blueprint is the country's Policy Framework Paper (PFP), 1991/92 - 1993/94 and the Rolling Plan and Forward Budget 1993/94 - 1995/96. The major handles for structural adjustment have been institutional reforms, parastatal reforms, financial reforms and liberalization of the economy in both the capital and final goods markets.

One principal objective of structural adjustment is the mobilization of resources over the long term to raise rates of economic growth and living standards, in particular for the poor. It is this latter objective thus provides the standard for measuring the effect of public policies.

The Concept of Poverty: Meaning, Measurement and Controversies

About three decades of active debate have seen major refinements on the concept of poverty (Orshansky, 1965; Townsend, 1979; Sen, 1983; Barries, 1985; Kanbur, 1987; to mention but a few notable contributors to the debate). A reasonable definition characterizes a poor person as "one whose standard of living falls below a minimum acceptable level". There has been greater agreement along the nutritional requirements (since these vary little across time and societies) but less on non-nutritional requirements like clothing, shelter and the like. Operationally two possibilities are used: one is to specify minimum requirements for both food and non-food items and then to calculate the amount of income necessary to purchase these at current prices thus obtainning the poverty line.

The other approach is based directly on food requirements. First a calculation is made to derive the minimum expenditure necessary, at current prices, to attain minimum nutritional intake. The minimum food expenditure calculated should then be "grossed up" by an appropriate factor to take account of non food requirements. An acceptable factor has been the "average ratio of food expenditure to total expenditure in the population as a whole". This captures the view of poverty which relates it to the "capacity to be able to participate in all of the activities of the community on average" (Kanbur, 1987, in an analogous way when he notes poverty as "enforced lack of material resources of a certain duration and to such an extent that participation in normal activities and possession of amenities and living conditions which are customary or at least widely encouraged or approved in society becomes impossible or very limited." Thus poverty is time and context specific and this is what makes international or intertemporal comparison rather difficult. Using the notion of poverty line various poverty indices have been proposed in the literature (Sen. 1976; 1983; Anand and Kanbur, 1985; Foster, Greer and Thorbecke, 1984; Barries, 1985.

Poverty Alleviation: Meaning and Measurement

Poverty alleviation refers to lifting the poor out of poverty (tautology?!). Typically two approaches have been discussed extensively in the literature: alleviation through growth and alleviation through redistribution. Under the first approach it is recommended that the government's and other actors' activities should concentrate on growth policies and the results of growth will "trickle" down to the poor through both primary and secondary incomes and thus alleviating their poverty. The latter continues to be tried through various processes of perfect and imperfect targeting or through special projects like SDA projects (common in many countries in Africa). Other initiatives are in public works programs and community-based social action programs, especially in areas where extreme poverty is associated with social problems like concentration of female-headed families, youngsters not in school, households on welfare and young males not in the workforce (see Oyen, 1992 Survey on the US cases).

The failure of the trickle down process to alleviate poverty within reasonable time frame has been amplified by some case studies like that in Kanbur, (1987.)[1] In Tanzania, as we note later below, there has been attempts to try both approaches (growth and redistribution).

Overview and Report Outline

Simple analytical frameworks with which to organize the discussion on Public policies and poverty appear variously in the literature. For Tanzania current public policies have their genesis in the attempts since the early 80s at restructuring the economy. In the early 80s stabilization was notable, followed by SAP and now the new wave of Reforms. It is also possible to trace both redistribution and growth approaches to poverty alleviation attempts in Tanzania as we do in the section below.

This chapter is organized as follows: in the section below (section two) the experiences of Tanzania, traced as the policies evolved since the 60s, are discussed, covering instruments of policy, the actual practices and the systemic response under the repressed regime. This is followed, in section three, by coverage of the new wave of reforms; again incorporating instruments of policy and the actual practices. In the final section (section 4) we consolidate the coverage of section Two and Section Three to characterize the role of public policies on poverty and its alleviation. A research Agenda on public policies and poverty is given at the end.

THE EXPERIENCE OF TANZANIA

Public Policies in the History of Tanzania and their Links to Poverty and Its Alleviation

Independence to Arusha

At the independence of Mainland Tanzania in 1961 the typical slogan of "Uhuru na Kazi" (Freedom and Work) was associated with the identification of three national enemies; "poverty, ignorance and disease". However, no explicit actions specific to poverty were made operational in the first three year plan 1962-64 and even the first five year plan of 1964-69. The period 1961-67 was a time of experimentation and the strengthening of machinery of government. In particular there was determined action in the civil service (following the Adu Commission Report) on creating a disciplined and trainable labour force. This was a period of high wages and it was noted that such wages were necessary to facilitate acquisition of requisite skills in the first post-colonial government.

Elsewhere in the economy labour was disorganized and most African workers were employed in the plantations. The wages were so low that the possibility of developing a disciplined and trainable labour force was threatened. A special commission (The Chesworth Minimum Wages Board) was set up and recommended in 1962 that in order to have a stable, well disciplined and trainable labour force the wages should be increased substantially. Minimum wages were raised and remunerations of many indigenous middle and high grades were also increased.

An immediate consequence of the increased wages was a reduction in employment[2]. However, even as the total wage employment was declining, the public sector (parastatal and civil service) employment was rising, mainly a result of the expansion and strengthening of the civil service. Between 1962 and 1967 public sector employment increased by 24.6%. Declines were mainly in the enterprise sector (25.9% decline in the period).

The Adu recommendations did not constitute a comprehensive Incomes Policy approach to Salaries since issues of price changes, tax instruments, etc, were not articulated in the Report. It was following the Arusha Declaration that a comprehensive Incomes Policy was worked out to, among other issues, address questions of relative poverty.

Arusha to Mid 70s: The First Report and the Incomes Policy

The Arusha brought with it the policy of Socialism and Self Reliance. The public sector grew large suddenly as a result of putting "commanding heights" in the public sector. With it the share of public sector employment in total employment grew suddenly too. The Government introduced an incomes policy (Government Paper number 4 of 1967, on Wages, Incomes, Rural Development, Investment and Price Policy). The new policy was based on an ILO Report produced under Professor Turner, H.A. (See Turner, 1967). The new policy would emphasize rural development to bridge the (perceived) incomes gap between the urban (mainly wage earners) and the rural poor (mainly small holders, peasant farmers) and also to reduce income differentials between the regions and among wage earners. Thereafter wages were to be restricted (and employment expanded).

To facilitate the fast change from a mere wage policy to a comprehensive Incomes Policy other instruments and institutions were created during this period, like the Permanent Labour Tribunal (to settle industrial disputes, to supervise production targets, to control payment by result schemes and to oversee collective bargaining agreements), the Price Commission (at the peak of its activities in the late 70s it was setting and controlling close to 2000 prices of commonly consumed commodities) and SCOPO (to oversee the Parastatal Sector), among others.

Turner was called upon again in 1975 on yet another ILO exercise. He came to evaluate the performance of the first policy and recommend on new a course of action.

The policies of 1967 to mid 1970s had the following impacts:

(a) Rapid increase in public sector employment (from 160,005 in 1967 to 239,261 in 1972, or by 49.5%)

(b) Creating a fast momentum for growth of disparity between the real wage and the cost of living (data in sections below).

(c) Building the basis of imbalances in the Budget (discussed below).

Tables in the next sections on employment, real wages and cost of living indices, and the budgetary imbalances discussed below attest to this.

Mid- 1970s to Early 1980s: Economic Instability

There is no hard and fast rule to distinguish the crisis and non-crisis period in the history of Tanzania especially with reference to the decade of the 1970s into the 1980s. However a chronology of events normally starts with the drought of 1973 and 1974, the oil crisis of 1973 and 1974 later to be compounded by another drought in 1975, then the Break up of the East African Community in 1977, then the War with Uganda in 1979, then another oil shock and depression in export prices in 1979/80, and so on. The Balance of Payments costs and budgetary implication of these various shocks have been quantified for some years (World Bank: 1984).

Economic growth was still sound between 1967 and 1973, at about 4.5% annual growth in GDP. However, recurrent expenditure growth had begun to outpace recurrent revenue growth between 1968/69 and 1972/73 (18% per annum versus 16% per annum, respectively). Between 1972/73 and 1974/75 expenditures grew at 39% due to increased pay, increased subsidies to parastatals and general expansion of Government programmes (including Ujamaa Village Schemes, villagization and the aftermath of decentralization, not to mention UPE, expanded schemes of water supply, etc).

By the early 1980s the new direction for economic survival was to be addressed by first NESP, then SAP before ERP I and II took over, to be blueprints of efforts until 1991/92. The major effort with regard to Incomes (and especially with some token reference to poverty and its alleviation) were to be reflected mainly in TURNER II Report.

The Turner II Report: The National Policy on Productivity, Incomes and Prices of 1981

This second Report was to result in the National Policy on Productivity, Incomes and Prices but it was not until 1981 that it became operational. The policy borrowed heavily from the earlier (Turner) Report of 1967, with the major objectives being:

(a) To reduce income differentials among groups, regions and between rural and urban areas,

(b) To promote socialist production and distribution.

(c) To raise efficiency in resource allocation and utilization, and

(d) To speed up national economic growth.

Because it was made operational at a time when other "package programmes" were in place (namely at the time of NESP in 1981 and 1982), followed by SAPs it was not successful. SAP and ERP I were subsequently to concentrate on growth, in some cases at the expense of this distributive philosophy and practice. The Turner II policy orientation was never heard of again.

The Instruments of Policy

The main instruments of policy during the time when the Arusha Declaration was still the blueprint were practices and regulations on salaries/wages, prices (both producer and consumer) and taxation. All these have been studied extensively, and only summary evidence is given here.

Salaries/Wages

It is well known that the ideals of salary and overall worker compensation include adequacy, equity and consistency as follows:

(a) *Adequacy or sufficiency*: that the salary should be adequate, to reflect responsibility, accountability and status. Decent salaries were never meant to be complemented with side payments and other formal and non formal earnings in a significant way. In this case the minimum wage ought to at least be a living wage.

(b) *Equity*: that extreme differentials horizontally or vertically should be minimized. Taxes and other nontax measures are typical measures for effecting this. Differences should reflect society's judgement about the premia it associates with specific skills, experiences, status, accountability and responsibility.

(c) *Consistency*: that account should be taken of comparable work/skill in comparable circumstances in parastatals, the private sector and in the non-civil service. If skills are internationally mobile then account should be taken of international wages in comparable circumstances.

Two recent studies (World Bank 1989, 1991), corroborated by others, have identified major problems relating to salaries and wages as being: extreme compression, falling real wages and non transparency and inequity. We note the data briefly below.

The World Bank (1989: Vol. II Ch.3) notes that public service pay was a significant component of public expenditure, (about 1/5 of total recurrent expenditures) and therefore issues of pay, productivity and numbers of employees are relevant to all sectors.

(a) On Pay levels

The World Bank's (1989) Public Expenditure Review PER summarized wage trends as follows:

Table 1: Wage Trend in Tanzania: 1969-1986

Year	Index of Real Wages			
	Minimum Wage	Middle Wage	Top Salary	Average Wage
1969	100	100	100	100
1975	103	68	44	108
1980	63	37	21	65
1986	30	n.a	6	19

Source: World Bank's (1989) PER Vol. II, Table 3.2

The table reveals more clearly what had been claimed to hold in the other studies; that nominal wages were falling fast in real terms, and higher wages even faster relative to the minimum wage. The average wage lost about 80% of its value between 1969 and 1986. This worked to increase absolute poverty of typical earners who considered such wages their primary income.

The reduction in differentials was also noted.

Table 2: Ratio of Average, Middle and Top Salaries to Minimum Wage

Year	Minimum	Middle	Top	Average
1968	1.0	6.7	28.8	1.7
1975	1.0	4.4	12.3	1.7
1980	1.0	3.9	9.6	1.7
1986	1.0	n.a	6.3	1.1
1988	1.0	2.4	5.2	n.a

Source: PER Vol. II, Table 3.3 and World Bank, 1991, Vol. I p. 23, Table 2.5.

The fall in the differential was a deliberate Government action, on equity consideration. In this case again the biggest casualty was the top salary, which was close to 30 times that of minimum wage but fell to a mere 6.3 times in the period from 1968 to 1986, then to 5.2 times by 1988.

The main refuge from the low and unrealistic pay was the increase in allowances and fringe benefits, especially in the higher grades of civil service and parastatals. This, as is well known, made pay structures overall to be less transparent, more inequitable and very costly to Government.

(b) On Productivity

The PER noted that productivity in the civil service and parastatals was very low. The main reasons were the low pay (as people worked less than full time) and under-provisioning of work tools and basic facilities. Mainly because of these reasons there were discernible trends in the public sector employment, like (a) brain drain of special and rare skills to private sector and to other nations (ii) increased incentive for officers to seek additional compensation within the system through formal and informal means, and (iii) increased informal activities outside office (moonlighting) but sometimes even absenteeism to attend to private matters (now commonly known as 'sunlighting').

(c) On Employment Levels

The World Bank study noted public sector employment trends for the period early from the 1970s 70s to the mid 1980s. A summary table is provided below.

Table 3: Public Sector Share of Total Formal Employment

	1970	1975	1989	1982	1984
Share (%)					
Government	35.9	31.5	37.1	44.0	47.7
Parastatals	22.5	33.6	33.7	29.3	29.3
Total Public Sector	58.4	65.1	70.8	73.3	77.0
Private Sector	41.6	34.9	29.2	26.7	23.0

Sources: Abridged from the Table 3.4 RER, Vol. II.

Several points can be made on the table, two are important:

(i)   That the public sector has been dominant in total formal employment, and the government was the critical actor,

(ii) The rise in Government share was more steady. So was the decline in the private sector share in total formal employment.

Other studies on Incomes and Employment, especially under Adjustment processes include Mtatifikolo and Naho (1988) and Mtatifikolo (1992). They reveal anomalies notable from the other studies.

Prices

The practice and mandate of controlling producer prices of traditional goods was vested in the crop authorities that were created almost "en masse" following the abolition of cooperatives in 1976. This was meant to guarantee incomes to farmers but since such prices were set very low relative to world market prices (in fact they were always set as "residuals" after all the "costs" associated with the operations of the crop authorities had been accommodated) smuggling became rampant. Official purchases of export crops stagnated or in some cases dropped even as total recorded production was known to be rising (coffee and cotton: see TET Vol 5 # 3 & 4, p. 94 cited as Economic Research Bureau Commission (1992, 1993).

As regard consumer prices it is known that the National Price Commission of 1974 (now disbanded) was responsible for setting such prices, and at the peak of its operations in the late 70s to early 80s it was controlling close to 2000 prices of consumables. Again, as a result of shortages amidst the economic crisis a clear wedge was drawn between parallel market prices and official prices. Attempts to trace data on parallel market prices are recent and for some staples there is some documentation in TET as cited above. For instance in January 1987 the official price of rice was 19/ = per kg whereas the parallel market price was 37/65. In December 1989 when the official price was Tsh.85/ = per kg the parallel market price was Tsh. 65/40 and thereafter the government liberalized the staple markets. Such paradoxes are to be noted also with regard to maize and wheat (see TET, Vol. 5, # 3 & 4; P 91).

Other studies on prices have been widely documented in our study of 1991 as contribution to the Social Audit (see Mtatifikolo 1992a). This is another case whereby public policies, possibly well meaning for purposes of addressing primary incomes of producers and consumers, were seen to negate the very objectives set out. Nothing yet can be traced about the actual beneficiaries of such policies in the absence of serious research, but it is important to note that since perfect targeting could not be guaranteed the role of the price policies in relation to both absolute and relative poverty could not be stated unambiguously.

Taxation

Some of the leading issues and important questions in tax policy revolve around burden sharing , equity, budgetary effects and cost.[3]

In Tanzania taxation was a subject of a number of studies, including more recently a Presidential Commission of Enquiry. It is observed in Mtatifikolo, (1990) as follows for the period early from the 1970s to the mid 1980s:

(a)   Over the same period tax revenues rose as a percentage of GDP. This is commensurate with economic theory and evidence in other countries.

(b)   There was a clear shift towards reliance on taxes which are regressive in nature (sales and excise taxes) from a contribution of less than 25% in the early 1970s to over 55% of total tax revenue in recent years.

(c)   Tax concentration had increased also. In the early 1980s over 95% of total tax revenue had been derived from the top three sources, rising from about 75% in the early 1970s. Two taxes alone: Personal and Income Tax (direct taxes) and Sales and Excise taxes (indirect taxes) contributed about 90% of total tax revenue by the mid 1980s.

(d)   The tax system in Tanzania was generally inelastic with respect to national income. Buoyancy was not high either. The low elasticity was explained primarily by the low response of the tax base to changes in the national income.

(e)   Over the period the highest rise in tax revenues occurred in sales and excise taxes and in PAYE.

(f)   Income taxation in Tanzania (PAYE and business income tax) showed anomalies, especially in the rates.   Rates were high and highly progressive, and over time they increased even for the same nominal incomes despite erosion of relative and real incomes as GDP and inflation grew, respectively.

Thus income taxation ate more into people's nominal income over time, implying possible attempt by government to keep real collections high by extracting more nominally.

(g)   The highest effort by government was noted in sales and excise taxes, and PAYE, and negative effort in business income. Since the latter (business income) constituted the larger component (but rising less fast) in the income tax revenue such negative effort suggested substantial tax avoidance and evasion in the business (self-employed) sector, and also challenged the claim of practical progressivity of income taxation in Tanzania.

(h)   Whereas business income responded highest to changes in national income its tax share responded least to its taxable capacity.   This suggested substantial undertaxation of the business (informal and formal) sector over time.

(i)   the high effort shown in the pursuit of PAYE and Sales taxes was explained by the high tax-to-base response. This implied obvious relative overtaxation of the taxable capacity relevant to the wage earning group in relation to other bases.

From these findings several conclusions could be made, two of the important ones being

(a)   The tax system of Tanzania showed all the basic elements of practical regressivity (The taxes yielding close to 60% of total revenues are regressive, the others yielding over 30% having anomalies of very high and rising rates and quite substantial tax evasion and avoidance, something akin to dynamic regressivity)

(b)   The wage earner in Tanzania was overtaxed relative to any other income earner. To the extent that tax effort implied the sacrifice the payer had to make, it was reasonable to conclude that the tax system demonstrated a real sacrifice the wage earning group was made to make to finance increased government spending. This questioned seriously notions of tax equity embodied in the tax legislation.

Overall, the conclusion was that the burden of taxation was badly distributed to the disadvantage of the wage earners. In the subsection that follows the manifestations that "not all was well" especially for the relatively poorer sections of the economy are highlighted.

The Repressed System and the Response Mechanism

We have remarked above that the mid 1970s to early 1980s saw the real beginnings of economic instability and erosion of living standards. Three important measures are singled out here to reflect upon crisis in delivery (to workers) and the manifestations of their refuge away from the formal system. These include the rising cost of living, an increase in the share of the "subterranean economy" and the falling trends in productivity in the Civil Service.

(a) On Cost of Living:

Data were given in the previous sections for the trends in the CPI for the period from the late 1960s to the mid 1980s (World Bank Reports cited above). Here we report only on trends in the 80s into the early 1990s.

Using 1977 = 100 (i.e. as base year) the December indices for food for urban dwellers in Mainland Tanzania rose from 547.7 in 1984 to 3127.7 in 1992 or by about 5.7 times, that for transport from 424.4 to 4153.7 or by about 9 times. Rises in such items erode the lower incomes more than the higher incomes (fuel, light, water, furniture, etc., rose less modestly). In terms of average quarterly changes, in 1982 it was 153.9, rising to 2972.2 in 1992 or by more than ten times within ten years. Inflation rates for 1982-1992 are given in Table 4.

Table 4: Inflation Rates in Tanzania: 1982-1992

82	83	84	85	86	87	88	89	90	91	92
28.93	27.07	36.13	33.28	32.43	28.95	31.19	25.86	19.7	22.3	22.1

Source: Planning Commission

In terms of purchasing power of, for instance, the minimum wage (using 1985/86 as base) a day's minimum wage could purchase 4.85 kgs of wheat in 1973, this falling to 0.76 kg by 1989 (or 4.85 kg of rice in 1973, this falling to 0.73 kg by 1988).

It is not meaningful to also consider the higher wages since by definition they are spent less proportionately in food; however, the point is made about rising inflation, rising cost of living and declining purchasing power (even using official prices) for the low income urban earners.

(b) Falling Civil Service Productivity

Labour Productivity Indices: These are used to compare the Civil Service's current productivity with that of previous years or that of the base year. Fixing a reference point (base year) enables us to analyse the trends in productivity changes. The labour productivity index is defined by the formula:

$$LP_t = \frac{Q_t/Q_0}{L_t/L_0} \quad \text{or} \quad \frac{Q_t}{L_t} \cdot \frac{L_0}{Q_0} \quad \text{expressed as a percentage}$$

where,

LP_t = Labour productivity index in year t
Q_t = Output in year t
Q_0 = Output in base year
L_t = Labour input in year t
L_0 = Labour input in base year

Notice that the index of output is obtained by dividing each year's output by that of the base year. This gives a measure of change in real production between the base year and the subsequent years. The index of labour input is similarly obtained by dividing each year's labour inputs by those used in the base year. This is in turn gives a measure of real changes in labour input between the base year and the subsequent years.

The base year we use for Tanzania is 1976. This is known to be a generally "normal" year in the turbulent history of Tanzania, and moreover, it is still used as a base year for national accounts purposes. The measure of output is GDP from Public Administration (measured in Million TShs) whereas the measure of input is employment in Public Administration (in numbers). Table 5 provides the computation of productivity indices.

Table 5: Labour Productivity

Year	GDP (PA) Q_t 1976 Prices Mill. TShs	Employment in PA L_t Thousands	$\frac{Q_t}{Q\ 1976}$	$\frac{L_t}{L\ 1976}$	LP_t
1976	2342	110.8	100.0	100.0	100.0
1977	2497	127.3	106.6	114.9	92.8
1978	2797	141.0	119.4	127.3	93.8
1979	3145	180.7	134.3	163.1	82.3
1980	3188	182.0	136.1	164.3	82.8
1981	3551	209.2	151.6	188.8	80.3
1982	3556	223.8	151.8	202.0	75.1
1983	3547	220.9	151.5	199.4	76.0
1984	3549	217.9	151.5	196.7	77.0
1985	3616	239.9	154.4	216.5	71.3
1986	3225	265.7	137.7	21.7	59.4
1987	3243	258.3	138.5	233.1	59.4
1988	3343	258.8	142.7	256.7	55.6
1989	3475	255.3	148.4	230.4	64.4
1990	3552	275.7*	151.7	248.8	61.0
1991	3619	297.8*	154.5	268.8	57.5

Source: Computed from GDP and Employment Data from *National Accounts*: Planning Commission.

NOTES: GDP (PA) = GDP, Public Administration; Employment in PA = Employment in Public Administration Other variables as defined earlier. *Estimates

It clear from the trends shown that labour productivity in the Civil Service declined very considerably between 1976 and 1991. The most conspicuous period was between 1982 and 1988 (for which data are reasonably reliable), and for some years (e.g. 1986, 1987 and 1988) productivity was less than 60% of what it was in 1976. Even the temporary reversals of 1989 do not seem to suggest clear recovery (if anything the continued fall in 1990 and 1991 would indicate a worsening of the problem). The measure used by the National Productivity Council (see their 1988/89 Annual Report) reveals the same trends, of a generally declining trend in Civil Service Labour productivity.

(c) Increased Share of the Subterranean Economy

The growth of the subterranean economy, especially of the less-legal kind, is usually linked to either shortage of goods and services (excess demand in the economy) which is associated with some official controls on prices and/or quantities, or to the general criminal activity level in the economy (which may in turn be a result of some social 'discontent' with political malpractice). At macro level excess demand may be a function of shortage of foreign exchange to import the needed domestic deficiencies. Under such conditions exchange control, especially under fixed exchange rate regimes, has been common place. Smuggling, rent-seeking and parallel markets (illegal connotation) have proliferated in economies repressed by shortages and official controls. In Tanzania, post-independence traces of parallel market and related illegalities can be found as documented in Mtatifikolo (1990) on the Subterranean Economy. The objectives of that study related to, among others, providing annual estimates of the subterranean economy and its components: A summary table of the relevant annual estimates is reproduced below (Table 6).

Table 6: Annual Estimates of the Subterranean Economy

Year	Current Prices GDP (fc) Bill TShs	Subterranean money Bill TShs	Subterranean economy Bill Tshs	Subterranean Economy as % of Official economy (GDP)
1978	28.582	0.34	1.496	5.2
1979	32.317	1.19	6.296	16.4
1980	37.454	1.79	7.590	20.3
1981	43.906	2.30	9.062	20.6
1982	52.546	5.19	13.430	25.6
1983	62.608	3.19	15.248	24.4
1984	78.143	4.32	20.736	26.5
1985	108.083	5.47	30.523	28.2
1986	140.793	8.45	44.616	31.7
1987	192.969	11.74	64.805	33.6

Source: Mtatifikolo, (1990, p. 35).

Thus by this study the subterranean economy (measured by GDP) grew from about 1.5 billion TShs in 1978 to almost 65 billion in 1987. As a share of official GDP it rose from about 5% in 1978 to about 34% in 1987.

There have been other comparable studies in this area and the interested reader is referred to Bagachwa (1993) and the relevant references in Mtatifikolo (1990).

The new wave in policies is covered next.

THE NEW WAVE

Toward a Credible Income

In the section above we have noted that the main policies around which notions of primary and secondary incomes could be discussed with specific reference to Tanzania are traceable, until the early 1980s, to an evolved Incomes Policy. The main instruments of Policy were Taxation, Wages and Salaries, and Prices. All these were noted to have resulted in eroded living standards and falling incomes, possibly magnifying absolute and relative poverty. The main manifestations have been declining real wages, falling productivity and increase in the size of the subterranean economy as the main refuge.

As further manifestation of increased absolute poverty as measured "as if one relied on the official salary" there have been attempts to establish a meaningful minimum (living) wage along various approaches as follows:

(a) Using a market basket or a poverty line based on an assessment of what constitutes a typical and realistic expenditure. Appropriate setting and decompression of structure is then made to design a minimum wage to atop salary package. Field survey is normally the first critical input.

(b) The preferred salary approach. Under this approach information is sought and obtained objectively from the employees themselves about what they think are their "premia in society" and therefore what they ought to be paid, given government capacity. Appropriate weighting and averaging out may be necessary to obtain realistic scales. This normally is more demanding in terms of field work data and objectivity in the search for such normally subjective information.

(c) Indexation to private sector and/or international wages. If the private sector has operated more freely and the wages in that sector are deemed to be more realistic the civil service and parastatal wages are indexed accordingly. In a country like Tanzania the prime mover has been the Government wages which provide the relevant standard for private sector wages. Where personal emoluments have been higher in private sector (as they have in practice) they mainly took the form of non-wage payment and thus they were less transparent. Appropriate weighting would again be necessary to take account of tax policies if such other benefits (e.g. non-monetary) are monetized and explicitly included in Salaries (and thus became taxable when they would otherwise not be). International wages or donor community wages may provide the index but account of tax and other policies would have to be taken.

(d) Restoration of some base year real wages. A year is picked, that is considered average and reasonable for remuneration purpose (i.e. year in which pay was considered adequate and affordable by government). Current pay is then indexed to the base year. Sometimes when no single year is considered typical a weighted average of some years may have to be used. If structural changes are in progress too distant years would be unrealistic; but then also too near a year would be unreasonable too on account that it may have been a year belonging to the critical crisis and/or the actual structural changes.

(e) Budget share reference for indexation. Here instead of indexation to a base year real wage it might be more meaningful to index to a year (or some weighted average of some years) in which the share of the budget going to personal emoluments was considered realistic (and the budget was "meaningful"). The share is then used to compute the needed changes. It works if emoluments are known to have suffered relative to other expenditure items; but if the total budget itself has shrunk without significantly affecting shares then this approach need not help emoluments as such.

Attempts have been made to establish meaningful yardsticks for Tanzania. It is noted for instance, in Mushi and Wangwe (1991) and Mtatifikolo and Katabaruki (1992) that using any of the above measures the minimum wage would have had to be at least 10,000/= in 1991 in order to keep up to the mere purchasing power of the late 1960s (not to mention accommodation of new tastes, aspirations, etc). Other corroboration is notable from Kapunda (1992) who approaches the discussion from a nutritional perspective. Allowing for realistic wage decompression would have meant a top salary of about 160,000/= in 1991.

In what has become a classic conclusion it is noted that the Incomes Policy resulted mainly in shared poverty, not so much on enhanced income. There are, however new efforts which appear to reverse the direction, and for all practical purposes are diammentrically opposed to the practices inspired by the Arusha Declaration. We turn to these now.

**The Current Blueprint; The Policy Framework Paper (PFP) 1991/92-93/94
and the Rolling Plan and Forward Budget (RPFB) 1993/94-1195/96**

Since 1982/87, the Government's main economic policy objective has been to
bring the economy to register a balanced and sustained growth. Two economic
recovery programmes (ERP I: 1986/87-1988-89 and ERP II: 1989/90-91/92)
aimed at:

(a) raising GDP growth to an average of 5 percent:
(b) reducing inflation to below 10 percent.
(c) restoring internal and external balances in the economy, and
(d) improving social service delivery.

The most current thinking in Government circles in relation to reforming the
economy is reflected in the Policy Framework Paper, 1991/92-1993/94 and the
Rolling Plan and Forward Budget for 1993/94-1995/96.   The major
recommendations from the Policy Framework Paper that are of direct bearing
on the discussed by this report address (i) Fiscal Policies and Budgetary
Management, (ii) Civil Service Reform and, (iii) Parastatal Reform. Most of the
recommendations relate to expenditure reforms to effect savings which can thus
contribute toward enhancing incomes and possibly alleviating poverty (Para 28-
36 of the March 22, 1991 draft of the PFP deal with Fiscal Policies and
Budgetary Management; Para 46-47 deal with Civil Service Reforms and Para
48-50 deal with Parastatal reforms).   On the other hand The Rolling Plan
mentioned above addresses institutional Reforms as being the cornerstone of its
setting for the relevant period. Thus the RPFB states that: "During Economic
Recovery Programmes I and II, the need to bring about institutional changes to
match the economic policy changes became increasingly obvious. Government
has set up several Commissions to examine the activities of a number of key
institutions within financial services, co-operatives, public revenue and
expenditure and recommended how those activities could be pursued in a
restructured economy. Many of the Commissions' recommendations have been
accepted by the government, and their implementation has either started or is
envisaged". (Rolling Plan, p.5).

To attain the main policy objectives two kinds of reforms in the Public Sector
are explicitly cited, Parastatal Reforms and Civil Service Reforms. Some
highlights, in summary form, for these are given below.

**Macroeconomic Reforms, Parastatal Sector Reforms and Civil Service
Reforms**

The Parastatal Sector Reforms

According to the Rolling Plan and Forward Budget the reform programme for parastatals is required because the parastatal sector has not been subjected to the competitive pressure needed to stimulate efficiency. Consequently, while skills have been generated and employment created, this has been done at an unacceptable cost to the economy. The system has misallocated resources, led to inefficient production and caused severe drains in the government budget.

In order to achieve the parastatal reform objectives outlined, the government has taken a number of steps. These have included institutional, legislative, policy and implementation action. The parastatal Sector Reform Commission (PSRC) was set up in early 1992, charged with coordinating the reforms and ensuring transparency in the process of such reform[4].

Complementing these legislative and regulatory reforms have been some revisions of a number of laws relating to the business environment including the Companies Ordinance, Land and Labour law, and to enact capital markets legislation in order to promote private sector development. Related commitment has also been repeated in the 1993/94 Budget.

The other main areas of focus included limiting Treasury Financial assistance to parastatals, limiting bank credit and restricting, and ultimately eliminating, Inter-enterprises arrears.

The Civil Service Reforms

The need to restructure, revitalize and strengthen the public sector management institutions is underpinned by the Government's broader policy objectives of:

(i)   drastically reducing direct involvement in the national economy, through the liberalization of the economy and privatization of non- strategic public enterprises; and

(ii) creating an enabling environment for enhanced private sector participation in the provision of social services, with a corresponding reduction in the role and functions of the Government in the direct delivery of these services.

Major Problems in the Civil Service in Tanzania

Overstaffing: During the past three decades, civil service employment grew at an average annual rate of about 8.6 percent. This rapid growth in civil service employment reflected a socio-political philosophy that in the past committed the Government to:

(i)   maximize public provision of both social and economic services; and

(ii)   alleviation of the unemployment problem through recruitment into public service of relatively large numbers of graduates from training institutions.

Recent Government sponsored studies of civil service structures and manning levels have confirmed that the level of overmanning is in the order of 50,000 employees, i.e. equivalent to about 15 percent of the total current number of Government employees.

Decline in real wages: In the period spanning late 1970s and the 1980s, there was severe erosion in real wages and salaries for civil servants. In constant prices, it is for example, estimated that on average the direct pay of level in 1972. It has also been independently confirmed that for a majority of Government employees the current level of remuneration is insufficient to properly feed and clothe an average size household.

Wage Compression: Following the promulgation in 1967 of the Arusha Declaration, the Government decided not only to control wage levels but also to adjust the relative level in favour of junior civil servants. Consequently, there was a decompression of the formal pay structure and the erosion of basic pay was persistently more severe for the senior civil servants. Salary adjustments since 1988 have, however, gradually halted both the erosion of real direct pay and the compression of the basic salary scales.

Sub-optimal Organization and Management of Functions: A common denominator to all the issues underlying the need for civil service reforms is the observed non optimal organization and management of Government functions. A macro-review of Government functions has indicated the need to reduce duplication of roles and functions by closing or merging (some) ministries or departments, and laying-off some employees. It is also recognized that improvements in organization and work methods within Government departments could result in significant efficiency gains.

Reform Components

In the context of the need for reform as outlined above the Government has determined that a civil service reform programme should comprise the following four complementary components, supported by two others of an Institution Building Capacity Enhancement nature viz:

(a)   Manpower retrenchment and redeployment;
(b)   pay reform

(c)   personnel control and Management system reforms; and
(d)   Organizational and efficiency reforms.

The other two are:

(e)   Training for the civil Service; and
   (f)   Institution and Capacity Building for the Civil Service Department.

The six components were initially addressed by a Government Project called "Strengthening Management in the Public Sector" (Project URT/90/031). This and some other emerging initiatives are gradually being addressed by a comprehensive project linking the Government, the World Bank, UNDP, and ODA. Other actors are expected to join these efforts in due course.

From Subdued to Reemergence of the Formal Economy:

It clear from the discussion above that the economy is drifting toward a market system. With it many instruments of direct government intervention in the economy have ceased to operate: SCOPO disbanded, the Price Commission disbanded and discontinued control over wages except for the minimum wage. A combination of policies are all working to produce, gradually, a market economy. These are cited in the various reform components such as (a) reducing the size and role of the civil service through such measures as personnel retrenchment and hiring freeze while at the same time trying to increase work tools, productivity and remuneration (b) privatizing and/or reforming parastatals, including liquidation of budget-drainers and (c) financial sector reforms that address exchange rate, interest rates and specific aspects of banking or financial operations.

There have been attempts to trace the systemic response of the economy. Devaluation seems to be working (a) to create conditions for a more "Mixed Economy" especially in as far as the traditional exports are expanding fast despite the constraints (See TET Vol 5 # 3 and 4 mainly devoted to the theme of non traditional exports) (b) facilitating a move towards a more market-determined interest and exchange rate regime, as primarily reflected in the narrowing of the gap between official (now unified in an overall interbank determined exchange rate) and non-official rates. A more liberal system in exchange and other regulations was initially credited with the reemergence into the formal economy of previous "subterranean" money (manifested in increase in official own funded imports). The proliferation of informal activities is more a result of search for better or greener pastures, not so much a refuge from a repressed system. Between 1991 and 1992 the value of exports increased by about 14% while imports increased at about 2.2% only. The official exports-imports ratio was only 27.5%.

Recorded growth in 1992 put GDP growing at 3.6%, a fall from 3.9% in 1991. The falling rate of 1992 was mainly a function of stalled crop production and industrial performance. However, construction (a normal sign of economic recovery/slump) grew at a comfortable 3.1%. It is noted, for instance, that compared to other countries in Sub-Saharan Africa, Tanzania's GDP growth for 1992 was 2.4 times the average GDP growth rate of 1.5% for the low income countries of Sub-Saharan Africa. The 1992 GDP growth rate was also, as has been in the past five years, higher than the country's estimated population growth rate of 2.8%.

We assemble all these pieces and bits of information on public policy trends and link them to poverty and its alleviation in Tanzania.

PUBLIC POLICIES AND POVERTY: A RECONCILIATION

It has been the purpose of this chapter to provide an outline (and to provoke discussion) of the link between public policies and poverty generally, and using the context of Tanzania as a special case. In this section a reconciliation and sum up is done. The research agenda on the implications of public on poverty is given at the end.

Governance and Public Policy on Poverty

It is well known in the theory of Governance that from a policy perspective the primary objective of any modern government is in the welfare of its people, particularly the poor. Typically a desirable approach is to seek to alleviate poverty through distributing the scarce resources in a way that reduces poverty the most for the country as a whole. A common way to do this is to allocate "welfare" benefits to the poor. If targeting is feasible this innocent concept can be operationalized, however, it is generally the case that any welfare benefits in partial targeting "spill over" to the nonpoor and the government must accept some costs associated with this. It is also noted that due to limited resources any enhancement of welfare to one group (the poor) shall impose costs on some others (the rich) and as we have noted in the case of Tanzania the afflicted groups shall take their own steps to effect even further redistribution, sometimes even more than compensating for their earlier loss. Budgetary rules under partial targeting that minimize cost to society (efficiency costs, distortions and costs associated with resource redistribution to "less productive" groups, etc) have been proposed in Thorbecke and Berrian (1992) and Foster, Greer and Thorbecke (1984), among others.

We have remarked in section one above that in as far as the poor are economically active a potential exists for increasing their primary incomes, and in crisis periods such incomes are complemented with secondary incomes.

In the aftermath of the establishment of the new post-colonial state in Africa it was typical to read about Declarations (Arusha Declaration, The Common Man's Charter, African Socialism, and the like) which explicitly specified the need to enhance incomes, particularly for the poor, and in many cases practical instruments of policy were put in place. This is what makes the case of Tanzania an interesting one to trace.

The Case of Tanzania Revisited

It has been noted that at the time when the new state was creating and strengthening the machinery of government prior to the Arusha Declaration only token reference (in the coined phrase about the post-colonial enemies "ignorance, disease and poverty") was made to the concept of poverty and its alleviation. Even the expanded employment and wages were mainly geared toward creating a disciplined and trainable labour force, rather than as part of poverty alleviation.

From Arusha Declaration to mid 1970s saw some determined (and possibly ill-advised) attempts to create an equitable and self reliant economy. The incomes policy evolved from the language of Turner (first Turner Report) and the Arusha Declaration. Thereafter equity considerations were to dominate, and assessments made about this "Nyerere Experiment", concluded that results were those of shared poverty rather than enhanced absolute incomes to alleviate poverty.

It has been remarked also (section 2.1.3 and 2.1.4) that mainly as a result of the crisis Turner was called upon again to "advise" government in 1975. When the government tried to operationalize some of the recommendations in 1981 (the 1981 Policy on Productivity, Incomes and Prices) it was too late, NESP was in place trying to salvage whatever was left of the economy under the economic "Survival" programme.

The primary instruments of policy were salaries and wages (and in this the Turner Report had significant inputs), prices (crop authorities mainly used to control producer prices while the National Price Commission was mandated to control most of the consumer prices), and taxation (The 1973 Income Tax Act and the 1976 Sales tax Act were critical influences).

In this chapter we have noted the various anomalies in all three broad instruments, many necessitating in the 1980s the creation of Commissions to reassess trends (The Nsekela Commission on Salaries/Wages; The Mtei Commission on Taxes, Public Revenues and the Budget) or the disbanding of the mandated organs (e.g. disbanding of SCOPO and the National Price Commission).

Evidence has been gathered above on the manifestations of the crisis in the economy: including increased cost of living, falling Civil Service Productivity and the increased share of the subterranean economy, especially of the non-legal kind.

The new wave is that of reforms: and the critical ones are those in the Civil Service, the parastatals and the Financial institutions. In aggregate variables there seems to be some recovery: in production, in productivity and the subterranean economy is "Rising from under" and becoming formal.

Concluding Remarks and Agenda for Research

Alleviation Through Redistribution

We have noted the practical problems of hoping for a "trickle down"effect. In view of the practical difficulties of trickle down policy makers have gradually designed direct redistributive strategies for alleviation of poverty, and the Social Dimensions of Adjustment Project (including concepts of targeting) in many countries in Africa seems to be the most elaborate donor-supported initiative for this continent. Under ideal conditions a "perfectly targeted" initiative would entail absence of the two primary costs of redistribution: that disbursing income/resources to the poor to help with poverty alleviation involves no leakage to the non-poor; and that raising the required resources from the non-poor involves minimal cost in terms of economic efficiency and growth. The resources required to eradicate poverty with perfect targeting provide the measure of redistributive effort required for poverty eradication.

However, perfect targeting of public spending programs to those below the poverty line is administratively costly, and any scheme which relies more on bureaucratic vetting of the poor (households or individuals) on a case-by-case basis is open to corruption and manipulation. A middle course is thus more akin to success, whereby broad population sub-groups are identified and support is extended to them with some understanding that there will be some (tolerable) leakages to those above the poverty line. For instance, price support for particular crops helps to enhance incomes of poor people who grow such crops, but is also supports the rich farmers engaged in the production of such crops. Subsidies on food and fuel help the rich and the poor alike.

A critical input for purposes of minimizing leakage is the identification of the poor and vulnerable and using the different income distribution characteristics of these different groups, particularly their different patterns of poverty and vulnerability, so that expenditures/support can be directed to them.

Mitigation Through Integration

In broad terms social action programs are of two types: those designed to protect or mitigate the effects of adjustment policies on specific target groups and those aimed at fostering greater participation by the poor and vulnerable groups in the process of socio-economic development. The first type deals with protection or compensation so that welfare and consumption levels of target groups are restored (or protected from deterioration). The second type aims at enhancing the productive capacity so that actors can more strongly participate in the emerging socio-economic environment. Generally the first type would be aimed at measures targeted to the groups directly affected by the policy, if such groups can be identified with ease. The second type aims at problem areas, whose solutions are consistent with long term aims of development, so as to maximize integration of the poor and vulnerable in the economic mainstream.

The 'vulnerable group' is another concept whose operationalization for policy intervention purposes is not without difficulty. The following groups in society are generally considered vulnerable (vulnerability defined in relation to "Welfare openness to shocks"):

(a) the youth: because the labour market to them is uncertain and they are generally still dependent, on parents and guardians.

(b) The children: tenderness, dependency and lack of income sources make them vulnerable.

(c) Women: in many societies where the 'bread-earner' is the man women are necessarily dependent. Many societies deny them ownership of productive assets too.

(d) The aged: many would be living on fixed incomes (like pensioners) and on assets which may be of low yield. Such incomes fall with inflation, just as their labour power diminishes from old age also.

(e) Others: especially wage earners in risky public sector jobs, in the informal sector, etc. Vulnerability results mainly from low returns and insecurity of employment, especially where budget cuts may mean retrenchment to save on costs. The disabled may also be considered especially where no social action programmes and facilities exist to their working environment conducive (no appropriate transport of office facilities to accommodate their disabilities, etc).

Emerging Evidence Poverty in Tanzania

Poverty in Tanzania has been widely documented; from the policy makers' fora that first established the Distributive philosophy of the Arusha Declaration in the mid 1960s to the current efforts that address specific questions like "What are the realistic poverty lines in Tanzania? How poor are the Tanzanians? How many fall below the poverty line(s)? and the like".

Wage incomes, the main official source of urban incomes, have been depressed, especially during economic crises and the adjustment processes. For instance, the minimum wage (which was less than the living wage anyway) rose in nominal terms from 380 TShs. in 1977 to 2500 in 1990; but when urban inflation is considered the 1990 value was only equal to 113 TShs. at the 1977 prices; and in terms of purchasing power a day's minimum wage could only buy 2.2kg of maize flour (sembe, a basic staple food in Tanzania) and nothing else! The nominal minimum wage in 1991 was 3500 TShs. and a day's wage could purchase no more than 1.3 kg of maize flour (see Kapunda, 1992).

The inadequacy of salaries has also been characterized through major surveys of expenditure patterns. In Mushi and Wangwe (1991) for instance it was reported that the actual monthly expenditure of a top executive in government ranged between 16 and 100 thousand Shs. per month (average 58 thousand in November-December 1990 prices, but the top salary was fixed at 22930 TShs; implying substantial gap between average expenditure and top salary. For the parastatal sector top executives spent on average 80 thousand Tshs per month but the top salary was only about 18,000 TShs. For semi-professional scales in parastatals (salaries not exceeding 15,000 TShs) average expenditure per person was given at 20,000/=.

Supplementary income have been surveyed too, and in a study cited in Mushi and Wangwe (1991) other forms of accruals included family contributions and secondary informal and formal earnings (via moonlighting). A low income for civil servants after all primary and secondary accruals was given at 9,460/= whereas a high one was given at 43,198/=, with a weighted average of about -13930/=. Lower scales of incomes (say about 10,000) would then have been the closest indicator of poverty lines in 1990. But these are sensitive to price changes, to geographical location and to social stratification.

Rural poverty continues to be researched too and the World Bank (1991) reports on some studies which indicate that the majority of rural people are not rich, and their incomes fell rapidly during the crisis and adjustment processes. Such income declines appear to have been arrested. Further research is in progress on poverty in Tanzania and the Social Audit of the SDA project aims at characterizing it in more details.

Research Agenda

From the discussion throughout this chapter it is clear that the government had policies on (absolute and relative) poverty alleviation in the period following Arusha. These took the form of the government Paper of 1967 following the first Turner Report and 1981 following the second Turner Report. In effect the policies were those of "direct intervention", and even the second five years development plan (1969-1974) was heavily biased in favour of basic needs provision, particulary for the poor and disadvantaged (regions and persons). Events in the 1980s reshaped the policies to those of an implicit nature, following macroeconomic malaise which (may have) necessitated the need for emphasis on economic growth. Policies on poverty alleviation for the period especially in the late 1980s to the early 1990s have been project-centred in practice even as government has continued to give some token emphasis that the poor and vulnerable must be protected. Initiatives exist in sectors of direct incidence to human development (food, shelter, clothing, education, health, etc) and a national project specifically addresses questions of poverty alleviation (The Social Dimensions of Adjustment Project).

Agenda 1: The various initiatives in poverty alleviation in Tanzania are not coordinated (except possibly at the macro level in discussions in IMTC and above). Any serious research on poverty alleviation in Tanzania ought to start from taking an inventory of the various initiatives in place (both as studies and as action programmes). In particular specific information is necessary on how these various initiatives (a) characterize the poor (b) provide for measures of poverty lines (c) attempt to help with poverty alleviation through methods of direct interventions and/or empowerment and (d) judge what it takes to say poverty is falling or rising.

Agenda 2: Public policies on poverty alleviation have evolved too; from the direct and explicit interventions of Arusha, to the extreme cases of trickle down under adjustment, and currently to a more "middle course" attempt through aspects of intervention, empowerment and integration. Whereas direct intervention had its limits when the economy was not growing, and the pitfalls of trickle down are clear, there is no knowledge about the emerging results of the middle course action. It is necessary to organize a research theme about (a) the various forms of middle course actions (b) the implied logic of such actions and (c) the optimal mix of initiatives of an interventionist (targeting) nature, those of trickle down and those of integration (empowerment).

Agenda 3: It has been remarked variously in this chapter and in the general literature that pressure groups may exert forces that can "disorient" good, purposeful government policies. We noted for the case of Tanzania the case of eroded salaries which affected the higher echelon disproportionately, etc. Information and analysis is necessary on poverty alleviation, in particular (a) is there discernible evidence that part of the problem on poverty may have been from the pressure groups or the higher echelon officials who need not have liked the notions of equity (hence the relative poverty)?, (b) is there evidence that the poor may have been too poor, too weak and unorganized as to have no exerting pressure to affect the course of government actions?. The question of pressure groups is thus a critical one.

Agenda 4: When the government used explicit interventions there were explicit instruments of policy. These included controls/manipulations of prices, taxes and wages. Such have been discontinued as instruments to effect policies on poverty alleviation as the government goes "market". Information and analysis should be done to examine possible alternatives under a market regime; in particular (a) what do we learn from some of the market "welfare" states that have explicit poverty alleviation policies, Such as the scandinavian countries Singapore and Switzerland? (b) what typical instruments exist for Tanzania to take the place of the earlier ones for purpose of poverty alleviation if prices wages are decontrolled? and (c) what transitory mechanisms need to be put in place to effect the move from the interventionist (targeting) approach of Arusha to the regulatory, market regime (involving the middle course approach) of the 1990s so that poverty does not increase?

Agenda 5: In the trace of historical development above there is evidence of a structural shift in both orientation of policy and in the structure of institutions to effect such change. The process is having dramatic effects on the social structure and property ownership in the country. The implications for both poverty and wealth (and their distribution) seem little understood. It is necessary to obtain information and do analysis on the various reform components and their impact on poverty and primary incomes (Civil Service Reforms; particularly issues of Pay Reform, Retrenchment and Redeployment; Parastatal Reforms, particularly privatization, liquidation and some imminent lay offs; Financial Sector Reforms; particularly aspects of liberalization of exchange rates, interest rates and the trade regime; etc). All these reform components have the potential of changing primary and secondary incomes and their distribution.

Agenda 6: There is increasing talk, under political pluralism and economic liberalism, that the past monopoly nature of the state in politics (on partly system) and the economy (control over commanding heights and some rigid controls) may have also added to poverty in this country, to the extent that divergent views, though well meaning, may not have not received sufficient consideration by the state. It is noted, for instance, that even the skinned pay (salary plus all cash and non cash benefits) in favour of the higher echelon in the party and Government worked to increase both relative and absolute poverty in the low echelon in the salaried segments other population. It is said remarked that the same could be said of rigid controls over agricultural producers prices which extracted significant "rents" to cater for the bureaucracy in the parastatal sector (especially Crop Authorities). This may have worked to magnify rural poverty. It is thus important to organize a research agenda around this cluster of claims to obtain: (i) the precise nature of political monopoly under one party as it existed in Tanzania; (b) the nature of the income distributive effects of the decision making in Government with reference to the management of the economy; and (c) how any divergent but well meaning ideas on poverty alleviation were "accommodate"

Agenda 7: Much of the literature about the trickle down effect take a stance that assumes the lower echelons in society (the poor) as the passive parties in development with government and big business being the "actors" whose spill over results trickle down. There is increasing evidence from grassroots that the poor can become self reliant if empowered with even the minimum of primary and secondary incomes. If this approach is to take root in bringing change, information will need to be sought and acted upon on the possibilities of "trickle-up" so that sufficient feedback is floated to these higher echelons about (a) what survival tactics exists and are used by the poor (b) What potential exist for further empowerment (c) what optimal mixes exist for mitigation through redistribution and that through integration (d) how best to keep the dialogue so that common Tanzanian are made to understand or aware of policies, institutions and facilities that exist to help them and other actors in the fight against poverty, and (e) what role to anticipate of NGOs especially in areas where incapacity of government and the poor themselves is conspicuous.

Agenda 8:   There has been a mismatch between the timing of various decelerations and their embodiment in legal language for constitutional operalionalization.   For instance, even as agriculture has historically been emphasized as the foundation of the economy since the 1960s it was not until the early 1980s that a national agricultural policy was worked out. The same could be said of land policies, population policy, health policy etc. Lacking such policies or their late enactment means that operationalization lacked the legal mandate and this may have led to laxity or haste in actions. Poverty alleviation may have suffered as a result. It is proposed to organized to organized a research cluster around the them of policies; both macro and sectoral.

There is no doubt the debate on poverty alleviation shall continue (unfortunately not necessarily involving a dialogue of the poor themselves and how their poverty can be alleviated).

NOTES

1. In a now classic example he assumes a scenario in which growth in real per capita income occurs without altering the relative distribution of income between receiving units. If (a) the poverty line remains fixed so that concern is only with absolute poverty in the income dimension (b) mean income of the poor is one half of the poverty line and (c) the annual per capita growth rate is 3 percent; then, it will take more than twenty years for the average poor person to be lifted out of poverty. He concludes that "explicit redistributive strategies may well be introduced in response to slowness of "trickle down - it is simply a matter of political arithmetic" (p.70)

2. It was observed, for instance, that in 1962-63 real wages rose by 48% and total wage employment declined by 13%. Another jump in real wage in 1964/65 (by 25%) resulted in a fall in employment by 5%. the average change in the period 1962 to 1967 was a rise of 18.2% in real wage per annum and a decline of 2.2% per annum in total wage employment.

3. (a) These are success of the tax system in imposing the tax burden on the group of persons or sectors intended and to the desired degree, (b) the effective realization of the concept of tax equity underlying tax legislation, (c) the success of the tax regime as a fiscal instrument for stabilization and growth via the budgetary process, and (d) the existence of a reasonable balance between the costs of administering the tax system (economic costs, compliance costs, administrative and other costs) and the yield of taxation. Thus when clamours for tax reforms are widespread in the economy, and cries of unfairness, injustice, inequity and instability are commonplace it is because the tax system is significantly at variance with one or more of these tax policy PRINCIPLES.

4. A Loans and Advances Recovery Trust (LART) was established by legislation to expedite the disposition, including liquidation, of parastatal enterprise in serious default of loans. An order was made through the Budget of 1992-3 effecting a *hard budget constraint* by ending tax exemptions for parastatals and enforcing payment of commodity import support counterpart (see Rolling Plan 1993/4-95/96). The financial restructuring of the banks has ensured that enterprise lending is exclusively for borrowers that are judged viable.

REFERENCES

Addison, T. and L. Demery (1986):'The impact of Liberalization on Growth and Equity', *World Employment Program Research,* No. 4, ILO, Geneva.

Anand, S and Kanbur, R. (1985): "Poverty Under the Kuznets   Process". *Economic Journal,*London, Vol.95, Supplement, March.

Bagachwa, M.S.D., *et al,* (eds) (1992): *Market Reforms and Parastatal Restructuring in Tanzania,* Economics Dept and Economic Research Bureau.

Bagachwa, M.S.D (1993): "Estimates of Informal Parallel and Black Market Activities in Tanzania" International Conference on Development Challenges & Strategies for Tanzania: An Agenda for the 21st Century, Dar es Salaam.

Barrieros, Lidia (1985):"Operationalizing Concepts and Measurement of Poverty and Basic Needs"; in the Institute of Social Studies: Planning for Basic Needs in Latin America, *Working Paper No.23,* July.

Bevan , D.L., A. Bigsten,: P. Collier and J.W. Gunning (1988): "Incomes in the United Republic of Tanzania During the Nyerere Experiment" in Ginneken, V.M., ed., *Trends in Employment and Labour Incomes: Case studies on Development Countries,* ILO, Geneva.

Demery, L and Addison, T. (1987):*The Alleviation of Poverty Under Structural Adjustment,* The World bank, Washington, D.C.

Government of Tanzania, The World Bank and the International Monetary Fund: *Tanzania: Policy Framework Paper* 1991/92-1993/94; Dar es Salaam.

ILO (1988):*Distributional Aspects of Stabilization Program in the United Republic of Tanzania, 1979.1984*; Report of an ILO Mission, ILO, Geneva.

Kanbur, R. (1987):'The Theory of Adjustment and Trade Policy' The Rockfeller Foundation. CPR/Commonwealth Secretariat *Project on Trade Development in Sub-Saharan Africa.*

Kanbur, R. (1987a):'Structural Adjustment, Macroeconomic Adjustment and Poverty: A methodology for analysis' *World Development,* Vol. 15, No. 12.

Kapunda, S.M. (1992):"The Urban Poor in Tanzania": *Input to Social Audit Study,* SDA Unit, Dar es Salaam.

Mtatifikolo, F. (1990):The Subterranean Economy in Tanzania: Mid 70s to Mid-1980s: Its Structure and Annual Aggregates. *Report to OSSREA,* January.

___, (1990a) "An Economic Analysis of Tanzania's Tax Performance: Expe-riences since the 1973 Tax Act". *Eastern Africa Economic Review,* Vol 6,#1.

___, (1992): The Social Context of Reforms: Poverty and Poverty Alleviation in Tanzania: in Bagachwa *et al* (1992) (eds): "Market Reforms and Parastatal Restructuring in Tanzania": DOE and ERB, UDSM, P 57-71.

Mtatifikolo, F and D. Katabaruki (1992): "Towards Realization of an Optimal size of the Government: A Review of Worker Compensation and Government Capacity" *Report to Project* URT/90/031 "Strengthening Management in the

Public Sector", Civil Service Department.

Mushi, R. (1991): "Review of Donor Policies on Remuneration of Local Staff, Local Consultants and Government Employees". *Report to the World Bank.*

Mushi, R. and S.M Wangwe (1991):Review of Comparative Compensation Policies in Tanzania". *Report to the World Bank,* April.

Orshansky, M. (1985):"Counting the Poor: Another Look at the Poverty Profile". Social Security Bulletin, U.S Government.

Oyen, Else (1992:) "Some Basic Issues in Comparative Poverty Research" in "The Americas: 1492-1992: The *Municiplicity* of Historical Paths and Determinants of Development" multiplicity; Blackwell Publishers/UNESCO.

Sen, A.K. (1976): "Poverty: An Ordinal Approach to Measurement"; *Econometrica,* Vol. 144.

___,(1983) "Poverty; Relatively Speaking". *Oxford Economic Papers,* Vol.35.

Stewart,F. (ed) (1983): *Work, Income and Inequality*: Payment Systems in the , Third World; London, Macmillan.

Tanzania Government, (1967): "Wages, Incomes, Rural Development, Investment and Price Policy". Government printer.

___, (1981): "The National Policy on Productivity, Incomes and Prices of 1981" Government Printer.

___, (1981): NESP: 1980/81-1981/82. Government Printer.

___, (1982): S.A.P, 1982/83-1984/85. Government Printer.

___, (1986): "ERP; 1986-1989". Government Printer.

___, (1989):"ESAP: 1989/90-1991/92". Government Printer.

Tanzania Government (Annual):*Economic Survey,* Various Years; *Budget Speeches,* Various Years; Budget Documents; various years; Statistical Abstracts, various Years.

Tanzania Government (1993): Rolling Plan and Forward Budget, 1993/94-1995/96. Government Printer.

Townsend, P. (1979):"Poverty in the United Kingdom: Survey of Household Resources and Standards of Living", Penguin.

Turner, H.A. (1967):"Report to the Government of the United Republic of Tanzania on Wages, Income and Price Policy", *Report of an ILO Mission* (Known also as the First Turner Report).

___, (1975):"Report to the Government of Tanzania on the Past, Present and Future Incomes Policy in Tanzania". *Report of an ILO Mission* (also known as the Second Turner Report).

World Bank (1984): *Country Economic Memorandum, Tanzania*; Washington.

___, (1989): *Tanzania: Public Expenditure Review;* in Three Volumes: Washington, D.C.

___, (1991):*Tanzania: Towards Sustainable Development in the 1990s:* In Two Volumes, Washington, D.C.

5

Environmental Issues and Poverty Alleviation in Tanzania

A MASCARENHAS

INTRODUCTION

Concern about issues on environment and poverty is increasing at the international level. In this context, as the countries of the South pay more attention to their national economies there is a rising consciousness of poverty, and to some extent of their environment. The focal point of this chapter is the situation in Tanzania. To what extent are the environmental or the social systems responsible for the real poverty in Tanzania? How does poverty manifest itself in Tanzania? What should be the components of the research agenda to better understand the relationship between poverty and the environment?

To put the subject in context, the global situation will be discussed briefly and this will be followed by a similar treatment for Africa. The bulk of the chapter will concentrate on the environmental background and social situation in which poverty occurs in Tanzania. With this background it is possible to draw a research agenda on environment and poverty alleviation in the country.

GLOBAL PERSPECTIVES OF THE RELATIONSHIP BETWEEN POVERTY AND ENVIRONMENT

Concern with poverty has been one of the main themes of all the three recent global commissions: Brandt, Brundtland, and the South. Brundtland starts with the environment and works on the premise that while we all depend on the biosphere for sustaining our lives: "The Earth is one but the world is not." The Brundtland Commission is explicit about the interrelationship between poverty and environment:

> Poverty is a major cause and effect of global environmental problems. It is therefore futile to attempt to deal with environmental problems without a

broader perspective that encompasses the factors underlying world poverty and inter-national inequality. (WCED, 1987).

The Commission underscored the need for the natural and social systems to be understood, and to work together so as to bring about sustainable development.

The global interaction of both poverty and wealth with the environment has resulted in a variety of environmental threats. The main ones are: degradation of the soil, water and marine resources which are essential for life supporting systems; pollution which is becoming health threatening; global climate change; and loss of biodiversity (World Resources Institute 1992). In this framework one can discern two major trends: the rapid increase in population, and great and increasing disparity in wealth.

Within the context of the great disparity of wealth, the South Report realized the importance of the environment and regarded the then forthcoming United Nations Conference On Environment And Development (UNCED) as a conference of *exceptional importance* (South Centre, 1992). The acceptance of the twofold "link" by the North and the interdependence of the issues and solutions opened up the possibilities of mounting an integrated approach to the global challenges of sustainable development (South Centre, 1992). Towards this end, negotiations were to be centred around two fundamental strategic objectives: First,

> to ensure that the South had adequate "environ-mental space" for its future development;

and secondly,

> .. to modify global economic relations in such a way that the South obtains the required resources, technology and access to markets .... which would enable it to pursue a development process...for its growing population (South Centre, 1992).

The nature of the link between environment and poverty was given priority by UNCED. The UNCED Secretariat commissioned UN agencies and SIDA to submit papers concerned with poverty, environment and development. The SIDA report concluded that:

> ..the relationship may not be quite that straightforward. Authors .. use a set of suppositions as their point of departure ... although there is a growing body of intuitive and field-related experience which has yet to command serious attention. The casual effects between poverty and environment are often more complex .... further, there is the potential for conflict in policies and programmes between the goals of poverty alleviation and environmental protection (Holmberg, 1992).

The assessment of the World Bank, in its annual report specifically devoted to the theme, environment and development, is that, "..the links between environmental degradation and poverty are as yet poorly understood" and that "improved understanding between poverty and environment remains a priority" (World Bank, 1992)

It is worth considering poverty in tangible terms. In 1985 there were 340 million people not getting enough calories to prevent stunted growth and suffering from health risks (World Bank, 1986). The number of people living in slums and shanty towns and who lack access to clean water is on the increase.

The degree of poverty is often measured by per capita income. The alarming element in these figures is not only the magnitude of differences in financial wealth but also in the implied capacity to meet the basic needs. The contrast is obscene: in 1989, there were 157 billionaires and perhaps 2 million millionaires yet nearly 2 billion people drunk and bathed in contaminated water (Durning, 1990).

However amidst all the wealth, destitution seems to be perpetuated by mutually reinforcing factors at the local, national and international levels that form a poverty trap, which among the poor is increasingly taking an environmental dimension (Durning, 1990). This does not imply that the rich have a positive impact on the environment. On the contrary, there is a persistent theme in recent studies that shows that the global environmental threats, such as polluted air and water and contaminated oceans are a result of affluence. (WCED, 1987, Brown *et. al.* 1990, Commission on Global and Human Settlements, 1992).

Measuring Poverty

The main reference point for measuring national wealth or Gross Domestic Product, although now disputed by some, has been the performance of the national economy. National wealth or the poverty which goes with it for most third world countries tends to be sanitized and abstracted, and tells one little about the nature and extent of poverty. For example, Measures such as GDP tells little about either the state of the environment or the state of poverty.

The concern by African governors in the World Bank about the crisis and lack of development led to the influential Berg Report. This and the subsequent reports from the World Bank have been preoccupied by national economies, their sectors and their external relationships. Yet, there is need to look at poverty in a multi-dimensional perspective such as regarding poverty in the context of:

> ... a simultaneous prevalence of sickness, malnutrition, indebtedness, hardwork, discomfort and poor food availability at certain times of the year, usually during

the rains. This period before the harvest - "the hungry season" is one of considerable stress for rural people, exacerbating their poverty. (Longhurst, 1986)

Conceptually the Institute of Development Studies in Sussex, especially Robert Chambers and his colleagues, have done much to draw attention to several dimensions of poverty in the Third World. To have tools of analysis and to better understand poverty, it is best to restrict the disadvantages to:

> ... lack of wealth or assets, and lack of flows of food and cash - to which it properly refers. To make a start, five clusters of disadvantage can be described - poverty, physical weakness, vulnerability, isolation and powerlessness. ... these clusters of disadvantage interlock. (Chambers, 1985)

These clusters lead to the viscious circle of poverty - leading to the syndrome of poverty or the poverty trap. The five clusters give twenty causal relationships (See Figure 1).

The professional ethos has been towards the "sophisticated" and the economic rather than to the "primitive" attributes or the uneconomic indicators of development (Chambers, 1983. See Table 1). To tackle poverty it is necessary to gain reversals in three areas: in space, in professional values, and in specialization. This means that spatially, there is more attention paid to the "core" rather than the "peripheries", urban rather than rural, centralized rather than the decentralized. The urban bias of development - be it as aid, policies or magnitude, is so ingrained that even when it is meant to assist the poor it frequently ends up enriching the wealthy. For this and other reasons, poor people remain poor (Lipton, 1976).

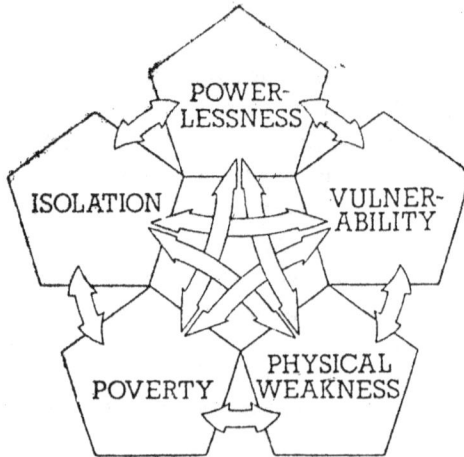

Fig. 1: Poverty and Casual Relationship

Table 1: Some Professional Values And Preferences

<u>Sophisticated</u>   <u>Primitive</u>

For Technology, Research And Projects

Urban	Rural
Industrial	Agricultural
High cost	Low cost
Capital Using	Labour-Using
Inorganic	Organic
Complex	Simple
Large	Small
Modern	Traditional
Marketed	Subsistence
Quantified	Unquantified
Geometrical	Irregular
Clean	Dirty
Odourless	Smelly

For Contracts And Clients

Rich	Poor
Influential	Powerless
Educated	Illiterate
Male	Female
Adult	Child

For Place And Time

Urban	Rural
Office	Field
Accessible	Remote
Day	Night
Dry Season	Wet Season

Based on: (Chambers, 1983, p.173)

Professionals are currently rewarded for focusing on the "cores". As a result all the professional attributes and values reinforces the trends to service the rich and the powerful in the cores. To redress the balance, professionals have to pay as much attention to the "primitive" rather than concentrating on the "sophisticated" column of Table 1. Specialization is also very much attracted to the core and to the first world. This results in many gaps and failures to bring change among the poor (Chambers, 1985).

It would appear that both environmental issues and poverty have a number of different dimensions. *The issue of poverty especially in Africa cannot be confined to finances only.* As Sen (1986) and others have pointed out, poverty is a matter of "entitlement" and not resources alone. The rulers have to set the norms. With this general background to the global environmental issues and poverty, we now take a specific look at the African crisis.

The African Crisis

As famines swept across Africa in the last two decades the full dimension of the ecological and social crisis became very evident. An entire continent seemed near to collapse. There was an annual decline of 4.1% of incomes from the 1980's (ECA, 1985). Since the period of independence, the continent has moved from food self-sufficiency to widespread hunger (Timberlake, 1985): by 1984, some 140 million or 26% of the population were being fed from grain coming from abroad (Brown & Wolf, 1985).

Through visualization and graphics the Ethopian famine, brought the full message of the human tragedy unfolding itself. Some have given ecological causes a large share of blame for this state of affairs. One such interpretation puts it that:

> .. Africa has taken too much from its land as well. It has overdrawn from its environmental accounts, and the result for much of Africa has been environmental bankruptcy. (Timberlake, 1985)

Where authors have tried to quantify, the losses are astounding. A USAID (19..) estimate was that Ethopia was losing through erosion over a billion tons of top soil per annum, and the Ivory Coast has lost most of its forest cover. In addition, as African countries imported more food so too did the debts grow.

It must not be forgotten that there were natural calamities especially drought and floods and insect pests that destroyed even the little crops that had survived. The relevance of drought cannot be exaggerated.

There is no country in Eastern and Southern Africa which has not, at some time or another, experienced problems related to drought. The duration, extent and intensity of the droughts vary considerably. In Botswana, since independence there have been at least two major national droughts which have virtually covered the whole country, lasting for several seasons. These droughts were severe enough for policies to be drawn to combat drought.

One of the major contributors to African ecological instability has been drought. Overall, the areas under severe drought account for about 17.6% of SADCC. This varies from a low of 1% and 5% in Zambia and Angola respectively, to a high of 23% and 65% in Zimbabwe and Botswana respectively. Tanzania has 19% of the land in this category (Gomez; Mutambenege & Moyo: 1987).

There is a close link between production and rain dependent agriculture. In the past there were efforts by nearly all communities to have mechanisms to cope with drought. These mechanisms have been greatly weakened by the attrition of traditional knowledge, the introduction of new food crops, the penetration of markets and unequal exchange. Droughts are also linked with several other environmental factors, including floods, fires, decline in water tables, erosion, etc. They have an impact beyond their immediate border. As an environmental hazard, droughts are persistent and affect countless people in sub-Saharan Africa.

Whatever the reasons, the cost of food imports rose from $600 million in 1972 to over $5.4 billion by 1985, and food costs and debt repayments absorbed over 40% of the export earnings (ECA, 1985). Also there have been political instability in several countries - in Angola, Ethopia, Mozambique, Somalia and Sudan - and this has led to poverty and the loss of countless lives. It is interesting to observe how African governments responded to the multi-dimensional environmental problems.

Environment And The African Governments

Environmental issues and problems have been so severe that major regional and continental conferences have been held to discuss them. The outcome has been an official perception about the main environmental problems and issues faced by African governments. The first African Ministerial Conference On the Environment (AMCEN) was held in Cairo in 1985.

The 1989 Kampala Conference of Ministers of Environment was partly in response to the Brundtland Commission and to the 'Environmental Perspectives To The Year 2000 and Beyond' (UNEPGC, 14/26). The eight issues identified by the WCED were accepted at the Kampala Conference, including urban challenges, food security and desertification. There was a realization of growing environmental problems which led to some continent-wide decisions being made.

Between Cairo (1985) and Kampala (1989) there were reforms at least organizationally. Most African countries now have ministries of environment which are suddenly called to shoulder an enormous degree of "environmental and developmental" responsibilities. In the preparatory phases of UNCED, a great deal had to be done by officials and others to keep to tight schedules, and there has been little time for implementation. Environmental issues have been globalized to the extent that there has been little action.

Eastern And Southern African Sub-region

The environmental issues in the sub-region are very complex. Perception about the environmental issues vary from nation to nation, and from community to community; and between the various social groups. The real environmental issues are those situations where both biological and social systems have been threatened.

Yet, it is tempting to examine the environmental issues in conventional terms. Were the droughts in Botswana since the 1960's any less severe than they have been in Mozambique and Ethiopia? The social system in Botswana minimized suffering. In Mozambique and Ethopia the failure of the social system extenuates the impact of drought to tragic proportions. Social systems concerned with the masses can considerably minimize environmental problems.

Poverty, Environment & Economic Revival

Despite radical economic reforms and social adjustments programmes engineered by the international financial institutions, the economic situation in Africa is still pathetic. The SADCC and Eastern Africa Region is among the poorest region in the world. According to the World Bank classification by income and region, 15 out of the 25 countries in the region are in the low income category. The major exceptions are Reunion, Seychelles and South Africa which are in the upper middle income group respectively (World Bank 1992).

Are the rural areas being impoverished because of the macro-economic policies? Macro-economic policies imposed, adopted or devised by African countries which promote the expansion of export crops run a great risk of perpetuating both the environmental and developmental crisis. Prices of most of the raw materials have now touched rock-bottom in addition to the risk of opening new lands.

Overall there is no reason for the majority of people to be optimistic. For instance, despite following most of the recommended reforms, and even improving its credit ratings with the donor community, Tanzania has continued to slip further and is now regarded as the second poorest country in the world! The situation is not better in Zambia, Uganda, Sudan or for that matter Zimbabwe! This macro-economic stagnation and its links to agriculture do not augur well for the environment.

Environment & Agricultural Development

In most of the SADCC Region, agriculture contributes to about 34% of the region's GDP, employs about 79% of the total labour force, and overall accounts for 25% of the total foreign exchange earnings (SADCC, 1987). About 70 per cent of the population is dependent on agriculture.

The agricultural resource base is at present underutilised. Out of the total of 477 million hectares suitable for cultivation only 5% is under crops, 41% under ranch land, 33% under forests and woodland, and 21% is considered unsuitable under the current technology and marketing conditions (Mkandawire, 1991). However, these gross figures have to be used with caution.

The pattern of agricultural development was set during the colonial period and an ecological base. It is worth considering to what extent perceived environmental stability, the excision of natural endowment from the majority of indigenous people helped to shape and perpetuate economic patterns and development. For instance, a striking feature is that in nearly all well-watered, highland areas, from Angola to Zimbabwe, European plantations were established particularly for high valued plantation crops like coffee, tea, tobacco, etc. Do these remain the main bastions of economic development?

In drier areas where there was a risk of rainfall deficits, the main crops grown included sisal, cotton and cashew. In such areas of high population densities and less desirable for white settlement, smallholders were encouraged to grow crops like cotton, groundnuts and robusta coffee.

In nearly all ecological areas African communities in the past grew a variety of food crops which reflected the environmental parameters - sorghum and millet in dry areas, maize in better watered areas and rice and bananas where water was abundant. These subtle micro insurances of the past have given way to increasing "mono" subsistence agriculture centered around maize.

Over large parts, the marginal areas are covered by miombo woodlands or bush. Such areas are tse-tse infested, and in extreme cases are arid. These marginal lands can be used by pastoralists, nomads, hunters, and agro-pastoralists. The first impression is that it is in these marginal areas that poverty and environmental degradation occur side by side. Can one conclude that there is an ecological basis for poverty, or are there other reasons? It is tempting to ignore the antecedents of present-day crisis. The economic and social base even before the tragic developments in Somalia, Mozambique and others are well summarized thus:

...The drought and famine in Africa are but symptoms of a massive economic, social and eco-logical crisis .. It has the world's lowest incomes, the lowest growth rates, and the lowest levels of employment, literacy and life expectancy... Malnutrition and starvation touch the lives of millions each year even when there is no drought (World Bank, 1989).

The Social Systems & Environmental Management

There are no immediate technical fixes. As has been recommended in a recent report there is need for national scientists to take a multi-disciplinary approach in tackling the environmental and developmental issues (CDCGC, 1992). In the context of the growing liberalization African scientists and researchers can gain important concessions *by taking innovative approaches.*

Economics is also about politics. There have been efforts to explore the interrelationship between the two way processes - how ecological stress leads to political conflicts; and how political conflicts lead to environmental degradation (Hjort af Ornas and Salih, 1989). While it is apparent that political conflicts lead to land degradation, more work is needed to establish the converse linkages. Development strategies and their detrimental impact on the local communities also need to be stressed.

There is need to go beyond awareness. For instance in Uganda despite there being 27 laws, 9 amendments and 16 repeals of laws pertaining to land ownership there were soil loses (Kamugisha, 1992). Yet, conservation of soils was a secondary goal and the first soil conservation ordinance No 33 of 1958 applied to non-Africans. It has remained in the statutes even after the expulsion of the non-Africans in 1972. There is little link between social priorities and critical technical and management responsibilities.

The importance of informed management approaches relies on policy and institutional flexibility, integrated planning long term perspectives, and knowledge-intensive planning practices (Kiriro and Juma, 1989). Ecological information has emphasized reductionism which is dominated by scientist with knowledge in specialized areas.

Macro Economic Issues, Environment And Poverty

At a global level, thanks to GATT, there is some useful information about economic issues and environment. Some of the issues will be dealt with in other chapters. However, it would be logical to think that the integration of the poor into the world economy has meant that the poor have had to extract more and more from the environment because their food comes directly from the soil and plants around them, water from rain and from the ground, fuel from the trees, etc. Every primary export crop makes the same demand on the soils, on the nutrients and on water and land.

Already in a number of places the present generation has begun to suffer. In 1988, nearly half a million children died in the world because of the slowing down of progress. (UNICEF, 1989) The extent to which this figure can be extrapolated for Tanzania should not be taken for granted.

From The Global To The Tanzanian Perspectives

The Tanzanian perspectives can best be appreciated against the global and African framework which has just been described. To cover the national aspects, there will be an attempt to describe the status of poverty in Tanzania and to specify some of the prevailing environmental issues.

Generally the African environmental and socio-economic situation previously described is to be found in Tanzania without any extremes or excesses, but including all the contradictions, complexities and opportunities. Nevertheless one of the major anomaly is Tanzania's official position as the second poorest country in the world. This position was arrived at during the very time that the economy was supposedly recovering.

The origin of Tanzania's poverty can partly be explained in its recent historical past. Tanzania's colonial heritage left a slender veneer of infrastructure, miserable living conditions in some areas, and a human resource base that was barely developed. For instance, it was estimated that the under-five mortality was over 300 for Rufiji District. Life expectancy was in the lower forties, famines and food shortages were frequent. The social statistics were similarly miserable: illiteracy was rampant, and access to basic social services uncommon.

In an attempt towards egalitarian development, notable gains were made over the next two decades and the social indicators improved very significantly. However, by the mid 1980's it was becoming apparent that despite a reduction in imports, there was an increasing deficit in the external trade balance, the GDP was declining, as was the production in both agriculture and manufacturing sectors.

While the debate to increase national wealth continued (at times acrimoniously), between the all-righteous proponents of the ujamaa ideology of the Party and the Government on the one hand, and the all-knowing international financial institutions on the other, life for the ordinary people worsened. There is an emergent class of very rich people but also growing signs of poverty.

Towards Increasing National Wealth

In 1986, an agreement was reached with the IMF and a start was made of the Economic Recovery Programme. In its various forms this led to increasing levels of liberalization, reduction of social services, ascendency of the private sector, and the deconfinement of domestic trade. There has been an improvement in the prices offered to farmers, and there have been some notable increases in the production of some of the crops. However, given that the international price of some of the primary crops has ebbed to the lowest in the postwar period, the real gains to producers is marginal.

Currently, the nation derives most of its income from the sale of primary products. There is little application of science and technology here, and the majority of people are occupied in the subsistence economy. In such situations, the influence of the natural factors of production, especially precipitation and soil quality are critical. Yet, the environment or natural resources have not really entered into any serious analysis.

Measured in conventional terms of national wealth, Tanzania has a place among the poorest countries. However, for the purpose of this study, the national poverty measured in GDP is not evenly spread among the Regions (See Table 2). The immediate impact of the ERPs on the GDP was not positive, but how were the various Regions affected? A persistent pattern is the poverty of the Coast Region, compared to the relative affluence of Dar es Salaam City Region. Other Regions at the bottom of the list, in 1980 and 1990 were Singida and Lindi. Is there an environmental basis for this poverty?

The administrative regions are too large to serve as units of analysis. In the three regions mentioned the disparities between districts maybe larger than between the regions. Indeed the poorest districts may not be in the poorest regions. Therefore, the exercise on poverty in Tanzania could well start by tracing the fortunes or misfortunes of the regions, and to find out whether there is any environmental basis for this poverty. If in this exercise the data could be disaggregated to a district level it would be more useful.

Official Environmental Issues

Even during the colonial period concern about the environment was a reoccurring theme. The major landmarks for ecological concerns were during the depression of the 1930's and immediately following World War II which brought about failures in large colonial projects in East and West Africa. In East Africa, the Groundnut Scheme fiasco led to the Royal Commission Report which paid attention to the natural resources, especially land, population, and on the need for research.

As a result, the critical base was established for research and the institutions that were needed to carry out the work. This is best exemplified by the creation of separate East African organizations to cover topics such as meteorology, agriculture, forestry, fisheries, etc.

Table 2: Regional Per Capita, GNP, & GDP

REGION	GNP per cap. in T.Shs 1988	Estimated GDP In Million Shs
Tanzania	5221	285,155
URBAN		
RURAL		
Dsm.	16063	40,921
Mbeya	6420	12,915
Arusha	6322	20,954
Mwanza	5753	27,811
Iringa	5718	18,220
Ruvuma	5224	15,285
Rukwa	4947	10,749
Mara	4488	22,616
Kigoma	4326	9,950
Morogoro	4242	10,637
Tanga	4218	16,634
Kagera	4014	9,215
Singida	3923	8,986
Mtwara	3569	8,671
Shinyanga	3486	9,856
Tabora	3183	14,470
Kilimanjaro	2967	4,666
Dodoma	2668	8,094
Lindi	2541	11,727
Coast	1945	2,776

Source: URT (1990)

All this set the stage for better understanding of the environment and the resources. Unfortunately, the collapse of the East African Community had a very negative impact on the organizations which were created.

For several reasons the environmental issues, important as they are, have until recently not received the attention they deserve, or they have been conveniently ignored by the government. Thus in the exigency of trying to hasten independence, all forms of protests were seized by TANU, to gain political capital. There were protests against destocking, and generally against conservation. Although independence was won relatively peacefully, in a few instances protests became violent, best exemplified in the Ulugurus and in the Usambaras, by the anti-conservation stand of TANU (Young & Fosbrooke, Cliffe 1972).

The era of using short term economic and political gains over environmental concerns is not over, as has dramatically emerged in the recent events over land allocation in Loliondo. The historical antecedents to down-playing environmental issues and its subsequent implications to development merit attention. In most such cases the issues at hand are not only "environmental" but also pertain more to ethics and the rights of communities to benefit from the natural resources or to maintain a relatively more secure livelihood pattern. This is not to suggest that these livelihood systems are perfect in a Rousseauan sense.

Despite all the environmental warning signs such as floods, droughts and famines throughout the 1960's and 1970's, the policy and decision makers spent little time on these manifestations. By the time of the preparation of the Third Five Year Plan, regional plans which made some efforts to consider environmental issues were quietly forgotten. Subsequently, after 1975 the environmental issues and the use of natural resources were at best taken for granted, and became very subservient to the economic planning and eventually to political consideration. This trend continues with the difference that the "environmental lobby" is now slowly emerging in Tanzania, and added to this is the creation of a dedicated Ministry of Tourism, Natural Resources and Environment.

Global environmental concerns leave their imprints on national statistics and priorities. Two such recent figures are the estimates of United Nations Sahelian Office (UNSO) which assessed that by 1986 about one-third of Tanzania was affected by desertification; and a Government of Tanzania/FAO report which alleges that by 1980, 45% of the country suffered from problems of desertification. Basically, the problem is that terms like "desertification" and "land degradation" are processes which have be used interchangeably in a social and physical context, thus compounding the uncertainties (Blackie, 1989). More often than not environmental issues are not neutral. Even a seemingly non-partisan topic like soil erosion is socio-politically loaded:

> .....Usually this recognition come 'from above' either literally, in the case of a foreign advisor from a light aircraft, or by policy-makers, politicians... Whoever, recognizes soil erosion, it is then publicised by those who have access to political power...after soil erosion has become .... an object of discussion and debate by those who have political power, then there arises the question of intervention usually by ....the institutions of the state.... conservation requires quite fundamental social change.. (Blackie, 1989)

Interventions in nearly all cases involve socio-economic costs which have to be borne not too infrequently by "the victims" themselves. There are excellent case studies which can be developed around the topic of conservation and poverty. There is need to be cautious against the all-too-willing acceptance of global plans of action, such as those envisaged in the Tropical Forest Action Plan, for they may not always be in the interests of the local people.

BOX 1

LIVELIHOOD PATTERNS & POVERTY

The livelihood patterns of the pastoralist, hunters and gathers deserves special attention not only because of the large area they cover but because of a number of critical problems that have begun to emerge. The so called marginal areas can sometimes be some of priceless real estate in the world.

In the Ngorongoro Conservation Area, wildlife and domestic animals and the action of the pastoralists has created a landscape that has to be subtly managed by movement. Interventions to, change, protect, control or promote certain land uses have not only brought increasing malnutrition (Arhem 1984, Homewood & Roger 1989) poverty in all the meanings of the word and even outright violations of human rights (Lane 1991, Mustapha 1992,). Basically, there is an unwillingness to recognize that the pastoralists have knowledge about the environment and resources. Expropriation has been without adequate compensation for the pastoralists for loss of resources or their rights. They have been marginalized because of their isolation and lack of information.

Towards Reality: Environment And Poverty

In a biblical sense the poor we will always be with us. What makes it unacceptable is that the biblical passage will be accepted as dogma. Poverty is not pre-determined, it is a state that others allow to happen and therefore can be reversed.

The whole issue of environment and poverty in Tanzania can generally be approached by considering four important environmental parameters: population, deforestation, land use and degradation, and the use of resources such as water. All four parameters must be looked at dynamically as they help to give some reality of the link between environment and poverty. There is also a socio-economic dimension to poverty.

One should add "development" to the socio-economic list, because development activities and policies may accelerate the use of resources, including fishing, mining and land use. Economic policies, trade and industrialization, can at times lead to pollution, deforestation and land degradation. A broad scale meaningful agenda on poverty alleviation and the environment can be developed in the context of the four areas identified above, as well as in the socio-economic framework.

POPULATION IN TANZANIA

Ever since Malthus, the spectre of geometric population growth has been a recurrent theme worldwide to try and explain poverty, disease and war. It has become very fashionable to describe the people-environment relationship in Africa in terms of concern and alarm. The argument starts with statements that the population growth is so rapid, that there is:

> .. a steepening spiral of degradation and, ultimately, desertification. Africa is
> on the brink of ecological collapse (Bell, 1987).

Not surprisingly Tanzania's population has also been regarded as a constraint to its development. The latest manifestation of this view is to be found in the review of forestry. The TFAP noted that Tanzania already has 23 million people growing at 2.8%. Consequently:

> From being a food exporter in the late nineteenth century Tanzania has become
> a net importer. ..By the year 2010, the population of Tanzania is estimated to
> reach 48 million .. Feeding this population will be a difficult, not to say
> impossible, task. (TFAP, Vol 1 TA)

The catastrophes predicted very seldom occur because of the assumptions made. There are so many dimensions to the population issues and variations at different levels that it becomes imperative to carry a robust analysis of population and environment.

The statistical base on population in Tanzania has been improving and is relatively good but is tied to the administrative framework. There are a number of problems related to their use, such as the relation of the figures to the biophysical world, to other social statistics, and their spatial and temporal variations. Above all there is need to better use some of the demographic data which tell considerably more than the population figures.

The Growth of Population In Tanzania

The population of Tanzania has now been on the increase for several decades. Since independence in 1961, the population has grown from slightly over 9 million, to over 24 million in 1990. Some estimates project that by the year 2000 the population would be approximately 34 million. Even without AIDS, it is unlikely that the above figures will be attained by natural population growth within the time specified.

The growth of population must be viewed in a proper perspective. The important relationship which is frequently ignored is that while the population grows, the land, with its varied potential is fixed (Table 3). The average national population density has steadily increased from about 8.5 in 1948, to 25 per square km in 1990. Therefore, for several decades there has been a steady decline in the per capita availability of land. If land set aside for National Parks, Game and Forest Reserves, is deducted, the densities would be 25% higher.

Apart from these considerations, the national averages also mask considerable sub-national disparities. Given these limitations there is need for studies which focus on the social and technical mechanisms needed to make the necessary adjustments for the well-being and sustainable use of resources.

Population is not equally distributed. On the Mainland, the regions with high rural densities are Mwanza (96) and Kilimanjaro (83), with Lindi and Rukwa trailing the list with 10 per skm. The unevenness of distribution is reflected in that 65% of the population occupies 36% of land. At the district level, about 65% of the population occupied about 29% of the land. Below the district level densities are even more skewed.

Table 3: Population Growth And Density

Year	Population Mainland	Growth Rate Per Annum	Density Per Skm	Hectares Per Cap
1913**	4,100,000	*	*	*
1921	4,300,000	*	*	*
1931	5,300,000	*	*	*
1948	7,480,400	1.69	8.5	11.8
1957	8,788,500	1.79·	9.9	10.1
1967	11,958,654	3.08	13.5	7.4
1978	17,036,499	3.22	19.8	5.0
1988	22,533,758	2.8	25.5	3.9

** German East Africa, consisted of present day Mainland Tanzania as well as the Republics of Rwanda and Burundi. The 1913-48 figures are estimates. Since World War I the boundary for Mainland Tanzania has been stable.

Land Pressure At The Sub-District Level

For operational reasons, there is need to examine densities below the district level. In North Pare District, while the district density was only 18.9 psk, at the Enumeration Area Level the density more than doubled and was as high as 50 psk, and dramatically rose to over 632 psk if only the cultivated areas were considered (Thomas, 1970). In some EA's staggering densities of 1057 psk were reached, and hillsides with slopes of 20 degrees or more were cultivated. Even with these very high densities the classical example of land degradation is uncommon either in the Pare or the Ukara. In contrast there are relatively more serious environmental problems in the medium density areas such as in Kondoa and Shinyanga.

Population growth or increase in densities on their own tell us little about the level of land degradation or deforestation. Nevertheless, there is need to examine the distribution of population in Tanzania in the biophysical dimensions because it gives an indication of the kind of pressures to anticipate.

Population and Landforms

Following the 1967 Census, efforts were made to account for people in Tanzania by landforms rather than by administrative units (Thomas, 1971). The three main landforms - mountains, hills and plains - were subdivided into 9 units on the basis of geology, altitude, location, etc. Densities were calculated, for 1957 and 1967, for each of the landform units. Most of the increase took place in the hilly areas. The highest density changes and intensification of land use were in the volcanic areas, in the flat lands around the lakes, and on the coast.

The study gave the trends and the broad changes which were taking place within the physical domain. It forms a baseline undertaken before the major socio-economic changes took place. These include villagization, growing urbanization and policy decisions which would fundamentally alter the shape of the spatial pattern of population distribution and developments in Tanzania. A repeat of the exercise is almost a prerequisite.

Biophysical Factors of Population Distribution

Looking at population distribution in an administrative framework masks the strong influence of biophysical factors in the distribution of population in Tanzania. Like other Third World people, Tanzanians living in the rural areas are critically dependent on natural resources for their basic needs especially food, water and shelter.

This direct dependency, reflects that capital and other inputs are scarce, and the level of mechanization and technology is low. This dependency on natural resources indicates that there is no reason for complacency. For instance, based on existing land use practices, a study in Tabora reveals how even in areas which are lightly populated, there was already overcrowding in 30 out of the 76 wards of the region (Mitchell, ed. 1984).

The natural resources are varied and unevenly distributed. Also the opportunities to exploit them have differed, and they have been subject to all manner of legislative control. The relationship between the use of natural resource and population is a dynamic process which is becoming even more complex. Therefore, understanding the circumstances and ways in which natural resources are used is important to reveal the different options which can be used to bring sustainable use of resources. In theory it is possible to plan for proper use of resources, but in practice there are problems.

The Social Factors Of Population Distribution

Broadly speaking, social factors have always had a powerful influence in the distribution of population, but its impact is even greater now. In the past a considerable amount of population movement took place by displacement to the adjacent areas which were regarded as favourable for settlement. Villagization slowed and almost put to an end that pattern of population dispersal.

Villagization

The saga of villagization in Tanzania is a very important episode in the history of the country. There are many studies on the topic (Freyvold, Hyden 1980, Mchenry, 1975, Cliffe 1972). However, the definitive one has yet to be written. In the meantime there are several contradictions. For instance while there are many studies on the topic, they are so diverse that a consensus is not possible. Did villagization, for instance, contribute and distribute poverty? While some portray villagization as something recent, there are historical antecedents in several parts of the country where attempt were made to cluster population in order to spearhead development.

The dispersed nature of population distribution was regarded as a disadvantage by most administrators, planners and politicians. In a dramatic "civilian" exercise, between 1974-75 millions of people in Tanzania, voluntarily or through coercion, were shifted from their homes. As a result since the mid-1970's the majority of people in rural Tanzania began to live in villages. In the rush issues pertaining to management, organization and land use were simply ignored or overlooked (Mascarenhas, 1979). Villagization affected Tanzania differently - it may have impoverished some, but it also gave others new opportunities.

The dramatic efforts at villagization at first put a great deal of pressure on resources. The resources themselves are not uniformly distributed, yet there were efforts to uniformly settle people in units of 250 families or "kayas", and at times the numbers were larger. In the semi-arid areas the availability of fuelwood and building materials availability posed problems. Journeys to collect fuelwood become longer, and building poles of the desired length could not be easily obtained. Adjustments had to be made along several fronts - including within official circles. Therefore, not surprisingly, "village forestry" "community forestry", and other approaches become important in Tanzania.

Urbanization

There has been unprecedented urban population growth in recent years especially to the coastal cities and towns including the commercial capital - Dar es Salaam. During the last four decades the urban population growth has been two to four times higher than the national population growth rate. In 1948 only a mere 197,300 people lived in towns. At present nearly a fifth of the population, comprising about four million people, live in urban areas. The environmental and social impact of this growth is very different from rural population increase.

The movement to urban areas is not for resources - it is for opportunities, imagined or real. Since the number of jobs available are few and the pay has been very low, there is a growing subsistence employment in the urban areas, and this continues to exert undue pressure in the rural surrounding. Due to the congestion in the large urban areas and the monetization of transactions, the poor can more easily be defined in urban areas, and they are also more visible.

Demography for Poverty Indication

One very powerful indicator of poverty is the use of demographic data, especially the Infant Mortality Rate (IMR) and the Under 5 Mortality Rate (U5MR). These figures at a national level easily separate the rich from the poor countries (See Table 4). If this conventional wisdom is true, could a similar analogy be used to separate the poor from the wealthy regions of Tanzania? Unfortunately, as Table 2 reveals there is little correlation between incomes and IMR, and the mortality rate of the under-fives. There have been notable improvements between the various censuses.

The regional GDP and the per capita amounts can vary considerably from year to year. The differences between the wealth of the regions is striking. There are major anomalies in the co-relationship between the IMR and the regional wealth (Table 5). Another feature is that the IMR has not fluctuated as much as the GDP.

Table 4: International Comparison of National Incomes and
Infant and Child Mortality Rates

Country	GNP per cap in US $ 1988	Estimated 1988 IMR	U5MR
Tanzania	160	104	176
Malawi	170	149	262
Bangladesh	170	188	188
Sweden	19,300	6	7
USA	19,840	10	13
Japan	21,020	5	8

Source: UNICEF/URT 1990

Table 5: Regional Per Capita GDP and IMR & U 5MR

REGION	GNP per cap in T.Shs (1988)	Estimated 1988 IMR	U 5MR
Tanzania	5221	115	191
URBAN		104	179
RURAL		138	249
Dsm.	16063	105	173
Mbeya	6420	124	209
Arusha	6322	75	119
Mwanza	5753	115	192
Iringa	5718	130	220
Ruvuma	5224	113	188
Rukwa	4947	131	221
Mara	4488	125	211
Kigoma	4326	115	192
Morogoro	4242	125	211
Tanga	4218	106	176
Kagera	4014	130	219
Singida	3923	96	157
Mtwara	3569	138	233
Shinyanga	3486	110	183
Tabora	3183	101	166
Kilimanjaro	2967	67	104
Dodoma	2668	132	222
Lindi	2541	140	236
Coast	1945	113	189

Source: (URT 1993)

Furthermore, both GDP and IMR vary a great deal within the region, and even more within the districts. In Iringa Region the district with the highest rate of malnutrition had 7.7% with severe cases in this category, but the lowest had 3.4%. At the divisional level, in Njombe District the percentages were 4.1 and 1.5 respectively (UNICEF, 1990).

Contrary to expectations, the drought prone areas have lower mortality rates than some of the surplus grain growing areas such as Rukwa, Mbeya, Ruvuma and Iringa. Is it the diet, or are environmental factors more important? From cause of death statistics and other data kept in hospitals and dispensaries, it is possible to analyze and begin discriminating the underlying from the immediate causes of IMR.

If the seasonal dimension is also added, which for instance determines the workload of the mother, the availability of food, the prevalence of disease and related phenomena, one can get a composite picture of the problems faced in rural areas (Bantje, 1983). Such research can also contribute to a multi-dimensional image of poverty in Tanzania.

In the urban areas macro-economic policies have favoured the rich. Even in the wage sector, the minimum wage buys less and less even of the basic food. In 1966 a day's minimum wage purchased 11kgs of grain, while in 1993 only 2.4kgs! Poverty in the urban area now increasingly means that even the basic needs are not met. The poor in these areas are easier to define and identify.

Most people still live in the rural areas. The changes to the environment are relatively slower and there is room for adjustments. An intriguing research issue is how have people in the rural areas adapted to diminishing resources.

VEGETATION COVER IN TANZANIA

An important feature of the biophysical world of Tanzania is the vegetation cover. Apart from land, it is one of the main wealth of the people. The extent of the different types of vegetation is determined by geologic history, the land, the climatic factors, and human interventions. Its long geological history, including rifting, has created plateaus and the remnants of ancient mountains on which are superimposed recent volcanic features, found in the southern and northern parts of the country.

Both rainfall and temperatures have an important role giving vegetation common to desert-like conditions, in the plateaus of northern and central parts of the country. In contrast are the mountainous areas with their lush patches of tropical forests. In extensive stretches experiencing prolonged dry season some form of grasslands and bush dominate. Apart from the broader climatic regimes, micro-climatic factors can also be very critical.

Table 6: Land Use in Tanzania

Category	Area in '000 Hectares	Percentage
Total Area	94 260	
Inland Water	5 900	
Total Land Area	88 360	100.0
Cultivators- Smallscale	3 880	4.4
Plantation & Largescale	585	0.7
Grazing	44 245	50.1
Forests/Woodlands	38 050	43.0
Urban/others	1 600	1.0

Source: Berry, Mascarenhas, Steward 1982, Tanzania Bureau of Statistics, 1986.

Human activities directly and indirectly had, and continue to have a profound effect on the vegetation through the use of fire, land use and the introduction of plants and animals. The interaction of the natural system and the socio-economic system gives an extremely complicated pattern. Table 6 summarizes the main types of land use and a general picture of vegetation types in Tanzania.

Type And Extent Of Vegetation

The status and extent of the vegetation, including forest cover in Tanzania, is not precisely known. The single largest category of vegetation cover is some form of thicket, bush or grassland.

The Miombo

There are three main types of forests in Tanzania. The wide varieties of woodland called *miombo*, constitute over 96% of the forests. The woodlands are not uniform because of their location in areas of varied geologic composition, geomorphic history, and soil types. Rainfall also differs between 800mm - 1200mm of per annum. Not surprisingly agricultural development and pressure on the miombo is not uniform.

The remaining 1.48 million hectares scattered away from the centre make up the invaluable moist forests, including the mangroves. The extent and coverage of the main types of forests is summarized in Table 7.

The critical factor regarding closed forests is that they make up for about 3% of Tanzania's forests, and while being the most invaluable they are also the most threatened. The "Eastern Arc" chain of mountains stretching from the Pares in the north to Uzungwas in the south consist of three clusters of scientifically valuable forests based on: the Usambaras in the north, Ulugurus, and Uzungwa Mountains. The forests of East Usambara Mountains probably constitute what is one of the richest biological communities in Africa. Out of the 2000 plant species, 500 are endemic (Hedberg, 19?, IUCN, 1989).

These forests have been under threat for some time. The most recent onslaught, beginning in the mid 1960s would have eliminated the forests. Local and international concern arrested the threat at the very last moment. The significance of the Usambaras is now well documented (Hamilton & Bensted-Smith 1989). Despite the very small area that they now cover, they are extremely valuable because of their biodiversity.

There are four other clusters of closed forests. These include: a scattered chain of coastal forests; Southern Highlands of Iringa and Mbeya Regions, the highlands in the north stretching westwards from Kilimanjaro, Ngorongoro and including the Mahale Mountains on the shores of Lake Tanganyika, and finally forests found in the foothills of the mountains.

Table 7: Estimates of the Type, Legal Status and Use of Forests

Types/Use/Status	Rounded to 1000 hectares
Type of Forest	
Woodlands	42,800
Closed Forests Excluding Mangroves	1,400
Mangrove Forests	80
Use of Forest Lands	
"Net Productive" areas	34,600
"Unproductive" areas	9,700
Legal Status	
Public forest lands	29,000
Forest Reserves	13,000
Forest/Woodlands in NP* & GR*	2,000

*NP = National Parks,   *GR = Game Reserves

Source: Adopted from TFAP (1989)

Mangrove Forests

The 80,000 ha. of mangrove forests of Tanzania cover less than 1% of the forested area, and their significance as a habitat is disproportionate to the area they cover. In the past all the five administrative regions along the coast of Tanzania had mangroves. More than half of the mangroves are to be found in the Rufiji Delta alone.

Trends In Deforestation

From the perspectives of foresters, the forests in Tanzania are under threat. Already at the turn of the last century there was concern by German foresters about the rate of tree felling, mangrove exploitation, and the decline of the forest cover (Schabel, 1990). There was fear that the "scarce forest of the protectorate" which are constantly subjected to damage and destruction by human interference... of the local people... and the forests in the vicinity of Dar es Salaam were described as "almost completely devastated", due to burning, overcutting and overgrazing. By 1898, it was even reported that the "magnificent" forests of eastern Usambaras had "largely vanished" (Schabel, 1990). The current concerns are only slightly different.

As part of the ongoing global concern for the environment, the "destruction" of the tropical forests have been earmarked for special attention through the Tropical Forest Action Plan, (TFAP). The objectives of the TFAP is simply that deforestation must be halted in the interests of the present and future generations. Like other governments, Tanzania has been convinced that forest protection must be given top priority. The basis of this conviction is that:

> There is ample evidence of deforestation, of diminishing possibilities of satisfying the needs for forest products, of serious environmental damages and ecological hazards. (Mnzava & Riihinen, 1989)

Furthermore, while the TFAP acknowledges that there are no reliable rates of deforestation, there is a doomsday scenario created with the assistance of the projected growth of the population. The TFAP gives the main reasons for deforestation as being:

> ...clearing for agriculture, overgrazing, charcoal burning, woodfuel harvesting, bush fires for various reasons and harvesting for industrial wood. In many areas land is extensively burned for the eradication of tse-tse flies. (TFAP, 1989)

Appraising Deforestation.

An important area of research is to verify or appraise the scenario being painted by the foresters for nearly a century. Part of the problem is the persistence for over two decades of misleading statistics that about 300,000 -400,000 ha. are cleared in Tanzania each year.

The above figure needs re-examining because of the doubling of the population, villagization and the increased use of wood-based energy. Although the Germans administratively took the first steps to halt deforestation, measures to preserve trees were taken by tribal authorities long before the 19th century (Kjekshus, 1977; Schabel, 1990).

There would be no forests left at all if the above figures were true. A great deal of the overgrazing is not in forested areas but in grasslands and thickets. How does one interpret, without qualifications, clearing for agriculture as a problem? Additional evidence for the rate of deforestation should be derived from various sources, and these should be used to assess and to give new dimensions to the problem of deforestation in Tanzania. For instance, the Wachagga retain an average of about a dozen different types of trees, and their agroforestry is a one good example of High-Intensity Tree-Management System (Munslow, Katerere et. al., 1988). Under what circumstances does agriculture prove to be destructive?

As part of the exercise of poverty alleviation, research could focus on how traditional agricultural practices have attempted to remain sustainable. It could well be that small additional improvements to traditional agricultural and agro-forestry practices, and the participation of people would be the most cost effective way of ensuring sustainability.

One of the major areas linking the environment-poverty debate is the occurrence of the specific crisis related to the biomass energy crisis. Because it is a feature that is almost confined to the third world, it is worth examining its manifestations in Tanzania.

The Energy Crisis Of The Poor

The relationship between energy and poverty needs to be researched again because of the extreme heterogeneity and genesis of both the problems and the tendency for the literature on the subject to be biased. There are two types of energy crisis - the oil price crisis, and the biomass crisis.

Studies in the former - which have dominated in the recent past - are more concerned with macro-economic issues including trade, balance of payments and technological; while the latter focus on the households and technologies associated with biomass conservation. Over recent years, conservationists have taken keen interest and spread doomsday messages about the future of biomass energy use in Tanzania (see TFAP 1989).

Since "energy" is term used both in the social and natural sciences there are difficulties in the use of energy in analysis (Greeley, 1987). A strong case has been made for the study of the urban energy needs because it falls under both crisises, and it is tied to welfare and distributional justice (Leach, 1987).

Calculations made in 1986 revealed that Tanzania requires 18.16 million tons of oil equivalent (MTOE), out of which 14.4 m. tons was in final use. Wood alone provided 16.9 MTOE. Crude oil and petroleum products provides only 0.89 MTOE (World Bank, 1986). Oil imports which account for only about 7% of the total energy needs gobbles up over a third of the export earnings. HEP generation provides about 2% of the needs but the potential is very large. Basically, 90% of the population is dependant on biomass energy. The environmental and economic aspects of this dependence are therefore critically important. It is best to consider rural and urban energy issues separately even though they are linked.

Aspects of Rural Energy Needs

For a long time the rural energy needs and the implications of these needs was largely simply ignored or overlooked. Villagization accelerated the awareness that the country had another energy crisis. Starting in the late 1970s, officials, assisted by research studies, became conscious of the magnitude and dependence of the vast majority of people on biomass energy. (Nkonoki, 1980).

Rural households all over Tanzania collect their own biomass energy from the vicinity of their own homes, their agricultural plots, communally held bush, woodlands or even forest reserves. The task of collecting wood and carrying it as a headload is largely left to women and children. Therefore there is a threefold relationship in the issue of rural energy: wood (use or substitutes), environmental status (degradation or sustainability) and its impact on women. There are also links with the labour chain, health nutrition, and other aspects of the welfare of the households. As a first step on the research agenda, an index should be devised and applied for the districts of Tanzania which depicts the energy situation, using the threefold relationship described above.

Another possibility is to focus on the labour demands of energy collection. There are three aspects related to the collection which require attention: time, distance, and the load factor. Differences in Tanzania in this aspect vary a great deal. At a village level the average distance travelled varied from 2.5 - 4.2 kms, while individuals in households carried loads over distances varying from.5 kms to over 10 kms each way (Kikula, Mascarenhas, Nilsson 1983). The collection time also differed from a low of 17 to a high of 70 wood collecting working days per year (Nilsson, 1984).

Domestic woodfuel and related studies have to be approached with care. The efforts of the people to respond to scarcity is important, and in this respect it is not only the opinion of the foresters which matters. There is considerable controversy about the real supply and demand situation in the region (Leach & Mearns, 1988).

In Tanzania it is estimated that the rural households require some 42 million cubic metres of wood per annum. Given that plantation forestry can only replenish forests at the rate of 20,000 ha. per year, how can sustainability be achieved? Are there parts of rural Tanzania where the annual population increase is higher than the biomass production per annum? In which part of the country are women seriously constrained in obtaining domestic fuel? In the semi-arid areas? In areas adjacent to game parks?

Wood is not only used for domestic purposes but is also required for rural based industry: brewing, fish smoking, making utensils, and importantly, for construction purposes. While there is still some wastefulness, there have been significant efforts to contain the rural energy situation. Basically this means paying more attention to the social dimension of energy use in the rural areas. For instance, in many parts of Tanzania households cannot afford to pay cash for labour and resort to brewing. This requires logs which in several places are difficult to obtain. What are the alternatives?

The Urban Domestic Fuel Needs

Some of the major statements about deforestation come from wood fuel surveys that have been launched. The "gap model" assumptions are used. Towards this end, the main objective of the World Bank's Fuelwood/Forestry Project Proposal in Tanzania is to reduce existing and future woodfuel deficits, and the countryside around Dar es Salaam, Mwanza and Arusha (World Bank, 1988).

In the period 1967-1990, the distance from which the supply of charcoal for Dar es Salaam comes has increased from about 30 kms to over 130 kms. Extensive areas around the city have been cleared of trees because of the annual requirements of about 250,000 tons of charcoal. For Iringa Town, with a population of about 125,000, it is stated that:

> The pressure on wood energy sources from the town is such that it is a major cause of the serious deforestation which now extended in a radius of 40–60 km around Iringa. (COWINSULT, 1987).

At the present rate of fuel consumption in Iringa, about 87,500 cubic metres (m³) were required in 1986, and this figure will rise to 450,000 by the year 2006. From a positive balance of 100,000m³ there will be a deficit of over 500,000 (m³). Annual clear felling will have to rise from 2,000 ha. to 11,000 ha. In practice, two to three times more land will be degraded because only superior species are used (COWICONSULT, 1987).

Given Tanzania's resource base in which both coal and gas are available in strategic areas, the time has come to make deliberate choices to safeguard biomass and make available alternative domestic energy sources.

In departing from the convention, there is a caution against high-cost measures, such as peri-urban plantations to meet projected deficits (TFAP, TA Vol.1). Should there be subsidies or other forms of inducements to enable the low income in urban areas to obtain more fuel efficient stoves or switch to alternatives, gas or coal?

Could the poor be helped to learn that the continuing use of traditional fuels are expensive? If a small *night time research* project could be funded along Morogoro Road, in the vicinity of Manzese-Magomeni, what would one learn about energy efficiency? Given the known substantial efficiencies by moving from open wood fire to electricity, what type of policies would help? The poorest of the poor in urban areas are faced with intractable energy problems which are "non-market" related, such as the varied size and types of energy sources which encourage open fires, lack of secure or fixed abode (Leach, 1987). How true is this for Tanzania?

A focus on communities charcoaling and their impact on the environment, their own incomes, pre- and post-land use studies, etc., could be investigated. For instance, a recent study tentatively suggests that as the urban areas spread and land gets cleared, land values increase leading to the intensification of land use (Mascarenhas, 1994).

The "energy" subsector fits well into the overall framework of this study. It is worth to move into new fields which need attention. For instance, over much of the high plateau country, both in the south and northern part of the country, area heating for warmth is a necessity. Warm clothes is one way to address the problem, but in other cases the open fire is the best alternative. What do these special needs mean to the workload of old and new families? Similarly, in developmental terms what does the absence of light mean to families in the rural area?

ENVIRONMENTAL INSTITUTIONS & POLICY

The creation of a new Ministry of Tourism, Natural Resources & Environment (MTNR&E) in 1991 has given environmental issues a national focal point. In many aspects the new Ministry has inherited and operates along sectoral lines. The "tourism" part of it comes at a time when government itself is disinvesting, but a change of policy may make a difference to the economy. The "natural resources" part is based on the traditional division of Wildlife and the Forest & Beekeeping Division. A new Directorate of Environment competes with the National Environmental Management Council (NEMC) which had already been established in 1986.

The establishment of any new ministry takes time, and the MTNR & E has yet to find its feet. It has to establish an identity, but notwithstanding this phase, the Ministry has already had to extricate itself from malpractices. Moreover it has been presently caught in the grip of trying to please the myriad of environmental interests, mostly international, and donors. Unfortunately, this comes at a time when there is need to take a clear, transparent stand in national interests. The arrival of the NGOs, opens a new front.

The Second Front

The majority of NGOs in Tanzania sprung up in the late 1980s with the watchful support of the government and the Party. Prior to this period most of the NGOs were either sponsored by the Party, the religious organizations, or were foreign based: Red Cross, WWF, or friendship associations or societies. Unlike in Uganda where NGOs were given a boost by the decline and withdrawal of the government, in Tanzania the NGOs continue to function parallel with the government.

Tanzania has its share of NGOs with environmental interests. Indeed a few NGOs were quick to add the current buzz words: "environment and gender" in their constitution. A few urban based NGOs have tried to take on an "umbrella" role. This has both a beneficial and a restrictive role. Unlike in Kenya, there are very few serious research, advocacy/activist or policy orientated groups in Tanzania.

Local volunteer bodies have also begun to be formed often out of the sheer frustration that individuals have experienced. These are noticeable in the areas dominated by pastoralists. Such groups rooted to the earth and with a cause have the potential to make a great deal of difference in areas where they matter. They need support to keep the democratic tradition alive.

Tackling Environmental Issues

People have been tackling environmental problems simply as a survival technique. Throughout the colonial period conservation and environment were tackled as administrative issues. By enacting laws it was presumed that the problems would be resolved. This trend continued well after independence. Who was to enforce these regulations and laws? Many of the laws were unpopular, and the protests that followed were linked to the independence movements. That phase is coming to an end, and several communities now participate in issues related to environment and management of natural resources. Who are the custodians, the main winners and losers in the development-environment nexus?

The main custodians of the natural resources are the women, men and children who make a subsistence living in the rural areas. It also includes the urban poor. The bureaucrats, the officials and the private commercial sector account and consider only some aspects of the environment. Because conservation was more concerned with law and order it was assumed in Tanzania that rural people had no rights.

The rural and urban scenes are beginning to change, and local governments, citizen organizations and various interest groups are being created, not to mention political parties. These could be important forces to harness in alleviating poverty and conserving the environment.

Charting The Course Ahead

Agenda 21 and the task of getting sustainable development are formidable activities. Development is a goal, it explores options and has a message of hope rather than despair. Since liberalization has a propensity to enrich the rich, there is even more reason to target benefits to the poor. This goal could be assisted if donors purposefully supported research on environment and poverty. Any such interventions must increase self-reliance, and the beneficiaries must be people in their own milieu.

In the earlier part of this chapter, mention was made about the poverty of the African region. However, within this poverty there is hope. The region has resources, indeed some of the most outstanding resources. One of the research goals should be to understand some of the anomalies. Why should a country which has some of the largest lakes in the world in its territory suffer from drought? How can people living in such diverse ecological zones be slaves to their environment? Can lessons be learnt from other countries in the South? For instance in mangrove ecosystems in parts of Western India population densities exceed over 500 per km. Why is it that in Eastern Africa, densities of less than 50 threaten the mangroves? Even if a fraction of the rates were attained, the Rufiji Delta could be more sustainable for a long time.

There should be a deliberate and purposeful effort to concentrate on women and children. A gender bias towards research on management of resources would shed a great deal of light about the poverty in the rural areas. Some of the demands on the labour of women make it impossible for them to get out of the poverty trap. Policy oriented research is badly needed. Such type of research should be collaborative. Research should build bridges between institutions, and between people.

Severe Environmental Degradation & Cases Of Poverty

There are certain parts of Tanzania, such as the semi-arid areas and the floodplains, which repeatedly have experienced environmental problems. At various times the culprits have been identified as nature, pastoralists or their cattle, or agriculturalists. There are other parts where rapid population growth has been held responsible for land degradation, as in the biologically important Usambara Mountains

Environmental problems came from various quarters. Are tse-tse less prevalent today or is this proof that creation of national parks and the like as well as anti-tse-tse campaigns have been very successful? Why is it that there is now silence in the nightmare areas of land degradation of yester-years: Ismani, the Ulugurus, the Usambaras? Has the overall productivity of Shinyanga been drastically reduced, and will this be the fate of Rukwa Region? There are gaps in our understanding of these areas. One could take a case study approach to research in certain areas in Tanzania (See Case 1-3)

Case 1 - Land Degradation in Drought-Prone Areas
Standing on top of the list is Dodoma Region. Repeatedly droughts and famines, which historically have been well described, have devastated the area (Brooks, 1967; Mascarenhas, 1969; Patton 1972). Cyclical growth and crashes, account for the poverty of the Wagogo (Rigby, 1969).

Parts of the region, such as Kondoa have been presented by successive administrations as an example of the devastation caused by irresponsible people and their cattle. There are parts of Kondoa, denuded of people, massive amounts of foreign assistance has been earmarked, and some of the areas have become show-pieces to demonstrate that if you invest funds and keep people and cattle out, mankind can restore land to its pristine splendour.

There is need to pay attention to the replicatability of such projects; there is need to examine whether this means "exporting" the problems to other districts; there is need to understand the processes at work (Mascarenhas, 1993). Zero-grazing is now allowed and there is a demand for grade cattle. Did the wealthy remain behind, did the poor migrate elsewhere?

Case 2: What Happened to the People

There are a diversity of problems in semi-arid areas. For instance the Kisongo area was the domain of the Maasai until 1945 when some of the Waarusha moved out of the highlands and settled as agro-pastoralists. The severe soil erosion started around this period. The reservoir built for the small catchment area in 1960 had a volume of 121,000m³, reduced to 69.1% and 59.6% of its size by 1969 and 1971 respectively (Murry-Rust, 1972). The dam was breached before it was silted, allegedly because of the activities of burrowing creatures! Twenty years later, what happened to the people in the small catchment area, to their cattle and to their cultivation? How and where did they go to adjust?

Case 3 - Sustainability & Poverty in the Rufiji Flood Plain

The delta of the mighty Rufiji has been considered as an area that could be developed to feed the whole of Tanzania or the river could be harnessed to make Tanzania one of the HEP giants of Africa! Even an institution, RUBADA, was specially created to harness this wealth.

Meanwhile, the area is known for the devastating floods that periodically hits the delta causing loss of property, crops and life. Eventually the Government became tired, and in 1969 the people were resettled away from the floodlands. The shift was unpopular - it meant long treks into the flood plains to cultivate and take advantage of the replenishment of the soils by the flooding, maturing crops could not be protected from the vermin, etc. The deep understanding of the environment had given the people in the delta a sustainable livelihood - even if the price was occasionally being flooded out (Ndulu/Angawazi, 1973; Sandberg, 1974)

Interventions exacerbated the situation. Cash crops, mainly cotton and cashew, declined. The cashew trees were cut down, turned into charcoal and sold to the urban market in Dar es Salaam. A characteristic feature is that the full income potential cannot be realized even if there were no labour constraints. At a time when the minimum rural wage was 280 Tsh per month the potential income for most of the crafts and trade was 100 Tsh (Havnevik, 1986).

Even more disturbing was the rate of malnutrition among the children and the seasonal stress on the mothers (Bantje, 1985)

The Present State of Environment

Generally the state of the environment in Tanzania is presented in terms of alarm and concern. The earlier parts provided the background to land use, population, biomass energy, etc. The horror projections have not abated: the last tree in Tanzania should have disappeared in 1992; 400,000 ha per annum have been deforested since 1972, and the 1987, FAO/GoT reports claims that 45% suffered from desertification and the another 35 % was under threat!

There is no reason to be complacent: land degradation is spectacular in parts of Kondoa; there is wind erosion in parts of Arusha and Shinyanga; several parts of the Coast-line are visibly disappearing, the waters of Victoria are polluted; the Ulugurus are becoming bald, and there are periodic droughts and floods. The real forests are now found in very small patches. They need to be protected because of their priceless bio-diversity. There is need to be concerned about life supporting habitats such as wetlands, the various types of thickets and woodlands and watersheds. There is need to conserve because reforestation and reclamation are expensive.

The unplanned and rapid growth of Dar es Salaam, coupled by very low investments has outstripped the infrastructure. The overall standard of housing for the great majority has gone down because of poverty. Unemployment has increased manyfold, yet the drift to the city has actually accelerated. The life styles and expectations of the young has become a matter of concern. Poverty in the urban areas is measurable and more site specific. The children in Oysterbay live in larger homes, consume more, have more access to knowledge, are protected, have leisure. The children in Bugurini have to struggle for the basics. The chances are high that the water is polluted, that they are exposed to disease, and that they do not go to school.

Conserving makes a lot of economic sense. For instance, there is evidence that costly investments in dams like Kidatu and Mtera will be lost in a shorter time if the suspected rate of siltation increases. Declining soil fertility or the diminishing use of fertilizers leads to a drop in production. But it is necessary to sound a note of caution - productivity declines can be caused by factors other than land degradation. The decline of cashew production in the late 1970's could be attributed to a number of factors including disease, villagization, and the age of trees. If trees yield more by spraying sulphur based compounds this risk will have to be taken.

The major problems of poverty and the environment may come from unsuspecting sources such as doctrinaire certainties concerning the environment, unbridled market forces, and policies which distort the ownership of land and access to resources, as well as an anti-change lobby. But there are also difficult decisions to be made - should Tanzania stop building dams, using its vast coal reserves, prohibiting all women in rural areas from using fuelwood? At the end of the day Tanzania will have to take calculated environmental risks.

The present national poverty of Tanzania is more a question of terms of trade, problems in the management of its financial resources, indebtedness, the slow rate and undirected growth of its scientific and technical staff, and related issues. The loss from this sources is many times higher than loss through environmental mismanagement. At a national level it may well be that the concern should be the economy. In contrast, at the grassroots questions of improved livelihoods and sustainability depend not only on economics, but also on the environment and the management of natural resources.

TOWARDS A RESEARCH AGENDA

Although the earlier parts of the chapter raised many questions which could be developed into a research agenda, efforts will be made to be more systematic in this section. The first part of the agenda starts at the desk, in the library, in the institutions. The second part is more related to the field, and demands that it be carried across seasons.

For any meaningful research agenda on the topic of poverty alleviation and environment to evolve in Tanzania there are several basic prerequisites. First, the global perspectives on both environment and poverty need to be understood, and then contained in a national and community context. Secondly, there is need to consider the various dimensions and status of poverty in Tanzania. Thirdly, there is clearly a need to collect environmental data in a social context. It is essential to do this in order to design, plan and put into place programmes that will alleviate poverty and make the environment sustainable.

The Desk-Top Start

From the global perspectives it may make sense to focus on other African countries. There is increasingly more information now being made available to assess priority areas in the study of poverty. For instance, in several African countries unemployment, population growth, land scarcity, food insecurity, violence, etc., have begun to be portrayed as the leading causes of poverty.

A start could be made by paying more attention to the parameters that have a strong influence on the environment. Is the population of Tanzania actually moving away from the highlands to the coast? Are some villages growing larger and faster than the others and threatening their resource base? In relation to household environmental problems, where in Tanzania do women spend most time to collect wood, water, or have to walk the longest to get services?

Revisit Past Studies

The four case studies outlined show that it is possible to gain considerable insight into the nature of poverty and some of the mechanism of adjustment both in a social and environmental sense. Its only then that the more costly field work studies should be undertaken.

The Unit Of Analysis

Studies on poverty and environment are best carried out at the district level, with a focus on the village and on the communities. The University of Sussex studies on poverty in Indian villages generated a greater understanding of poverty than if the unit of analysis were larger. It is only at this level that one can begin to understand poverty in terms of insecurity, deprivation, real demand on labour and time; and also to discriminate the social from the environmental causes of poverty. The larger the area of analysis the greater the externalities. At the same time it is necessary to be conscious that the problems may well not be in the village itself. Maasai pastoralists, for instance, can be made paupers overnight because of gun-trotting rustlers from neighbouring areas.

Conflict Resolution

Overall, there is a fairly large area for research to be centered around poverty and conflict resolution, both at the global and penetrating below the national level. Unless these are resolved a situation for violence and even greater poverty can be predicted. The first signs have begun to manifest themselves in Tanzania in obvious and violent ways - in both rural and urban areas.

In the cluster of research for conflict resolution two areas of concern which have been annotated: are the rights of the pastoralists, and the impoverishment of the peasants.

The Rights of the Pastoralists

Nowhere is the necessity of conflict resolution more evident than among the pastoralists. The contribution of the agro-pastoralist and the pastoralists to the national economy have been underestimated. Large parts have been annexed from the pastoralists and hunters, and carved out as national and game parks, or conservation areas. As tourism is now considered as a desirable growth industry, new pressures will be felt by the people. Improved earnings have largely benefitted groups foreign to the area.

The traditional users of these areas are regarded as incapable of managing their resources. There is a very large gap in the thinking between people who inhabit such areas, and those who have control over them. Conventional ideas continue to persist. In the Ngorongoro Conservation Area, the number of cattle necessary for survival have been diminishing, but the refrain about the damage done by livestock continues.

The conflicts are basic. Pastoralist have knowledge about their environment. The commonsensical traditional knowledge serves the people in many specific needs. Modern scientific knowledge on African pastures needs to be more purposeful to address issues that pastoralists have to confront. Meanwhile, the environment which could be used in a sustainable manner is being compromised, and the Maasai continue to become poorer.

The wildlife and conservation lobby - both international and local - have always been more powerful than those which support the pastoralists. Livestock keeping and wildlife conservation is compatible. However, all in the name of conservation large tracts of land have been appropriated by the state, promises have been made and flouted, and the benefits previously enjoyed by the pastoralists have been violated.

Is The Peasantry Being Impoverished?

The situation among the peasants is not too different from that of the pastoralists. Rural households in the past could keep poverty at bay largely by the presence of extensive family networks, and access to resources - especially land. Reforms in land tenure and customary rights and market forces are threatening social security.

It is not always possible nor necessary to turn back the hands of the clock. However, where the systems alleviated poverty or suffering they need to be revived. The sheer size of the selective movement of people from rural areas to urban centres indicate that not all is well in the rural areas. For many parts of Kisarawe and Rufiji Districts there is a disproportionate number of the very old and the very young who are left behind. What impact does this have on agriculture? How favourable are the rural urban terms of trade?

Can Ethnoscience Bridge The Knowledge Gap?

Many of the problems concerned with environment and development arise out of our imprecise knowledge about the environment. Livelihood practices in the past considered both the ecological and social context of production. There was a range of agro-ecological practices which were versatile: this included the irrigation practices of the Wachagga and the Wapare; the flood cultivation of the Warufiji; and the hunting practices of the Hadzabes.

There have been changes and there is now need for people in the rural areas to integrate the best in modern science and traditional knowledge to improve the quality of life. Where this has been tried, such as in Kilimanjaro, the standard of living is appreciably better. Research should examine the dynamics of change which permit or inhibit change.

Such local level development has been the mainstay of most of the livelihood systems in Tanzania. Without them the scale of social and economic problems would have been immense. In several parts of Tanzania these traditional livelihood systems were sustainable and not environmentally damaging even with population growth. In the high potential areas especially in the highlands, astute traditional forms of agriculture combined with modern commercial agriculture have helped to maintain a good level of sustainability.

Learning From Anomalies

There are anomalies and much could be learnt from them. For instance, on the slopes of the Kilimanjaro, the agriculture is a modification of traditional agroforestry practices: many indigenous trees are left, food and cash crops are grown together, livestock are stall-fed, manure is used, and there is careful use of water. Therefore, despite very large growth of population the destruction to the environment is relatively mild. In theory we are examining Bosrupian forces at play!

But not all mountain areas in Tanzania are treated in the same way. In the Usambara Mountains agricultural adjustments are an ongoing process which is made more difficult because of the need to preserve the rainforests with its high endemicity. In the Uluguru Mts or in Meru Juu, degradation goes on. Under what circumstances do people conserve in mountain areas? One could carry out such studies in a range of environments and livelihood systems such as among fishing communities and among hunters. The objectives of these studies is to learn - not simply perpetuate. Have others become interested in the resources which people use, and will this threaten their sustainability? For example, what is the impact of foreign trawlers on the shared Lakes of East Africa.

The Institutional Context

Another large area of research is the institutional aspects of poverty and environment. The perception of the administrators, their priorities, and national policies are as significant as the physical environment. In recent months the abolition of customary land rights may have started the run to deprive many in Tanzania of their land and means of survival. What is the role and impact of a MTNR&E?

In the emerging Tanzanian situation there is a cluster of research centered around institutions because of major shifts in policy. Traditionally, the Ministry concerned with natural resources legally and directly controlled, through national parks, forest reserves, etc., more than 25% of the country. The mandate of the newly created MTNR&E has widened to include "environment". This is also the time when the country has opened up and there are various non-governmental and other institutions and associations which have started to operate. Therefore, research is needed to assess the impact of the different institutions.

The Role Of The Ministry

In the context of the WCED and UNCED which should be the lead agencies to promote environment and development activities at a national level? What is the impact of the creation of the MTNR & E, NEMC and the Directorate? What will the impact of government withdrawal from a monopoly situation mean to the different communities? The newly formed Ministry has the advantage of starting on a new slate, but it will have to earn its credentials. There are many uncertainties in this exercise. At the international level it will have to adjust and attune itself to the growing North-South debate. At a time when there is retrenchment, will staff for the MTNR&E be considered as a priority and recruited?

Will the success of UNCED in up-fronting environment now push development in the background? Are donor driven environmental conditionalities beginning to emerge? On paper all ministries will now claim to be environmentally friendly, but there is a difference in reality.

Why was the MTNR & E created at all? Apart from all the good reasons one must not exclude the wish simply to please the donors, and herein may lie one of the problems. How effective have the Ministries of Environment(MOE) been in developed countries themselves? If even under the best of circumstances they have been very dependent on activism by the public at large, it is unlikely that in Africa where MOE which are weak, understaffed and uncertain about their role, can be effective. The real test may arise when the next HEP dam has to be built, or a proposal for a railway across Serengeti has to be considered, or simply an application is lodged for a hotel site on the Ngorongoro rim.

The problem is even deeper. One could question the effectiveness of the Ministries of Finance in alleviating poverty in African countries. Perhaps as effective as the IMF/World Bank wanted them to be? Who then sets the terms and conditions for MOE's - UNEP, WWF, IUCN, World Bank, Greenpeace, or other NGOs? So far the Ministry has responded mainly to the lobby of the rich and powerful. The message in RIO was clearly that lifestyles were not a matter for negotiations but that may not apply to Tanzania and the third world countries. A research project could aim to examine the implication of various life styles, including one in which urbanization dominates.

There is need to take environment to all ministries and to portray the real environmental issues at that level, and to specify the various options available. Strong coordination is necessary and cannot be dictated by doomsday rhetoric. Even merely incorporating the environment in development activities has many components, and the integrating elements are challenging. There is the whole question of awareness and choice. For instance, in a study to examine the role of public policy and institutions in promoting genetic resources conservation in Kenya, it was found that although the country has made great strides in the field of environmental conservation, there was need to deliberately focus on the conservation of biological heritage and diversity.

In Tanzania too, the current institutions and legal instruments are not well suited for the imperatives of long term conservation of, for instance, germ-plasm. The setting up of such institutions requires skills in law, biology and ecology. There is also the serious problem that the stakes in this particular field are very lucrative, and knowledge tends to be in the hands of a very few people. The necessity for law is also brought about by abuse of human rights in areas considered to be marginal in the arid and semi-arid areas of Tanzania. The main text of this chapter has drawn attention to the dangers of paying attention to one-sided perspectives.

The Emergence Of Local Governments

A strong case has been made for understanding and analysis at a district or lower level. Local governments have been restored for some time now, and citizen organizations, various interest groups, including political parties, are being created. Do the Tanzanian local governments have the means or the resources to meet the changing circumstances under which resources must be managed? To what extent are the incidents in Loliondo or Ngorongoro based on weaknesses of the local government system?

The Role of NGOs

In 1990, at a time of rapid expansion of the NGO sector, an appraisal on the role of NGO's in Tanzania on environmental issues was undertaken. There is need to carry out a reappraisal again given the complexity of the problems that are emerging.

What New Institutions

There is a strong case to be made for the creation of new institutions. Among the pastoralists it has been pointed out that institutions set up to take their interests have been weak because they lack consideration for the traditional rules of management, there is insufficient socio-economic concept of space, and too much strictness in the land tenure system (Sylla, 1993). There could also be outright contradictions between government objectives and the understanding of the pastoralists (Government of Tanzania, 1992)

The Government and Biotechnology

A strong political will on conservation and science and technology needs to be translated into actions through institutional innovation and reorganization (Juma, 1989). In development terms what are at stake are the concerns for food security, and the growing importance of biotechnology and its impact on the economy of agriculturally dependent countries. In Tanzania, there is now an urgent need to pay attention to the whole issue of biotechnology. The change of the sourcing of the raw materials for the markets of the developed world would be catastrophic. Already there are patents for cotton seeds, and others will follow.

As yet there are no effective institutions which can cope with this problem. Bio-technology will affect the lives of many who are poor. With vigilance and negotiation there is hope. Otherwise the poor will get poorer. Therefore there is urgent need to do research on the kinds of institutions that are needed at a government and NGO level.

Components of Poverty in Tanzania

The narrow concept of poverty focusing on finances has got to give way to a broader viewpoint. What are the local perceptions of poverty? How do local communities respond to them? Could they be assisted to be more effective?

The Need For Methodologies & Integration

As has already been stated in the initial part of this chapter, the links between environment and development - and for that matter poverty - are imperfectly understood both at the global and national level. There is clearly a need for ecologists and economists to develop methodologies which examine the issues in an integrated manner. The conventional efforts which push for the sectoral approaches are inappropriate. At present there are fewer studies in Tanzania than in the past by the Ministry of Agriculture which state the nature of land degradation, or which give any idea about agricultural productivity. There is need to share information.

One of the glaring areas of weakness in methodologies is that national accounts have been left to economists who have generally ignored natural resources as component of national assets. Already there are a few countries in the world which have attempted to incorporate natural resources and environment as part of national accounts. Tanzania could gain from the experience in Botswana, in which the environmental dimension in conservation and development were utilized. Similarly, work on natural resource use in the Philippines and Indonesia could also form a useful background (Repetto, 1988; WRI, 1990).

The Ecological Basis of Economics

There is an urgent need for economists to be oriented towards ecology. Once natural resources are "priced" correctly there may be less wastage and destruction. The interface between the biological and social systems is important to be understood. As will be soon noted, criticism of economists is not a defence for environmentalists.

Thus, differences between practice and reality is not confined to economists alone, but is pronounced even among environmentalists themselves. It is noted that:

> Most environmental thinking in the development field remains remote and idealistic, and there is a large and serious gulf between development theorists and development practitioners, both in their frameworks of thought and their scale of analysis....communications between them is poor and learning from past mistakes is slow, uninstitutionalised and ineffective. Questions about the environment in development are left unanswered and frequently unasked. (Adams, 1987).

One research activity connected with this agenda item would be for two or three specialists to be commissioned to write a position paper. This should be the basis for holding a national technical seminar to get some sort of national consensus of what items to include in the national accounts. There is a useful group of individuals with some exposure to the problems and issues.

Privatization & Poverty

There are other changes which need monitoring. For instance, as government participation in the economy begins to weaken, what is the critical minimum necessary to ensure that the excesses of the private sector and privatization do not create even more problems than they resolve? Since privatization is more for the rich and not for the poor it will be of concern and interest to note whose interests the Ministry will serve.

Assessing Poverty Inducing Environments

Basic problems like drought and food security have many dimensions - they are not simple problems with simple solutions. For instance, in the SADCC region a six-year research programme on food security, with some excellent work, will still need as much work again to resolve problems. The basic approach of that work was the efficiency of "market forces". Ironically, in a situation in which the majority of households are subsistence oriented, there may be factors other than the "market" which operates and ensures food security.

Are the environmental problems more severe in the lowland areas than in the highlands? Have populations grown more rapidly with the consequent increase in the vulnerable populations? How 'have the economic islands' changed in character, and what have the environmental consequences been?

Is there a seasonal dimension to poverty? What impact does population increase or decrease contribute to this seasonal stress? The main custodians of the environment and natural resources in many parts of Tanzania are the women and children. The kinds of adjustments that they have had to make should be educative to planners and decision makers.

Learning From TKS, TMS & Modern Scientific Methods

Since ecological management is facilitated by institutional change that experiments, retains and diffuses, it is necessary to understand the traditional knowledge and management systems (TKS &TMS) of various communities in Tanzania; and to see the limitation of traditional and modern methods in agriculture, livestock keeping, fishing and forestry. For instance, most of the increase in maize production in the "Big Four" maize regions took place with subsidies in fertilizers, massive use of pesticides, and improved seed. Studies in Rukwa region question the sustainability of maize cultivation using these methods. (Bury, 1983; O. Mascarenhas, 1985)

While scientists have considerable data and knowledge about the environment, its application in social settings and transformation into information pose serious problems. There is no single way to manage resources. In a project in operation in Africa, evidence from 27 case studies shows an array of management practices (Veit, Mascarenhas and Ampadu-Agyie, 1993), from the simple to the sophisticated. There is urgent need to carry out such research in the diverse socio-ecological setting of Tanzania.

ENVIRONMENTAL PROCESSES AND POVERTY

It is impossible not to be struck by the fact that certain processes in the environment cause loss of wealth, misery, illness and even death. The impact of drought, floods and land degradation has to be studied longitudinally.

On could of course pose the specific question whether:

> ...As the soil erodes, so do Africa's living standards. Bankrupt environments lead to bankrupt nations - and may ultimately lead to a bankrupt continent

How relevant is this statement to Tanzania?

REFERENCES

Anderson D. & Grove R. ed. (1987) *Conservation In Africa People, Policies and Practice,* Cambridge University Press, Cambridge.

Arhem K. (1986) "Pastoralism Under Pressure: The Ngorongoro Maasai", In, Boesen, J; Havnevik J; et.al. pp.239-252.

Barraclough, S. & Ghimire K. (1990) "The Social Dynamics Of Deforestation In Developing Countries: Principal Issues and Research Priorities," UNRISD Discussion Paper 16, Geneva.

Bell, R. (1987) "Conservation With A Human Face: Conflict And Reconciliation In African Land Use Planning", in Anderson D. & Grove R. Cambridge University Press p.79-102.

Berry L, Mascarenhas O, Steward S, (1982). East African Country Profiles, The United Republic Of Tanzania, International Development Program, Clark University, Worcester, Ma.

Blaikie P. (1986). *The Political Economy Of Soil Erosion In Developing Countries.* London, Longmans.

Brown L. R. & Wolf E. C. (1985) Reversing Africa's Decline, Worldwatch Paper No. 65, Washinton.

Brown L, *et al*, ed. (1990) *State Of The World, 1990,* Worldwatch Institute Report, Norton, New York.

Chachage C.S.L. and Mvungi (1989) "Village Participation Survey," TFAP Working No 18, Summary Report, Dar es Salaam.

Chambers R (1985) *The Crisis Of Africa's Rural Poor*, DP 201, Sussex.

---- (1985) *Rural Development, Putting The Last First*, Longmans 1989, London 246 pp.

Cowiconsult (1987) DANIDA/URT Iringa Soil Conservation And Environmental Protection Project, Project Proposal, Main Report, Virum, Denmark.

Durning A.B. (1990) "Ending Poverty," in Brown Lester, *et al* ed., Norton & Co, New York, pp 135-153

FAO (1988) An Interim Report On The State Of Forest Resources In The Developing Countries, Rome.

Gomes M.I; Matambenengwe M; Moyo H.(1987) "Research On Sorghum And Wheat Flour," in Rukuni M. & Eicher C., University of Zimbabwe, Harare, 341- 359

Hamilton A.C. & Bensted-Smith R. ed., (1989) Forest Conservation In The East Usambaras Mountains Tanzania, IUCN, Nairobi.

Holmberg J. (1991) *Poverty, Environment And Development,* SIDA, Stockholm,

Homewood K. M. & Rodgers W. A. (1991) *Maasailand Ecology - Pastoralist Development And Wildlife Conservation In Ngorongoro, Tanzania*, Cambridge University Press, Cambridge.

Kikula, I. Nilsson P. (1982) Trees For Fuel And Building: A Preliminary Assessment In Two Villages Adjacent To The Southern Pulp And Paper Mill, BRALUP Research Report No 51 (New Series), Dar es Salaam.

Kjekshus H. (1977) *Ecology Control And Economic Development In East African History*, Heinemann, Nairobi.

Lane C. (1990) Barabaig Natural Resource Management: Sustainable Land Use Under Threat Of Destruction, UNRISD, Discussion Paper No. 12, Geneva.

Leach G & Mearns R. (1988) *Beyond The Woodfuel Crisis-People, Land & Trees In Africa*, Earthscan Publications Ltd, London, 309 pp.

Lipton M (1977) *Why Poor People Stay Poor - A Study Of Urban Bias in World Development*, Temple Smith, London.

Longhurst R.(1986) Editorial, in *Seasonality And Poverty*, IDS Bulletin, Vol 17, Sussex.

Mascarenhas, A. (1983) Ngorongoro, A Challenge To Conservation And Development, *AMBIO*, 12, Stockholm, p. 146-62.

---- (1984) The Relevance Of The Miti Project, in, Temu A.B: Kaale B.K; Maghembe J. A. Wood-Based Energy For Development in Tanzania, MNR&T/SIDA, Dar es Salaam.

---- - (1994) Social Dimension of Deforestation In Tanzania, UNRISD Discussion Paper No 50,Geneve

Mascarenhas A, Kikula I & Nilsson P. (1983) Support To Village Afforestation In Tanzania, Institute of Resource Assessment, Dar es Salaam.

Mascarenhas O. C (1985) " Adaptation or Adoption? Ecological and Socio-Economic Implications of Technological Changes in Smallholder Production Systems in Rukwa Region, Tanzania". Ph.D. dissertation, Clark University, 1986. 320 pp.

Mnzava E. M. & Riihinen P.(1989) Forestry And Land Use Policy And Administration, TFAP Tanzania, SRM Report No. 9; Forest and Beekeeping Division, MLNR & T, Dar es Salaam.

Moore, J.E. (1971) Rural Population Carrying Capacities of the Districts of Tanzania, BRALUP Report No 18. Dar es Salaam.

Munslow B, Katerere Y, et.al.(1988) *The Fuelwood Trap: A Study Of The SADCC Region,* Earthscan Publications Ltd and ETC Foundation, London.

Mwandosya M.J. & Luhanga M.L.(Ed) Proceedings Of The Seminar On The National Energy Policy For Tanzania, Sept 1990, Arusha, SEI, Stockholm.

Ole Parkipuny, L. (1981). On Behalf of the People of Ngorongoro: A

Discussion Of The Question, Does The Future Of The Ngorongoro Lie In Livestock vs Wildlife or Livestock And Wildlife, Background Paper For A New Management Plan, *BRALUP,* University of Dar es Salaam

Potkanski, T. (1992) The Social dynamics of Non-Market Cattle Transactions Among The Tanzanian Maasai, Warsaw.

Rigby P. (1969) Cattle And Kinship Among The Gogo, Cornell University Press, Ithaca.

Schabel Hans G. (1990) "Tanganyika Forestry Under German Colonial Administration, 1891-1919", *Forest & Conservation History,* Vol 34, (Durham, N.C.) pp 130-141.

Sen A. (1986) Poverty And Famines: An Essay On Entitlement And Deprivation, Oxford University Press, Oxford.

South Centre (1993) Environment And Development, Towards A Common Strategy For The South In The UNCED Negotiations And Beyond, South Centre, Geneva.

Sylla D. (1993) Towards New Guidelines For Pastoral Institution Building And Administration In Dynamic Ecological Systems, UNSO, Arusha.

Temple P.H. & Sundborg A (1973) The Rufiji River, Tanzania: Hydrology And Sediment Transport, BRALUP Monograph No 1, Stockholm, pp. 345-368.

Thomas, I.D. & Thomas, C.J.(1971) Comparative Population Data for the Divisions of Tanzania, BRALUP R.P. No. 10, Dar es Salaam.

Timberlake L. (1985) Africa In Crisis, London: Earthscan

UNICEF/URT (1990) Women And Children In Tanzania, A Situation Analysis, Tanzania, Dar es Salaam.

United Republic of Tanzania (1975) Villages and Ujamaa Villages (Registration, Designation and Administration) Act, No.2, Government Printers, Dar es Salaam.

---- (1982) Local Government (District Authorities) Act, No.7, Govt Printers, Dar es Salaam, pp. 43-120.

---- (1982) The Tanzania National Agricultural Policy, Dar es Salaam, Ministry of Agriculture.

---- (1982) The Livestock Policy of Tanzania, Ministry of Livestock Development. Dar es Salaam.

---- (1989) Ministry Of Lands, Natural Resources And Tourism (1989) Tanzania Forestry Action Plan 1990/91 - 2007/08), Dar es Salaam.

---- (1989a) Ministry Of Lands, Natural Resources And Tourism (1989a) Tanzania Forestry Action Plan 1990/91 - 2007/08), Technical Annexes, Vol. I and Vol II, Dar es Salaam.

---- (1993) Statistical Abstract 1991, Bureau of Statistics, President's Office, Dar es Salaam.

URT/UNSO (1990) National Plan Of Action To Combat Desertification In

Tanzania, NEMC, Dar es Salaam.

Veit, P.G., A. Mascarenhas & O. Ampadu-Agyie (1993) *Local-level Natural Resource Management: Lessons from the Ground UP* Washington: WRI.

World Bank (1989) *World Development Report 1989*, Washington DC. World Bank.

World Commission On Environment And Development (WCED), (1987). Our Common Future, Oxford University Press, Oxford.

World Resources Institute (WRI) (1990) World Resources, 1992-93, Towards Sustainable Development, Washington.

6

The Use of Technology in Alleviating Poverty in Tanzania

A.S. CHUNGU & G.R.R. MANDARA

INTRODUCTION

Background

Technology has been viewed by many development analysts as a strategic variable for socio-economic development. However the actual incorporation of technological considerations into national development planning in many developing countries is far from the required levels for poverty alleviation. One of the crucial reasons for this situation, as pointed out by The Technology Atlas Team (1987), is the fact that economic planners have been treating technology as an exogenous variable conveniently viewed as a "black box". Wangwe (1993) argues strongly that technological development is important not only as a major determinant of the level and pattern of national economic development but also as a major determinant of international competitiveness. According to Streeten (1975), economic development and technological advancement are highly correlated, and for this reason, technology can be treated as a substitute indicator for development.

If technology is so widely recognised as being a fundamental requirement for the successful advancement of civilization, some basic questions must be asked and answered in a way that can provide both a vision and a systematic method for managing a progressive process of development, questions such as:

(a) How should we perceive and understand technology?
(b) How should we measure technology and effectively incorporate technological considerations into the national development planning process so as to achieve a desirable scale and rate of socio-economic development?

This chapter aims to address these basic questions and elaborate a research agenda for guiding Tanzania towards a techno-economic development management approach.

According to the World Bank (1992), " Poverty is conventionally measured by the income or expenditure level that can sustain a bare minimum standard of living. Poverty can be measured in relative or absolute terms. The World Development Report (WDR) 1990 used an upper poverty line of US$370 (in 1985 purchasing power parity dollars) per capita as a cutoff for absolute poverty. People whose consumption levels fall below that level are considered poor. The WDR also used a lower poverty line, of US$275. People whose consumption levels fall below that level are very poor. When discussing poverty within countries, the WDR used country-specific poverty lines. But poverty is not just measured by income and consumption. Health, life expectancy, access to clean water, and so on are central dimensions of welfare. For this reason, the WDR supplemented consumption-based measures with others, such as nutrition, under-five mortality, and school enrolment rates." Similar national development indicators have been argued by NCC-CSPD (1993) for achieving similar goals for Tanzanian children by the year 2000 measured in terms of infant mortality, maternal mortality, level of malnutrition, access to safe drinking water and sanitary means of excreta disposal, access to school and enrolment rates, adult illiteracy, household income, and the extent of protection of children in especially difficult circumstances. The relationship between the income brought into a household by women from a technology driven project and the nutrition status of the member families' children were found by Chungu (1993) to be highly correlated. Chungu (1993) argues that so long as the technology used is appropriate and properly transferred, the income brought in from the project will benefit the children and member families, thus improving their nutrition status.

Tanzania, like so many other African countries, presents a paradox: how can a country so well endowed by providence with natural resources and a reasonable sized population demonstrate so many of the classic signs and symptoms of poverty? What is Tanzania's problem? "...Consider the facts: Africa has the highest infant mortality rate in the world at 120 for every 1,000 births; the lowest life expectancy, 34 years on average; and while our population growth is the highest in the world at over 3 percent per annum, our food production increases only by 1.5 per cent ..." (Museveni, 1992:169). Although Tanzania in some areas has performed much better than these African regional averages, having for example achieved a lower infant mortality rate of 111, and a higher life expectancy of 51 years than the African averages, the sustainability of these and other achievements is highly at risk due amongst other things to the high level of dependency on external aid for meeting national budget requirements (macro-level indicator of poverty) and the very low household incomes of the majority of its citizens (micro-level indicator of poverty). The per-capita income of the average Tanzanian, at US$ 100, is currently ranked as the second lowest in the world, just above the US$ 80 rate of neighbouring

Mozambique (UNICEF, 1994). According to UNICEF (1994), about 41% of the Tanzania national budget in 1991 was financed by Overseas Development Assistance (ODA).

Currently almost 70% of national development and recurrent expenditures are dependent on donor financing. The lowest income group (as pointed out by SADCC (1988)) uses inferior tools of production. What can we do about this problem?

> ... If you asked me what is the biggest problem the African people are facing today is, I would tell you that it is backwardness. But how do we define backwardness? We are backward or not depending on our capacity to harness nature for our own benefit. Once we have a reasonable capacity to tame and harness nature, then we can say that we are developed..... All these problems we are talking about - floods, drought, unbalanced budgets, rampant inflation, lack of commodities, lack of spare parts, and lack of raw materials - all go back to one thing: our lack of technology and science. " (Museveni, 1992:173).

This theme is also at the heart of the diagnosis of underdevelopment, dependency and poverty by the Technology Atlas Project in Asia. The UN-ESCAP (1989) argue that most developing countries may be rich in many ways in terms of resources, culture, etc., but they all suffer from one serious common weakness. They are all poor or very poor in technology. It can therefore be argued that the basic difference between the developed and developing countries is their relative technological strengths. Developing countries are in fact technologically underdeveloped. Such technological underdevelopment stems from the reality that the developing countries are, in general, weak and dependent on external sources for the major elements or building blocks which are essential for development, and these as pointed out by UN-ESCAP (1989) are:

(a) Modern facilities for production;
(b) Technical abilities and skills of the people;
(c) Extent and utility of available knowledge;
(d) Effectiveness of existing organization and management.

The inherited weaknesses and consequent external dependence in all the above four major elements appear to set in motion four different vicious circles in these countries (see Figure 1). The net result of these is the overall vicious circle of technological underdevelopment, dependency and poverty. If this overall vicious circle is to be broken, it is necessary, as pointed out by UN-ESCAP (1989), to understand the constraints and opportunities to be found in all the four component elements mentioned above.

With reference to Chungu (1993) and the preceding analysis, it should be clear that technology should not be regarded as a scapegoat, but as a strategic variable which, if properly managed, is at the heart of the practical work to alleviate poverty in Tanzania. Apparently, there is a gap in the reviewed literature regarding the relationship between technology and poverty in Tanzania. Some work needs to be done in this area. It is important also to note that technology should not be mystified as an independent and autonomous force; it is merely an instrument for problem solving. "It is up to the user to determine which problems to solve and how to solve them. If we can master its production and use, technology can be the "key" to a prosperous society for all human beings - including the poorest of the poor!" (UN-ESCAP, 1989:).

A FRAMEWORK FOR TECHNO-ECONOMIC DEVELOPMENT PLANNING

Science and Technology

The terms "science" and "scientific" are used in three ways. Firstly, they refer to the body of knowledge that has been collected in books and papers by the practitioners of science. This is known as scientific knowledge. Secondly, they are used to describe the activity of this scientific community. At the core of this practice is scientific method - the procedures of systematic observation and recording, hypothesis formulation and experimentation. Thirdly the words science and scientific are used to describe the individuals, groups and institutions who are practitioners of science, i.e. the scientific community.

There are basically two central aspects of scientific endeavour:

(a) Science aims at the discovery and understanding of natural phenomena;
(b) Science proceeds by means of a methodology based on observation, experimentation and reason.

It must be emphasized that science is not merely a set of operational techniques or laboratory procedures: these alone would render science no more than systematic empiricism. Scientific knowledge is distinguished from other knowledge by its theoretical base, where empirical research is based on theoretical understanding and hypothesis testing. However, it must be remembered that some activities practised by personnel educated in science have deficits of theoretical underpinning. For instance, in civil engineering, theory cannot predict for all contingencies and so models are used and tested. In the pharmaceutical industry too, due to the fact that effects of new compounds cannot be accurately predicted, complex trial and error techniques are required.

Science involves a spectrum of activities, and a distinction is often made between "pure" (or basic) science, and "applied" (or mission-oriented) science. Pure science is popularly considered to be concerned with the discovery of natural law and the description of nature. It has as its aim the understanding of nature; it seeks explanation. Applied science is considered to deal with the task of employing the findings of pure science to get practical tasks done. Another aspect that may be worth noting is that there could be a time lag between the development of a theory in pure science and its application to practice.

Having made the above statements about science, the first point to be made about technology is that it is not simply, "applied science". Technology is not only a body of knowledge concerned with the solution of practical problems but also includes the tools and artifacts which are used to achieve those solutions. Thus we may say that while the applied scientist is concerned with the task of discovering applications for pure theory, the technologist has a more practical problem which deals not only with *applicability* but also with that of *fitness of purpose and of economy.*

The interaction between science and technology has been a topic of lively discussion and debate. As pointed out by Ramanathan (1990), some researchers have shown the pervasive influence across all sectors of the economy (steel, electronics, food processing etc.) of the diffusion of technologies growing out of basic research in the sciences (physics, chemistry, molecular biology, etc). Others have shown that major contributions have also been made by technology to science. Technology has also made "indirect" contributions to science because in the course of pursuing practical ends, abstract principles of science hitherto unsuspected are often discovered. For instance, electromagnetism stimulated the development of differential equations, and hydrodynamics function theory. Likewise, the pure sciences of thermodynamics were found as a result of the effort to improve the efficiency of steam and other heat engines.

Some researchers belong to another school of thought and question the analytical usefulness of distinguishing between the content of science and of technology. For this they cite molecular biology, biochemistry and solid state physics as examples where the content of science and of technology has become indistinguishable. Based on these considerations, analysts are of the view that the nature of the relationship and complementarities between science and technology varies considerably among sectors of application and that this should be well appreciated by policy-makers.

The literature on technology management abounds with numerous definitions of technology, each focusing on the specificities relevant to the context in which the term technology is being used. Some define technology with respect to its generation, others focus on its application and some analysts look at both generation and application. Often technology has been identified with machines and processes. Cetron (1974) defined technology as "the application of knowledge to achieve practical ends". According to Schlie et al. (1987), technology is defined as "the knowledge and means to do something -- e.g. to

FIG. 1: VICIOUS CIRCLES OF TECHNOLOGICAL UNDERDEVELOPMENT(Source: UN-ESCAP,1989)

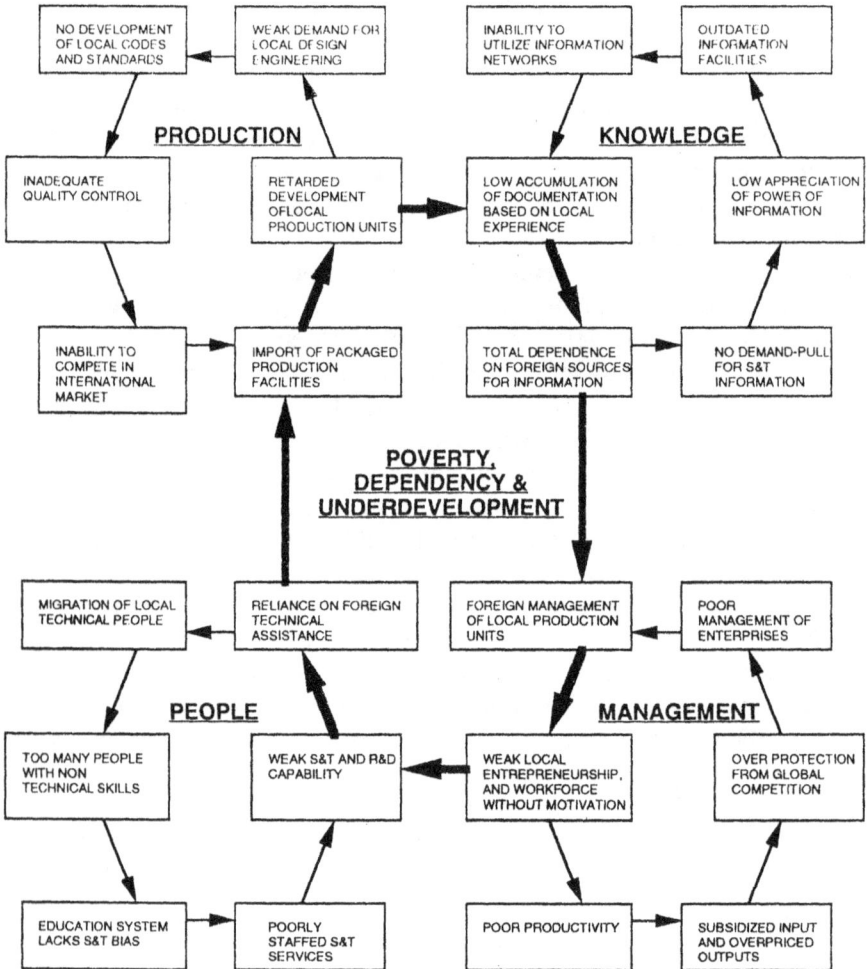

Fig. 1: Vicious Circles of Technological Underderdevelopment
Source: UN-ESCAP, 1989.

design and/or make a computer". Goulet (1977) defined technology as "the systematic application of collective human rationality to the solution of problem by asserting control over nature and over processes of all kinds". According to Hawthorne (1971), technology is "the application of science to the solving of well-defined problems". Some scholars [Stewart, 1978; Miles, 1982; Sharif, 1983] have defined technology as consisting of hardware (i.e. machines, equipment, tools, materials, etc.,) and software (i.e. know-how, skills, experience, information, management, etc.,). Wangwe (1993) has perceived technology as "embodied in people, institutions and networks and interactions among many types of information and agents". Sharif (1988) and his colleagues in the Technology Atlas Project Team (1987), have argued that either explicitly or implicitly the above and other previous definitions of technology really say that technology can be disaggregated into four totally interlocking embodiment forms:

(a) *Object-embodied form or "technoware"* - tools, capital goods, intermediary goods, products, physical equipment, machinery, physical processes, etc.,

(b) *People-embodied form or "humanware"* - understanding, capacity for systematic application of knowledge, know how, human capability, human labour, specialized ideas, skills, problem solving capacity, etc.,

(c) *Document-embodied form or "inforware"* - knowledge about physical relationships, scientific and/or other forms of organized knowledge, principles of physical and social phenomena, technical information, specifications, standards, computer software, etc.,

d) *Institution-embodied form or "orgaware"* - organizational work assignment, day-to-day operations of production, social arrangements, means for using and controlling factors of production, organization of products, processes, tools and devices for use by people.

According to the Technology Atlas Project Team (1987) and Sharif (1988), all four embodiment forms of technology (Figure 2) are complementary to one another and are required simultaneously for the production of goods and services. Such production can never take place in the complete absence of any of the four embodiment forms. Of course depending on the nature of the production activity, the relative importance of each of the four embodiment forms may differ. The use of the four embodiment forms concept has been demonstrated in Bangladesh to illustrate the policy imperatives of the non-farm sector [Haque, 1989], and also in other Asian countries such as India, South Korea and Japan (Ramanathan, 1988; Bowonder and Miyake, 1988).

Technology however does not operate in a vacuum. Its use takes place within an operational environment which may be called the "technology climate". The technology climate of a country has been defined by the Technology Atlas Project Team (1987) and Sharif (1988) as the national setting in which technology-based activities are carried out. The "climate" includes factors such as physical infrastructure (roads, water, electricity, banks, posts, telecommunications, market centres, etc.); support services (technical extension service, financial service, etc.); R&D institutions; and political systems at various administrative levels (for regulation, property rights, etc.). Hayami and Ruttan (1971) have argued that the "climate" (or "environmental") factors should be treated as endogenous to the technology development process, rather than as exogenous factors that operate independently.

The Concept of Appropriate Technology

The meaning of the generic term "appropriate technology" has been often used synonymously with terms "intermediate technology", "rural technology", "low-cost technology", "alternative technology", "village technology", "grass-root technology", "bare-foot technology", "progressive technology", or "community technology". Unfortunately, none of these terms on their own describe the kind of technologies that are most suitable for the needs of the poor anywhere in the world. The proliferation of such terms is due to the lack of a coherent conceptual framework of appropriate technology. Jequier and Blanc (1983) defined some of the above terms explicitly and clear difference from one term to another was observed.

Reviewing the efforts made in rural and urban development by various scholars in appropriate technology, it appears reasonable to state that, any technology is "appropriate", particularly at the time of development, with respect to the surroundings for which the technology has been developed, and in accordance with the objective used for development. The technology may or may not be appropriate at the same place at a different time, because the surroundings and/or the objective may have changed. Similarly, the technology may or may not be appropriate at a different place at the same time or at different times, because the surroundings and the objective may be similar or different. Thus, technological appropriateness as pointed out by Sharif (1988b), is not an intrinsic quality of any technology, but is derived from the surroundings in which the technology is to be utilized and also from the objectives used for evaluation. The appropriateness is, in addition, a value judgement of those involved in decision-making. Bruinsma et al. (1985) support

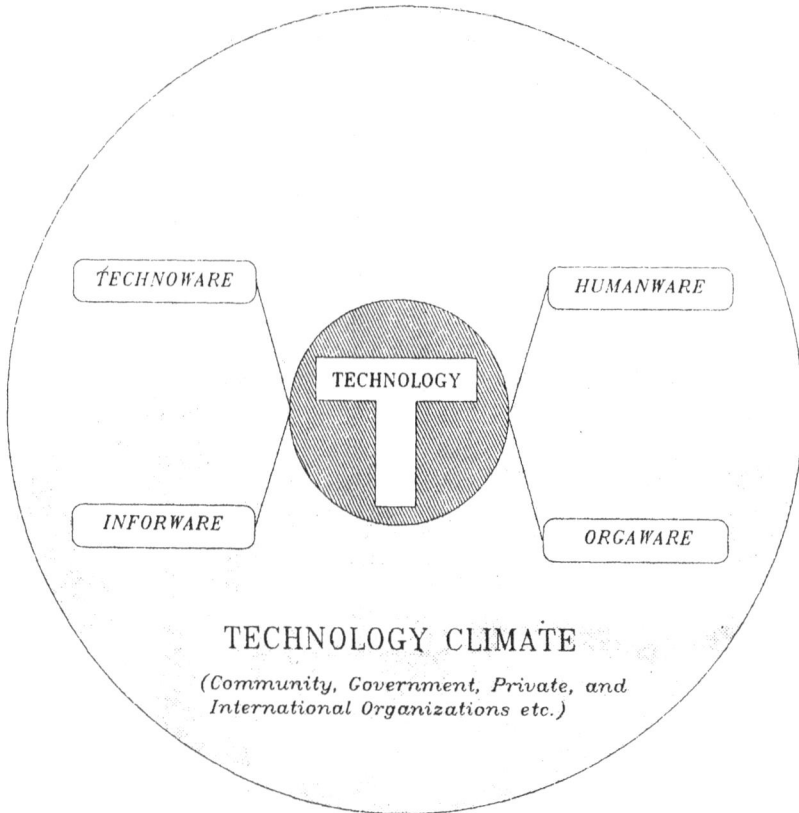

(Adapted: THE TECHNOLOGY ATLAS TEAM, 1987)

Fig. 2: *The Schematic representation of the four components of technology in a dynamic interactive technology climate*

the argument that appropriate technology in its broader sense should take into account the variations of the time horizon, place of operation, and the group which uses the technology.

According to this simple conceptual framework, any technology is appropriate at the time and place of original application. The technology is still appropriate at a later time and/or at a different place if the surroundings as well as the objectives are similar to the origin. The technology may not be appropriate at a later time and/or at different place due to three reasons:

(a) different or changed surroundings;
(b) different or changed objectives; and
(c) different or changed surroundings and objectives

The difference in surroundings between countries is quite significant. Even among districts or regions within a country itself, there are plenty of variations. These variations occur with respect to the individual components of the total surroundings within which technology has to function. The total surroundings can be divided into six components representing: population aspects; resource aspects; economic aspects; environmental aspects; socio-cultural aspects; and politico-legal aspects. Corresponding to each of these aspects there are innumerable variations. Population differences can be observed in terms of density and demographic structure. Resources are unevenly distributed throughout the country. Economic conditions vary from the very poor to the very rich individuals, groups and communities. There are different levels of degradation and disruption of the physical ecological environment. The socio-cultural factors vary widely from the most remote of rural areas to the most accessible urban areas. And, there are many different kinds of politico-legal systems in a country, especially with a decentralized government and multi-party systems. Likewise, the objectives of the group in maximization of opportunities and minimization of losses (threats) will vary also with surroundings. Therefore, when a technology is transferred from the transferor to the transferee, the objectives and surroundings of the transferee have to be thoroughly taken into account during the transfer process. However, how do transferees identify, select and choose technologies appropriate to their surroundings?

Some Perspectives on Technology Assessment and Choice

Technology assessment as reported by Martino (1983), can be of three kinds: reactive, corrective, and anticipatory. Reactive assessment is a reaction to currently recognized problems. The objective is to alter the technology, if possible, to prevent further damage. Corrective assessment involves tracing problems to their causes, and initiating research and development before it becomes severe. Anticipatory assessment is concerned with anticipating the future problems which would be posed by proposed technology. According to him, all the three aspects of technology assessment are important. Gotsch and McEachron (1983), have reported technology choice as a problem of choosing from among a set of feasible technological alternatives. Therefore, technology assessment provides the feasible alternatives where a choice can be made.

In the work of Chungu (1993), three distinctive criteria levels for technology choice are defined. These include the level of criteria for assessing the national priority needs, followed by the level of criteria for assessing the required type of industry, and finally, the level of criteria for assessing alternative techniques or "brands". The three criteria levels are named "socio-economic development sector criteria" for assessing the national priorities, "generic technology criteria" for assessing the industry priority, and "specific technology criteria" for assessing a suitable technique. Figure 3 shows in diagram form these categories of technology choice and their corresponding criteria.

The first category of choice from the socio-economic development sectors is encountered when a country wants to realize a particular objective, for instance, accelerated rural development, requiring an appropriate prioritization of national needs. This would involve the evaluation of the role of various sectors of the economy, such as food, health, afforestation, energy, mining, and communication, in rural development. Rohatgi and Rohatgi (1979), and Sharif and Sundararajan (1984) have made use of criteria C1 (Figure 3) for choosing priority sectors for socio-economic development.

The identification of the processes that should be used for the fulfilment of a particular need takes place at the second level. This involves the evaluation of the type of industries which will fulfil the needs of the country. This could include the assessment of vegetable oil processing, cooking stoves, milling, textile and other such industrial processes. Forsyth et al. (1980), Sharif and Sundararajan (1983), and Bagachwa (1991) have used criteria level C2 (Figure 3) for choosing generic technology.

The third category deals with assessment of specific technology to best meet either the need of the group, or community, or the country at large. This involves assessment of techniques or products represented by different brands, for instance, the "IPI" oil expeller, the "Bielenburg" oil press, the "TEMDO" oil expeller, the "KIT" oil expeller, the "IRRI" thresher, the "Komatsu" tiller, the "Caterpillar" bulldozer, etc. Mcbain (1977), Bowonder (1979), Gotsch and McEachron (1983), Sharif and Sundararajan (1984), Stewart (1985), and Francis and Mansell (1988) have used criteria level C3 (Figure 3) for choosing specific technology.

The Concept of Technology Transfer

The term technology transfer has been in use for quite some time. It is also referred to as technology flows, diffusion of technology etc.. The term technology transfer implies the movement of technology from one entity to another, and if the transfer is successful, a proper understanding and effective use of the technology by the receiving entity. If the receiver does not understand and use the technology effectively, the transfer is considered incomplete.

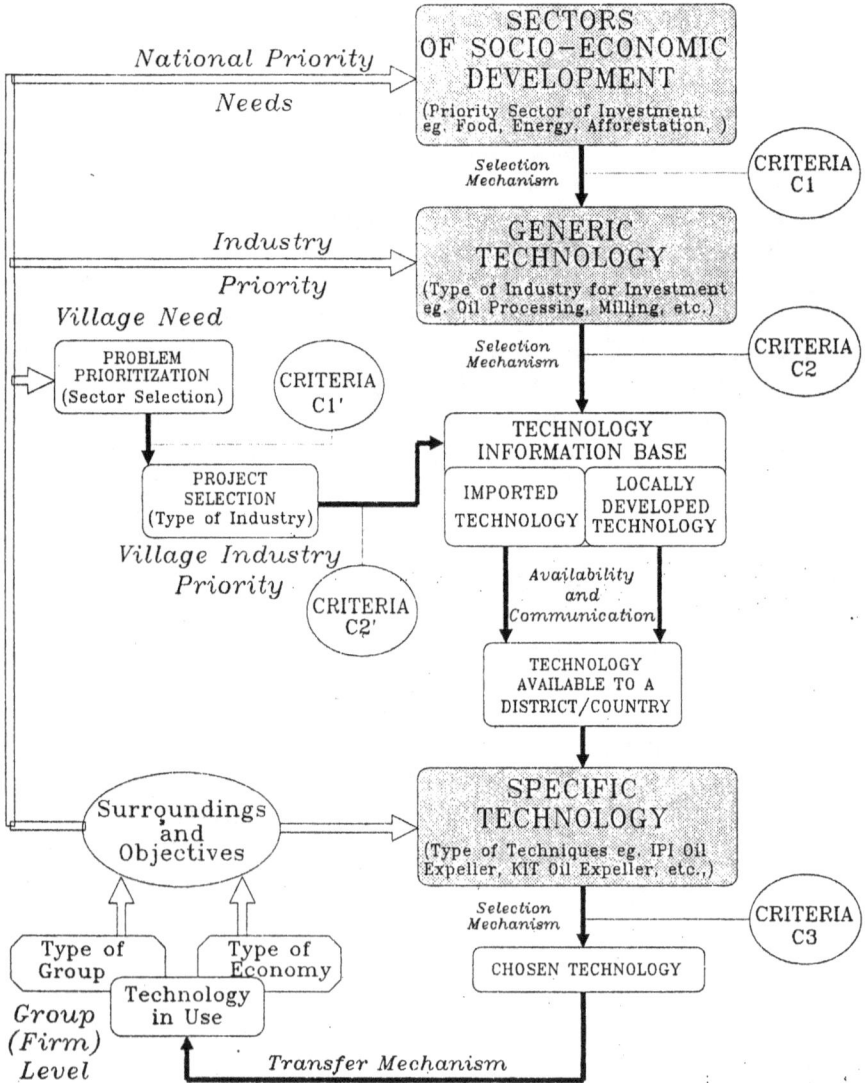

Fig. 3: Technology choice in a cascading process for national development

A synthesis made by Chungu (1993), revealed that the technology transfer framework presented by Schlie et al. (1987), contains almost all elements of technology transfer, with the exception of a "feedback" linking mechanism. However, Ofjord (1975), Shaw et al., (1982), Chambers (1983), and Chambers and Jiggins (1987), have pointed out that a "feedback" linking mechanism is a vital element of technology transfer. A comprehensive technology transfer framework consists of the seven main elements shown in Figure 4. These are the transferor (source of technology), the transferee (receiver of technology), the technology itself, the linking mechanism, the transferor environment, the transferee environment, and the greater (macro) environment.

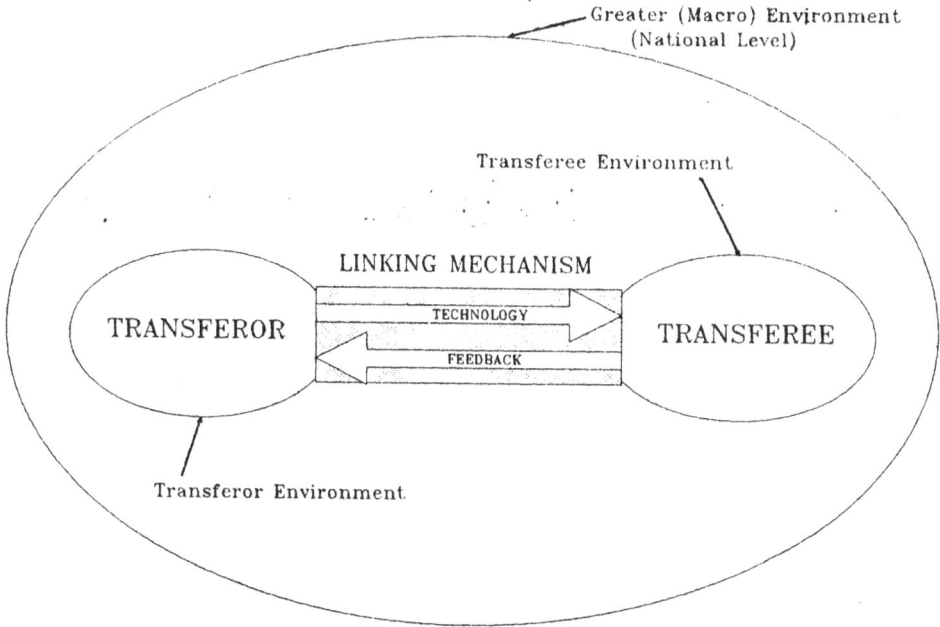

Fig. 4:   **Schematic representation of the technology transfer process for rural areas** *(Adapted:* SCHLIE *et al.,* 1987)

As seen in Figure 4, the socio-economic situational context of the transferor and transferee micro-environments are determined by and large by the greater macro-environment. It is in the transferor and transferee micro-environments where the transferor and transferee are located respectively. The linkage of the transferor and transferee micro-environments, depends to a great extent on whether the state of the macro-environment is conducive or not. A failure to examine the seven elements of technology transfer can easily lead to inappropriate technologies being transferred to the transferee.

A Conceptual Framework for Techno-Economic Development Management

From the preceding discussion, it becomes clear that there are a multitude of variables to be taken into account when striving to understand the nature of technology, and when working to manage technology effectively. It is perhaps the fact of this vast number of variables and their interlocking nature that has made the understanding and management of technology such a problem in the past, and numerous efforts have been expended in developing viable and practical approaches for effective technology management.

One of the leading edge approaches to technology management in recent years has been that developed by the Technology Atlas Project over a period of three years (1985 to 1988), implemented by the Asian and Pacific Center for Transfer of Technology (APCTT), a regional institution of the Economic and Social Commission for Asia and the Pacific (UN-ESCAP). This appears to the authors of this chapter to be the most holistic yet coherent conceptual framework they have come across, and they therefore recommend it as the entry point for guiding the identification of further research work in Tanzania on the subject of technology management for poverty alleviation.

Figure 5, drawn from the Technology Atlas Project Team's work, shows the relationships between the key elements of their model, with "Technology Content Added" (analogous to the economists "Value Added", but with technology-based considerations) being defined as the difference between the technology content of the outputs and the technology content of the inputs.

Table 1, adopted from the Technology Atlas Project Team, elaborates more comprehensively the relationship between conventional economic-based development planning considerations and techno-economic considerations, considered at macro, intermediate, and micro levels. The understanding of this "Framework for Techno-Economic Development" is essential in order to appreciate the implications of its use for guiding the development of a research agenda for technology management in Tanzania.

Table 1: Potential for Complementarity Between Conventional and Techno-Economic Planning

CONVENTIONAL DEVELOPMENT PLANNING	TECHNO-ECONOMIC DEVELOPMENT PLANNING
Firm Level Analysis (Production Aspects) Factors to production - Land Labour Capital Productivity measures - Labour productivity Capital productivity The value of capital incorporated by - Interest, Inflation, Depreciation, etc. Economic viability analysis (IRR, NPV)	**Firm Level Analysis (Transformation Aspects)** Factors of transformation - Naturally available resources Human abilities; Organizational arrangements Physical facilities; Documented information Contribution measures - Contribution of facilities Contribution of abilities Contribution of facts Contribution of frameworks State-of-the-art of technology incorporated by - Breakthrough, Performance, Conservation, etc. Technology contribution analysis (THIO, TCC)
Industry Level Analysis (Economic Output) Capacity utilization - output to capacity ratio Capital to output ratio Market situation Production and consumption (ISIC Statistics) Volume of import and export (SITC Statistics) Growth of output - manufacturing value added Quantitative aspect or production Employment generated by type and number	**Industry Level Analysis (Technology Content)** Technology status - Potential, Possible, Actual THIO Spread of production and innovativeness Technology content situation - Import content of inputs and technology Export content of outputs and technology Growth of capability - technology content added Qualitative aspect of production Innovations introduced by type and number

CONVENTIONAL DEVELOPMENT PLANNING	TECHNO-ECONOMIC DEVELOPMENT PLANNING

Sectoral Level Analysis (Structure of Economy)
 	
Sectoral contribution to GDP -
Gross output and value added by sector
  Agriculture
  Industries
  Informatics
Incremental capital to output ratio
Dynamics of the economy by sector -
Change in the relative contribution to GDP
Change in the labour force structure
	Stage Level Analysis (Structure of Technology)
	
	Stage contribution to TCA -
	  Technology content added by stages
	    Cultivating; Gathering; Preprocessing; Processing;
	    Manufacturing; Constructing; Assembling, Packaging;
	    Distributing; Supporting
	Incremental TCC by stages (SITC Statistics)
	Dynamics of technological transformation -
	Change in the technology content of stages
	Change in the labour force by stages

National Level Analysis (Economic Dimension)
 	
Size of the economy - GNP; GDP
Development status - Per capita income
Input-Output matrix
Growth if the economy
Income distribution
Shadow price (opportunity cost)
Balance of trade
	National Level Analysis (Technological Dimension)
	
	Size of technology - TCA; PCT
	Development status - Technology capability
	Technology flow matrix
	Growth of technology content
	Technology content distribution
	Climate factor (opportunity lost)
	Balance of payment for technology
	Resources and infrastructure profile
	Technology component planning -
	  Facilities needed
	  Abilities needed
	  Facts needed
	  Frameworks needed

Strategic Consideration Import substitution Export orientation (or export promotion)	**Strategic Consideration** Make-some-buy-some technology Three technology domains (import, evolve, export)

(SOURCE: UN-ESCAP, 1989)

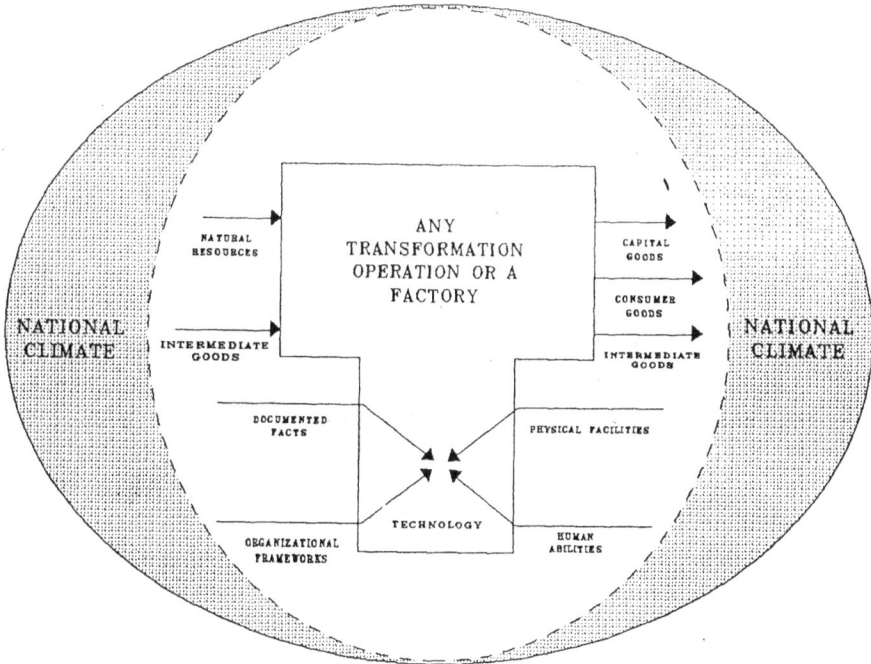

Fig. 5: The Concept of Technology Content Added

TANZANIA: TOWARDS A TECHNO-ECONOMIC DEVELOPMENT PLANNING APPROACH

Critical Issues for Techno-Economic Development Planning

Figure 6 is an adaptation of ideas from the Technology Atlas Project (UN-ESCAP, 1989). In this figure, several critical issues are graphically highlighted that are of particular relevance to a techno-economic based management approach. These include the following:

(a) the need to have a national techno-economic development policy that can provide a clear vision of how science and technology can be used to achieve national socio-economic development goals and objectives, and that can provide an adequate framework for developing and managing a perspective plan for a scientific and technological revolution;

(b) the need to derive explicit policy measures and instruments to effectively facilitate practical implementation of the national techno-economic development policy and perspective plan;

(c) the functional definition of empowerment as a measure of the degree of dependence on and control of own resources, leading to the need to plan for technology in three basic domains -importing, evolving, and exporting. This is in fact not only an issue at the micro-level (to which the term empowerment is currently popularly applied), but is indeed also a critical issue at national (macro) level;

(d) the complementary roles of both top-down and bottom-up development management processes, and the need to define the activities that should be implemented at each key level of control of resources, by specific agencies or key players, in order to put in place all the key elements of the national techno-economic development policy and perspective plan at all levels;

(c) the need to systematically apply "fitness criteria" and technology content assessments of specific desirable technologies at micro-level, and to make assessments of the technology climate, technology status, technology capability, and technology needs at the relevant micro, intermediate, and macro-levels as indicated in Figure 6. These assessments, when carried out with the appropriate participation of the concerned individuals, groups and/or agencies at these different levels, will serve as tools for integration.

Fig. 6: Implementation Schemes for Techno-Economic Development Planning
(*Source*: Adapted from UN-ESCAP, 1989)

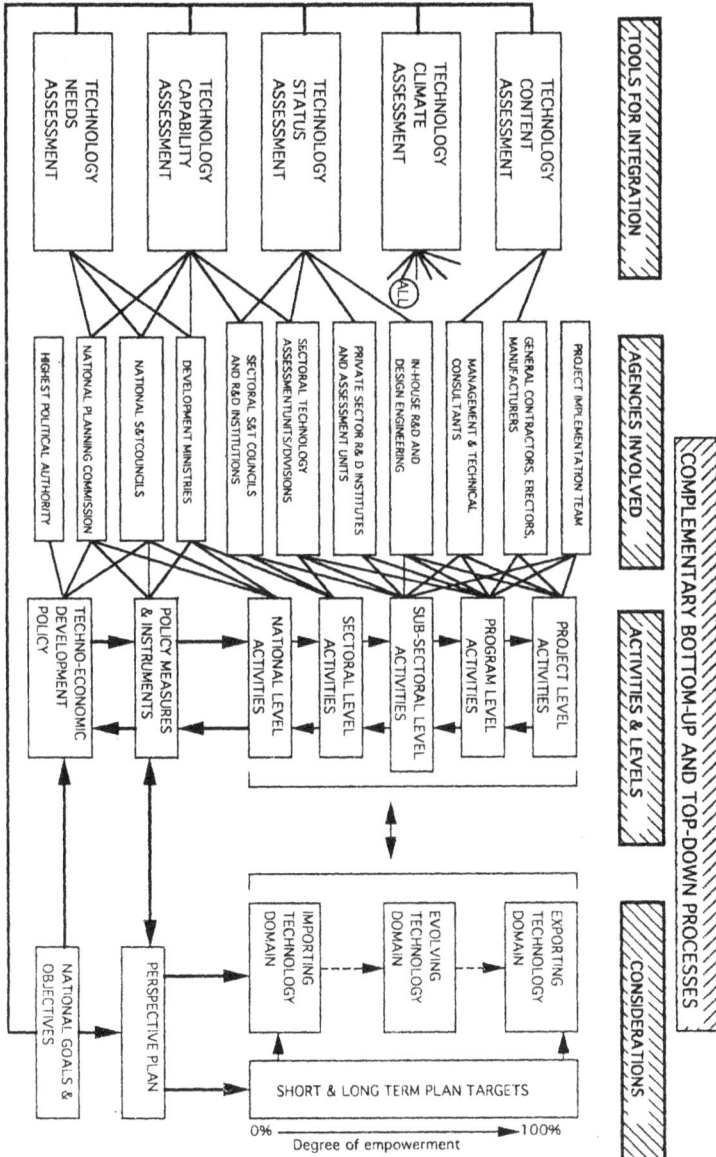

Technology Assessments as Tools for Integration

As an entry point for developing a comprehensive and improved national science and technology policy, and strategies, programmes and projects for the use of technology for poverty alleviation, this chapter recommends the adoption and adaptation to the Tanzanian context of the Technology Atlas Framework (UN-ESCAP, 1989).

The first significant effort in this direction is the work done by Chungu (1993), which is especially relevant to the issue of adapting the Technology Atlas framework to the rural Tanzanian context at the level of selection of techniques from an available range of options. The focus of his work was to develop a 'fitness criteria' for technology, to be used to determine the characteristics of a community based group which are most essential for enabling accurate choice to be made on the kind of technology which would 'fit' the group, selected from the available range of local and imported technology options on the 'technology shelf'. In his study, he found that the main factors affecting the adoption of oil processing technologies in the rural areas of Tanzania were 'technology climate, orgaware and humanware'. The technology climate was also found to be correlated to both orgaware and humanware at a significance level of 5 percent. This implied that any change in technology climate would also bring about a change in orgaware or humanware for better or for worse, depending on the direction of change. But the changes in technology climate did not appear to bring about any significant change in technoware and inforware. The conclusion therefore was that providing a conducive technology climate could significantly improve orgaware and humanware in a group or firm. *Thus, focusing on developing a conducive technology climate and thereafter concentrating on upgrading the humanware and orgaware of the group or firm (Figure 7), becomes the rational approach.*

The prime importance of the technology climate has also been put forward by Bagachwa (1992) and Moshi (1993), who report on how the post-independence to 1984 policies favoured public and large industries, resulting in a limiting of the choice of technology largely to that associated with medium and large scale turn-key projects based on imported technology with little or no consideration to the use and development of local technology capacity in practice, beyond the statements of intent in the industrial policy and plan documents. Even in the small industries development sector, most investments were directed into procurement, installation and operation of urban-based units with predominantly import-oriented inputs [Wangwe, 1993]. It was also found that there is an implicit rather than explicit process of technology choice by Tanzanian planners and policy makers [Bagachwa 1991]. This implicit process of technology choice, often done without an appreciation of the far-reaching and

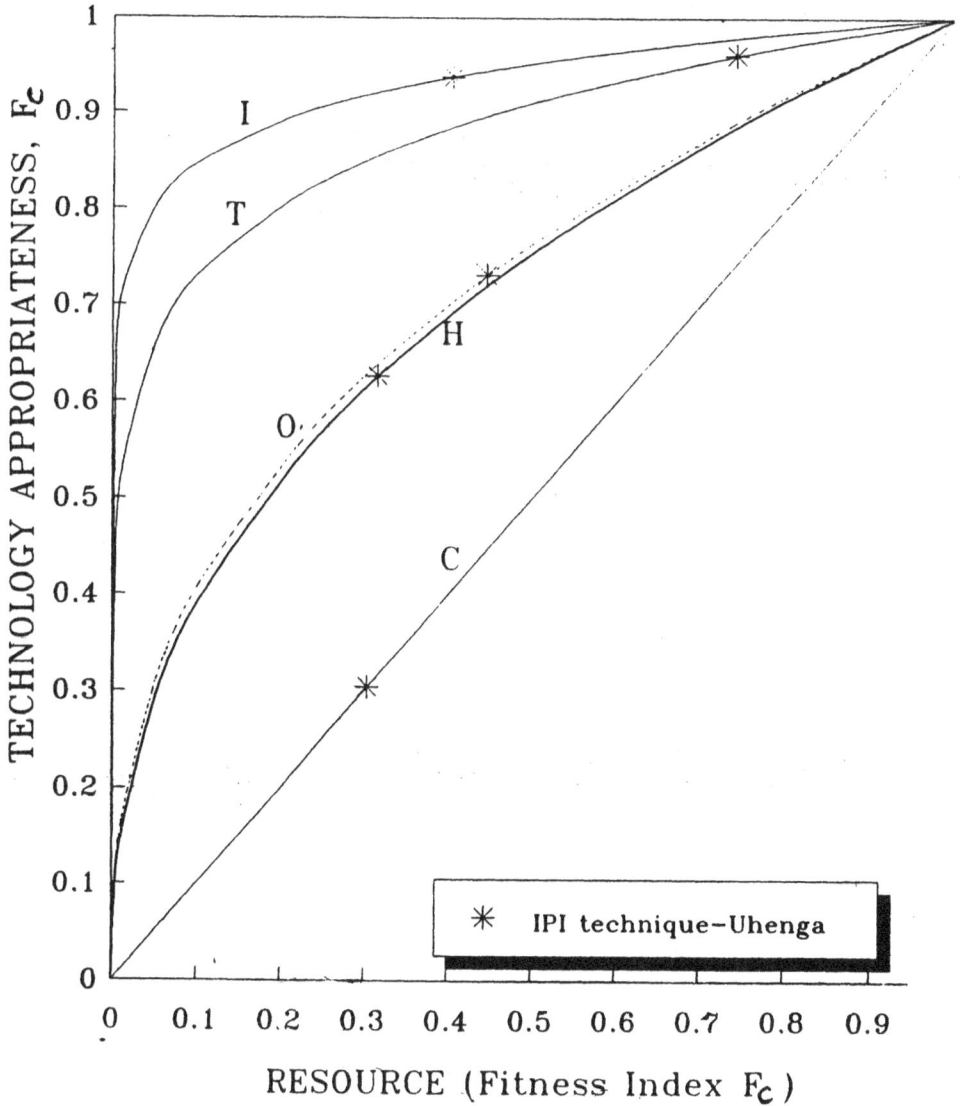

7: *Resource allocation as a function of the contributions made by the component to the appropriateness of technology*

at times devastating long-term consequences of the choice, is largely caused by the fact that our planning and decision-making machinery in Tanzania is dominated by economists and politicians, and also the fact that the proper implementation of some good decisions has been short-circuited as a result of overriding personal interests of implementers (the ten percent or more syndrome). This leads to inadequate planning and distorted implementation at the expense of important technological considerations, a fatal error in today's interdependent world in which technology is increasingly recognised as the master key to development.

The work of Chungu (1993), has adapted only two tools of integration for assessing technologies to be used in the rural areas of Tanzania. Included are technology content and technology climate assessment. Since the tools have been used to assess only oil processing technology, validation to other technologies have to be investigated. Likewise, adaptation of the other three assessment tools for integration, namely, status, capability and needs assessment, have to be looked into.

A Revolutionary Techno-Economic Development Policy

Most analysts of Tanzania's policy of Ujamaa and Self-reliance launched in 1967 agree that the goals and objectives articulated in this policy were visionary and revolutionary; but most now also agree that the implementation of the policy was unsuccessful, leading to the eventual acceptance of policy direction from the IMF and World Bank from the mid-1980's, inaugurating a period of economic liberalisation and political pluralism popularly termed 'mageuzi'(change). Paradoxically, the inward looking and protectionist policies implemented during the Ujamaa period served as an incentive for the development of local scientific and technological capacities, but also led to the ineffective utilization and non-sustainability of use of these same developed capacities due to some fatal errors in the translation of the policy into practice, such as the foreign investment protection act of 1963, the 1967 Party leadership code, the 1975 Ujamaa village act, and the 1967 nationalization act (Bagachwa, 1992).

The impressive expansion of the basic education system to achieve the goals of Universal Primary Education and improved adult literacy, the development of higher science and technology oriented education and training institutions like the University of Dar es Salaam and Sokoine University, the rapid development of local small and large scale industries and local Research and Development institutions, and other far reaching developments in practically all sectors, bears witness to the politically revolutionary spirit that animated national development efforts in the period from 1967 until late 1970's. However, from a technology perspective, the seeds of failure were sown during this same period. The politicians and economists who were guiding the ship of state did not pay adequate attention to the foundation requirements of the scientific and technological revolution that should have walked hand-in-hand with the political revolution. Granted that the oft quoted rhetoric in support of science and technology was impressive; but the realities of implementation - especially with respect to the empowerment of the scientific and technological professional community in Tanzania - told a different story, especially when viewed with the benefit of hind-sight and through the use of improved tools of analysis.

> Human resources ... constitute the ultimate basis for the wealth of nations. Capital and natural resources are passive factors of production: human beings are the active agents who accumulate capital, exploit natural resources, build social, economic and political organisations, and carry forward national development. *Clearly, a country which is unable to develop the skills and knowledge of its people and to utilise them effectively in the national economy will be unable to develop anything else* (Salam, 1989).

Over the years, a culture of superiority of roles and rewards for politicians has been cultivated, unfortunately at the expense of a more balanced recognition *in practice and not in theory* of the proper roles and rewards for scientists, technologists, and other local professionals. The respect and remuneration even of the foundation profession for science and technology - the teaching profession - has been eroded to the point where teaching, especially at the basic level where the roots of a scientific culture take shape, is a practically despised profession that does not attract the most talented members of society as used to be the case with previous generations when the title 'Mwalimu' (teacher) carried much honour and was also materially rewarding.

At the highest levels of scientific and technological capacity, Tanzania has witnessed the exodus of many of her most talented sons and daughters to greener pastures abroad, largely due to their frustration with poor facilities for work, and their perception and direct experience that their expertise is not recognised and rewarded adequately by "the system" in Tanzania. Many of these are performing well and receiving both professional honours and recognition as well as financial rewards in other countries of Africa (Kenya, Botswana, Swaziland, Zimbabwe, Ivory Coast etc.) and beyond. Their talents are therefore currently lost from the process of nation-building in Tanzania, the classic problem of 'brain drain'. Looking within the country, how many talents do we find being misallocated either through wrong assignment, or through being forced to underdevelopment for survival reasons - professors of mathematics, physics, engineering, biology, education, political science, as well as other well educated and talented professionals can be seen daily engaged in income generating activities unrelated to their professions, in order to make ends meet - the problem of 'brain in the drain'.

With respect to the kind of large and small scale transformation operations that were put in place during the Ujamaa period, reflection on the essential requirements for an investment process that will effectively lead to creation of wealth on a sustainable basis, shows the mistakes that were made by decision-makers and managers who were understandably out to get quick results, but failed to ensure a technology development and management process that effectively built upon local capacities and inputs. For various reasons - partly due to ignorance, but in some cases due to corruption and self-interest - industries were promoted and developed that depended too much on imported inputs and capacities, or were not located optimally, or were not scaled appropriately, or were simply not the right kind of investment in terms of the priorities that Tanzania should have been pursuing at her stage of scientific, technological and socio-economic development. Even the basic industrialisation strategy that was drawn up during the Ujamaa period was largely ignored in practice. With few exceptions, the climate was not conducive to the development of an indigenous industrial base, building systematically up from local foundations. Even today, the investment climate - with tax holidays and incentives for foreign investors, but not for local investors - clearly favours outsiders (CTI, 1993). The local entrepreneur has a hard time finding the resources to get started, and is then faced with the obstacle of a tedious bureaucracy to get registration, licensing, power supply, communication facilities, water, and other requirements for operation. Then he/she has to face the tax collector from year one, whilst still learning the ropes of business. Is it any wonder that few local entrepreneurs manage to succeed in such a non-supportive environment?

There are other elements that would need to be considered when developing a revolutionary techno-economic development policy, as highlighted both by the World Bank, and by the Technology Atlas Team. Even though the approach to poverty alleviation recommended by the World Bank (which apparently is the general basis for current national economic development planning in Tanzania), explicitly recognises technology as an important element in the whole process, there are some evident deficiencies in the understanding of the role of technology in the process, as evident in the statement that " ...The first element (of the World Bank strategy) promotes the productive use of the poor's most abundant asset -labour - through policies that harness market incentives, social and political institutions, infrastructure, and technology for broad-based economic growth..." (World Bank, 1992:   )   Thus the emphasis is on employment generation.

However, the conversion of natural resources to produced resources for economic growth as pointed out by UN-ESCAP (1989), is achieved through the production system of a country consisting of a series of transformation units which may be described in terms of four elements, namely the inputs (natural resources and intermediate goods), the outputs (consumer goods, intermediate goods and capital goods), the technology (the transformer and the core of the transformation activity) and the national technology climate which is the setting in which the transformation activity takes place (Figure 5). Technology which is the core of the transformation activity, has been disaggregated into four embodiment forms, namely: Object-embodied technology (Facilities or Technoware); person-embodied technology (Abilities or Humanware); document-embodied technology (Facts or Inforware); and institution-embodied technology (Frameworks or Orgaware). Any resource transformation can take place only when all four components of technology are present at a certain minimum level. Facilities need operators with certain abilities. Abilities have to be strengthened gradually from operation to improvement and generation of facilities. Facts representing accumulated knowledge need to be updated regularly, while the frameworks have to continually evolve to meet changing requirements. Therefore, the suggestions for the use of labour-intensive technologies in developing countries seem to overlook the fact that having a large population does not necessarily mean the existence of a high level of human embodied skills and knowledge, without which the physical tools are mostly useless. Technological appropriateness as pointed out by Sharif (1988b) is a dynamic concept and depends to a large extent on the use to which the technology will be put. For instance, if the purpose of acquiring a particular technology is to gain a competitive advantage in the international market, then labour-intensiveness might be of secondary importance. Therefore, the Technology Atlas Team categorically state that

> ...For meaningful integration of technological considerations with the socio-economic development planning process, it is essential that the analyses performed by economists and technologists be mutually supportive. Using the four embodi ment forms of technology as basis for enquiry, it is possible to achieve complementarity between conventional economic planning and technology-based planning at the firm, industry, sectoral and national levels (UN-ESCAP, 1989).

To be fully aware of the potential for technological advancement in an increasingly specialized and interdependent world, decision-makers in Tanzania need to have appropriate and timely information on the science and technology status of the country, to enable them to develop relevant policy measures and instruments to facilitate positive change. With respect to information for planning and decision-making, the tendency at present - as is evident in the national science and technology policy draft of May 1993 - is to select and adopt conventional indicators, such as the size of research and development expenditure, publications in scientific journals, number of patents, university/ student enrolment ratio, etc. These conventional indicators however were developed for the needs of the developed nations. It must be remembered that science and technology grew in what is the developed world today as an organic, *evolutionary* response to societal needs. Thus, the indicators developed in these countries are almost certain to carry within them the "genes" of such evolutionary development. On the other hand, this chapter is proposing that Tanzania today should attempt to use science and technology as the engine for a *revolutionary* socio-economic development process. In this endeavour, lack of endogenous scientific and technological capability inhibits rapid and sustainable development. Therefore the indicators which would be useful to Tanzania are those that can adequately capture this strategic perspective and provide the means for effectively and continuously monitoring short-term, incremental progress in the process of upgrading endogenous science and technology capabilities in carefully pinpointed strategic sectors and industries that hold the most promise for both macro-level wealth creation, and micro-level wealth creation for all population groups throughout the country.

Conventional science and technology indicators, useful as they may be, should therefore be applied with caution in Tanzania, with a proper understanding of the limitations of such indicators. These conventional indicators when applied to Tanzania will certainly show low values but will not adequately reflect the pertinent problems with respect to the science and technology status. As pointed out by (UN-ESCAP, 1989), some of these problems, among others are:

Under Research and Development

(a) The use of inadequate and outdated facilities,
(b) Inadequate facilities for unpackaging and adapting imported technologies,
(c) Inadequate emphasis on commercialization of research results,
(d) Lack of adequately motivated personnel who can facilitate innovation,
(e) Lack of qualified personnel, etc.

Under S&T Education

(a) Too many people with non-technical skills, and very few with required technical skills,
(b) Poor quality of education due to loss of skilled educators because of brain drain,
(c) Lack of science orientation in primary school education,
(d) Inadequate emphasis on vocational education,
(e) Inadequate emphasis on continuing education, etc.

The above problems show a need to conduct research to develop indicators suitable to the Tanzanian context, in order to provide appropriate guidance to the planning machinery.

The fate of Tanzanian industries in the post-trade liberalisation period which started from 1986 has been thoroughly discussed by CTI (1993). The focus of their discussion has been on the impact of various policy instruments on local industry. These include fiscal instruments such as custom duty, excise duty and sales tax; and financial instruments such as banking policies, special credit agencies, interest rates, and exchange rates. Tax evasion has been argued by CTI (1993) to affect the government by loses in revenue and domestic industry competitiveness. CTI has called upon the government to protect the local industries by creating a conducive technology climate such as tax holidays, temporary exemption on duties and taxes on industrial raw materials, strengthening of the monetary and fiscal management of the import trade particularly the own-funded imports, and also other measures elaborated in their report.

The sentiments in the CTI (1993), imply the promotion of trade in the products from local industries. Most of these local industries were built up based on a strategy of import substitution which however depended significantly on imported inputs. How long will these industries be protected? CTI has not looked into some of the crucial technological considerations which will sustain those industries. Given the resource base of Tanzania, one wonders why some of the industries cannot use locally sourced inputs. An assessment in this direction would be quite important and the technology policy instruments should be directed to enhance the use of locally generated inputs in the long-term. Of course, some protection would be required for a certain period of time, but this should be done in the context of active internal competition rather than the establishment of inefficient and ineffective local monopolies. Another issue which would be important in promoting technology but which is not dealt with in the CTI paper is the issue of legal instruments. This includes laws, decrees, regulations, by-laws, contracts and formal agreements. Some of these are concerned with intellectual property rights like patents, copyrights, trademark law and licensing rights in technology. As Wangwe and Luvanga (1993) points out, the existing procedures in intellectual property rights in Tanzania, inhibit local innovativeness and technology transfer. More research in this area is required to boost local innovations and investments.

In conclusion, if it is accepted that the basic goals and objectives of the revolutionary policy of 'Ujamaa and Self-Reliance' towards technological thinking are still valid, but that the implementation of the policy actually failed because of the lack of a complementary and equally revolutionary science and technology policy, then it becomes clear that one of the most urgent steps that must be taken now to bring focus, vision and energy back into the policy of Ujamaa and Self Reliance is to review, finalise and implement jointly revised versions of both policies, making full use of the lessons of the history both of successes and failures.

Research to support the development and articulation of a national techno-economic development policy, hand in hand with a revision of the national policy of Ujamaa and Self-Reliance, is clearly a key issue for attention. These complementary policies should jointly provide a clear vision of how science and technology can be used to achieve the stated national socio-economic development goals and objectives, and should further provide an adequate framework for developing a perspective plan with appropriate milestones and indicators that can delineate the road to a scientific and technological revolution in Tanzania.

Empowerment, and the Importing, Evolving and Exporting Technology Domains

Wangwe (1993) has commented on the low rate of absorption of imported technology in Tanzania, and on the slow process of technological learning. A major weakness he further points-out, has been the failure to utilize imported technology to augment domestic technological efforts and to selectively import appropriate technology.

Amongst the key considerations in the development of the short and long term targets of the perspective plan, as highlighted by the Asian experience, is the grouping of specific areas of technology into three domains, each reflecting a different stage of self determination. The importing technology domain reflects those areas of technology for which a country is dependent on an outside supplier. The evolving technology domain reflects those areas where the country has made a decision to acquire the technology, and is in the process of adopting, adapting and assimilation. The exporting technology domain represents those areas in which the country has acquired a mastery of the technology to enable it to compete with other countries in the world market-place. The same logic can be applied within a country, at micro-level. The two extreme domains (importing and exporting) can be seen to represent the two ends of the empowerment spectrum (Figure 6). Importing implies dependency on someone else to supply the technology, whereas exporting implies mastery and empowerment. Such a grouping, if done for Tanzania, will clearly serve to highlight the areas of technology in which the country is strong, and those in which the country is weak, providing a basis for more effectively implementing a 'buy-some, develop-some, make-some' technology development strategy.

Key Players, and Laws for Managing Technological Development

Though there is a clear recognition of the importance of science and technology in Tanzania as evidenced by the establishment of the Ministry of Science, Technology and Higher Education (MISTE) and also the Commission of Science and Technology (COSTECH), a widely understood and effectively working consensus on the specific roles of these and other key players at different levels of control of resources, from local to national levels, has yet to be arrived at, leading to a relative inertia and a lack of effective coordination and aggressive support for the promotion of national technological development. MISTE is one ministry among other ministries in the country, while COSTECH as originally conceived is supposed to be responsible for the formulation and coordination of technology related activities nation-wide and cross-sectorally. Since technology is required in all sectors, COSTECH should be able to advise, guide and support directly all sectors with regard to technology related issues. Unfortunately, placing COSTECH administratively under MISTE, hinders its cross-sectoral operational effectiveness due to bureaucracy. For effective operation of the mandate of COSTECH, it should perhaps be located in the President's Office - possibly in the Planning Commission - to contribute to the development and operationalisation of a better inter-sectoral 'techno-economic vision' for the country. The science and technology policy should be broadly conceived so as to provide a unifying framework for, amongst others, the country's education policy, industrial policy and trade policy. The past situation seems to be characterised by parallel rather than unified policies, leading to inadequate synergies between policies and lack of effective teamwork between key players in the socio-economic development enterprise.

The institutional set-up that propelled the South Korean scientific and technological revolution, although somewhat daring [Salam, 1989], is one model to learn from. The task of making specific and explicit decisions on who should do what with respect to science and technology development in Tanzania, and further, the enactment of legal and financial provisions to ensure compliance through applying the basic behavioral change principles of reward and punishment, based on reflection on the Korean experience, deserves critical attention. In this area, Tanzania has the great advantage of being able to learn from the successes of the newly industrialised nations as a "late-comer". In 1962 South Korea's GNP per capita was $100 (Salam, 1989) and in 1991 her GNP has reached $6,330 (UNICEF, 1994), while Tanzania's per capita GNP has been decreasing ending up at $100 in 1991, a value which Korea had in 1962.

Based on the above analysis, it can be concluded that the 'technology horse' of Tanzania is still blinkered and being dragged by the 'cart of circumstances', rather than taking the lead in pulling the country out of the mud of underdevelopment. Up to the moment, the country has no effective science and technology policy, and the one which is in use today is one which was formulated in 1985. The 1985 technology policy, as pointed out by Mawenya (1992) and Wangwe (1993), has a series of deficiencies, which has prompted a currently on-going revision. Even in the current science and technology policy, draft of May 1993 there is no definite demarcation of technology domains. Based on the comparative advantages of the resource-base in Tanzania, it should be possible to develop a pragmatic and effective "buy-some, develop-some and make-some" technology strategy which defines areas which will fall into importing, evolving and exporting technology domains in the short, medium and long term. These technology areas then have to be explicitly and systematically developed in all development plans, programmes and projects. The technology assessment tools proposed by the Technology Atlas Project (UN-ESCAP 1989), should prove useful in this regard.

It is imperative that in order to achieve a balanced techno-economic development planning, competent technologists have to be identified and posted in each strategic sector and area planning department. This should start with the President's office and Prime Minister's Office which are two of the most powerful offices in cultivating and sustaining a conducive technology climate. The May 1993 S&T policy draft document has put high emphasis on this issue.

Research Agenda

The effective management of a systematic process that can lead to the kind of technological and economic revolutions witnessed in recent times in the South East Asian "Tigers", according to the Technology Atlas Project Team involves certain basic steps:

(a) "Establishment of a "vision" and development goals;
(b) Formulation of a long term perspective plan which identifies strategic areas for development;
(c) Acceptance of technology as an important strategic variable;
(d) Classifying national development plans, programmes and projects into three technology domains -importing technology domain, evolving technology domain and the exporting technology domain;
(e) Establishment of public as well as private sector assessment mechanisms at appropriate functional levels for application of the analytical methodologies presented in this report in order to determine the:

(i) Technology Content at firm level
(ii) Technology Climate at different levels
(iii) Technology Status at industry level

     (iv) Technology Capability at industry/sector/national level
     (v)   Technology Needs at sector/national level;

(e) Clear identification of the technological gaps and opportunities revealed by the above analysis and prioritization of remedial measures based on overall development goals;

(f) Introduction of governmental intervention mechanisms in the form of legal, fiscal and financial policy instruments in order to bridge the identified gaps, explore the potential for the promote development in selected strategic areas taking into consideration all the four components of technology;

(g) Implementation of investment decisions to bridge the gaps, explore the opportunities and promote development;

(h) Introduction of review, monitoring and feedback mechanisms at appropriate levels.

Equity considerations, political overtones etc., are not explicitly stated in the above steps. Such considerations are implicit and should form an integral part of all planning processes, the modalities of integrating the technological aspects is the principal issue in this chapter. Based on the preceding discussions and the above basic steps stipulated by UN-ESCAP (1989), some questions are suggested which could be included in the research agenda for the relevant issues alleviating poverty in Tanzania including:

1. Cultivation and development of a revolution oriented science and technology culture and improving the education system in Tanzania.

2. Investigation of those industries in which Tanzania has a strategic, competitive advantage, either regionally (Africa) or internationally. Of these, which ones should Tanzania adopt for strategic, priority development?

3. Classification of strategic industries in Tanzania into the three technology domains: importing, evolving and exporting.

4. How best should existing industries with a significant proportion of imported inputs in their transformation processes be facilitated to optimise the use of local inputs?

5. Investigation for the applicability of the "fitness model" [Chungu, 1993], which was developed for a wide spectrum of technologies for assessing the suitability of these technologies in the rural areas of Tanzania.

6. Development of assessment tools which are suitable for Tanzania to assess the needs, status and capability of industry and/or country.

Adaptation of the technology assessment tools developed by UN-ESCAP (1989) would be helpful.

7.   Adaptation of the conventional S&T indicator for sustainable development in Tanzania.

8.   How can a techno-economic development policy (that is appropriate for Tanzania at the current time) be most quickly developed, adopted and effectively implemented in Tanzania? Due reference should be made to relevant work that has already been done in other countries, especially in Asia, but also in Africa. Technical assistance or cooperation should also be solicited from UN-ESCAP.

9.   Which specific policy measures and instruments (legal, fiscal, financial etc.) should be put in place to most dramatically improve the national "climate" or "environment" for facilitating a technological revolution in Tanzania?

10.   Which are the most critical "technology climate" factors that must be improved in the short term to most rapidly create an enabling environment for a technological revolution in Tanzania?

11.   How best should the agencies concerned with managing a national S&T revolution in Tanzania (highest political authority, national and sectoral S&T councils, R&D institutions, technology assessment units, etc. - ref. Figure 6) be organised, mobilised, empowered and coordinated to play their role effectively and efficiently?

12.   Study of the impact of new or emerging technologies such as biotechnologies, genetic engineering technologies, new materials technologies, etc., to the poor communities in Tanzania.

13.   Study of indigenous intellectual property rights in Tanzania to best meet the needs of the poor.

14.   Study of the dissemination, diffusion and commercialization of technological research and development results to reach the needy ones, the poor in Tanzania.

REFERENCES

Bagachwa, M.S.D., (1991). *Choice of Technology in Industry: the Economic of Grain-Milling in Tanzania*, International Development Research Centre, Ottawa, Ontario.

Bagachwa, M.S.D., (1992). "The Challenges and Potentials of the New Investment Promotion Policy", in Bagachwa, M.S.D., A.V.Y. Mbelle and B. Van Arkadie (eds), *Market Reforms and Parastatal Restructuring in Tanzania*, Printfast (T) Ltd., Dar-es-Salaam, :204-219.

Bowonder, B., (1979). "Appropriate Technology for Developing Countries; Some Issues". *Technological Forecasting and Social Change*, 15(1):55-67.

Bowonder, R, B. and T. Miyake, (1988). "Measurement of Technology at Industry level: a Case Study of the Steel Industry in India and Japan". *Science and Public Policy*, 15(4):249-269.

Bruinsma, D.H., W.W. Witsenburg and W. Wurdemann, (1985). "Selection of Technology for Food Processing in Developing countries", Center for Agricultural Publishing and Documentation (Pudoc), Wageningen.

Cetron, M.J., (1974). "Technology Transfer: Where we Stand Today", in Davidson, H.F., M.J. Cetron and J.D. Goldhar (eds),*Technology Transfer*, Noordhoff International Publishing, Leiden.

Chambers, R., (1983). *Rural Development: Putting the Last First*, Longman Inc., New York.

Chambers, R. and J. Jiggins, (1987). "Agricultural Research for Resource-poor Farmers Part II: a Parsimonious Paradigm". *Agricultural Administration and Extension*, 27(2):109-128.

Confederation of Tanzania Industries, (1993). "The State of Tanzania Industries - an Overview and Prescriptions", Dar es Salaam, 1993.

Chungu, A.S., (1993). "An Integrated Model to assess Technological Alternatives in Rural Areas of Tanzania", Doctoral Dissertation No. AE-93-1, Asian Institute of Technology, Bangkok, Thailand.

Forsyth, D.J.C., N.S. Mcbain and R.F. Solomon, (1980). "Technical Rigidity and Appropriate Technology in Less Developed Countries". *World Development*, 8(5/6):371-398.

Francis, A.J. and D.S. Mansell, (1988). "Appropriate Technology for Developing Countries", Research Publication Pty.Ltd., Victoria, Australia.

Gotsch, C.H. and N.B. Mceachron, (1983). "Technology Choice and Technological Change in Third World Agriculture: Concepts", Empirical Observations and Research Issues, in Lucas, B.G. and S. Freedman (eds), *Technology Choice and Change in Developing Countries:* Internal and External Constraints, Tycooly International Publishing Ltd., Dublin, :29-62.

Goulet, D., (1977). "The Uncertain Promise", Value Conflict in Technology Transfer, IDOC/North America Inc., New York.

Haque, M.M., (1989). "Promotion of Indigenous Innovations in the Non-farm sector for Achieving Sustained Rural Development". *Science and Public Policy*, 6(5):299-306.

Hawthorne, E.P., (1971). "The Transfer of Technology, Organization for Economic Co-operation and Development", Paris.

Hayami, Y. and V.W. Ruttan, (1971). *Agricultural Development: An International Perspective*, The Johns Hopkins Press, Baltimore, Maryland.

Hetman, F., (1973). *Society and the Assessment of Technology: Premises, Concepts, Methodology, Experiments, Areas of Application*, Organization for Economic Co- operation and Development, Paris.

Jequier, N. and G. Blanc, (1983). *The World of Appropriate Technology": A Quantitative Analysis*, Development Centre of the Organization for Economic Co-operation and Development, Paris.

Martiino J.P., (1983). *Technological Forecasting for Decision Making*, Elsevier Science Publishing Company Inc., New York.

Mawenya, A.S., (1992). Evaluation of the Institute of Production Innovation (IPI): Assessment of Recent Development in Tanzania's Science and Technology Policy and the Role of IPI, Design Partnership Ltd/GTZ, Dar-es-Salaam.

Mcbain, N.S., (1977). Developing Country Product Choice: Footwear in Ethiopia". *World Development*, 5(9/10):829-838.

Miles, D.W.J., (1982). *Appropriate Technology for Rural Development: The ITDG Experience*, Intermediate Technology Development Group, London.

Moshi, H.P.B., (1993). "Privatisation and Indiginisation in Tanzania: as Assessment", International Conference on Development Challenges and Strategies for Tanzania: An agenda for the 21st Century, Dar es Salaam, 1993.

Museveni, Y.K., (1992). *What is Africa's problem?*, NRM Publications, Kampala, Uganda.

Ofjord, A., (1975). "UNESCO Activities Related to the Transfer of Technology". *Technos*, 4(1):24-31.

NCC-CSPD, (1993). The National Programme of Action: Achieving the Goals for Tanzanian Children by the Year 2000, Government of United Republic of Tanzania, Planning Commission, Dar-es- Salaam.

Ramanathan, K., (1988). "Measurement of Technology at the Firm Level". *Science and Public Policy*, 15(4):230-248.

Ramanathan, K., (1990). *Fundamentals of Management of Technology*, School of Management, Asian Institute of Technology, Bangkok, Thailand.

Rohatgi, K, and P. Rapjatgi, (1979). "Delphi as a Tool for Identifying Future Appropriate Technologies in India". *Technological Forecasting and Social Change,* 14(1):65-76.

SADCC, (1988). "Women and Food Technologies in the SADCC Region", Report on the SADCC Conference on women and Food Technologies, Arusha, Tanzania.

Salam, A., (1989). *Notes on Science, Technology and Science Education in the Development of the South,* The Third World Academy of Sciences, Trieste, Italy.

Schlie, T., M. Radnor and A. Wad, (1987). "Indicators of International Technology Transfer. Center for the Interdisciplinary Study of Science and Technology", Northwestern University, Evanston.

Sharif, N.M., (1983). *Management of Technology Transfer and Development,* UN ESCAP Regional Centre for Technology Transfer, Bangalore.

Sharif, N.M. and V. Sundararajan, (1983). " A quantitative Model for the Evaluation of Technological Alternatives". *Technological Forecasting and Social Change,* 24(1):15-29.

Sharif, N.M. and V. Sundararajan, (1984). "Assessment of Technological Appropriateness": the Case of Indonesian Rural Development". *Technological Forecasting and Social Change,* 25(3):225-237.

Sharif, N.M., (1988). "Basis for Techno-economic Policy Analysis". *Science and Public Policy,* 15(4):217-229.

Sharif, N.M., (1988b). "Problems, Issues and Strategies for S&T Policy Analysis". *Science and Public Policy,* 15(4):195-216.

Shaw, R., R.H. Booth and R. Rhoades, (1982). "On the Development of Appropriate Technology: a Case of Post Harvest Potatoes". *Food Technology,* 36(10):114, 116-118.

Stewart, F., (1978). *Technology and Underdevelopment,* The Macmillan Press Ltd., London.

Stewart, T, F., (1985). "Options for Cement Production in Papua New Guinea: a Study in Choice of Technology". *World Development,* 13(5):639-651.

Streeten, P., (1975). "Industrialization in a Unified Development Strategy", *World Development,* 3:1-9.

The Technology Atlas Team, (1987). "Components of Technology for Resources Transformation". *Technological Forecasting and Social Change,* 32(1):19-35.

UN-ESCAP, (1989). *An Overview of the Framework for Technology- Based Development,* Asian and Pacific Centre for Transfer of Technology, Bangalore, India.

Wangwe, S.M., (1993). "Technology Development in Tanzania: Some Challenges for the 21st Century", International Conference on Development Challenges and Strategies for Tanzania": An Agenda for the 21st Century, Dar es Salaam, 1993.

Wangwe, S.M. and N. Luvanga, (1993). "Tanzania", in Patel, S.J., (ed), *Technological Transformation in the Third World, Volume II Africa,* Ashgate Publishing company, Vermont, USA, :95-142.

World Bank, (1992). *Poverty Reduction: Handbook and Operational Directive,* World Bank, Washington D.C.

7

Gender and Poverty Alleviation in Tanzania
Issues from and for Research

PATRICIA MBUGHUNI

INTRODUCTION

In a philosophical sense, poverty is part of the basic human condition, a relative term, best given meaning in a specific context. Looking at poverty from "outside", i.e. from the perspective of the "unpoor" countries, poverty is conventionally measured in aggregated statistics such as GNP usually coupled with socio-economic indicators related to health and nutrition (presence of services, calorie intake, life expectancy, infant and child mortality), education (number of schools, pupil/teacher ratio, percentages of formally educated population), employment and/or the structure of the economy (agriculture/ industry/service). From this point of view, the entire population of Tanzania is classified as poor, positioned among the poorest of the poor. Looking at poverty from "within" the perspective of the national development machinery, the measurement of poverty can be disaggregated on the basis of the main development units, region/district/village/household as well as rural/urban. In this context, some are labelled "unpoor" or relatively developed, others "poor" or developing. these labels may be based on economic and socio-economic indicators and often include household surveys of household income, economic activities of household members, acreage tilled, educational levels, fertility and mortality, presence of tin roof, sanitary facilities, radios, bicycles/cars and, in a recent joint study in which the Bureau of Statistics and the Planning Commission took part, parquet floors. Such studies make some economic differentials within the country visible.

At an individual level, the perception of poverty differs according to differing concepts of wealth as well as over time, in different situations. A man with many wives, or, perhaps if he is a Sukuma, many cattle, perceives himself as rich. A farming woman with a good harvest feels rich: "chakula ni uwezo" (food is power/capacity). Facing a village extension worker or one of the many types of obtuse civil servant wielding forms, many people perceive themselves as "poor".

In some contexts, poverty is not perceived in singulate, absolute or quantitative terms, but holds a constellation of meanings wrapped around different forms of power: economic, social, political. Thinking, for instance, of the Bagamoyo farmers (maskini - the poor things) locked in jail for not properly clearing the fields for the swaggering inspectorate, the man who calls himself "mimi mdogo tu" (a little fish) when pointing out "bwana mkubwa" (the big shot), the woman who calls working on her husband's farm working on "shamba la serikali" (the government farm).

From a gender perspective, power over resources, whether these are economic, social or political, is a key concept in poverty.

This is because the presence/absence of resources in themselves is not in itself an adequate measure of the wealth or poverty of a woman, but must include the level of her access to and control over those resources. These resources can include land, labour, credit, agricultural inputs, knowledge, - all associated as economic resources - necessary adjuncts to economic development.

In Tanzania, as in much of the world, women's access to and control over these resources is mediated by her subordinated position within patriarchal society. Specifically, they are conditioned by her subordinated but pivotal position in production and human reproduction.

It is this pivotal position which has also led many development planners and managers to ignore one or the other of women's roles with drastic consequences of making women poorer as a result of development efforts. Women's strategies and choices do not always fit neatly into one of those preassigned roles: producer or reproducer. She is sometimes not a rational economist, as for instance when she does not uproot food crops because they are less economic than export crops. Nor, as was so elegantly put by Diane Elson (1991b), can she uproot a child because the child is "uneconomic" to raise. Women may also not be "ideal" mothers, as when they keep children out of school to help in the fields or at home, or when they take the last food from the store to a funeral.

The attempt to "fit" women into one of these roles has therefore led to a misunderstanding of the scope and parameters of women's choices and strategies. It has also led to blindness to a whole pool of resources and capabilities utilized by women in reaching their goals. Social networks, whether neighborhood, kin or "professional", are a form of resource often utilized by women for labour or financial needs, particularly in hard times. But these are not solely economic: their accessibility depends on maintaining and building human relationships even over the "good" times. Similarly, a woman's harvest of sweet potatoes in Shinyanga, though unlike the cotton crop may never reach the formal marketplace, is a critical resource at her disposal to barter for labour, seeds or sell for emergencies/deaths/weddings. Children, for instance, are often cited as a measure of wealth or "mali", but they are not only an economic resource in the sense of being a future labour force. Children hold an intrinsic value; they cannot be uprooted like crops when they are not economically viable.

These situations throw a different light on our perception of poverty and wealth and women's varied strategies of resistance, accommodation, negotiation and resignation. In particular, the economic model "blankets" women with poverty and passivity as, not understanding the range of their choices and resources, it has not recognized their strengths or their weaknesses. In the same context, it has missed out on a area which is more complex and less quantifiable than straightforward economic explanations: the grey area of negotiated decision-making over allocation or household management of resources in a situation of conflicting priorities, the juggling of different priorities and roles, strategizing on how to "have one's cake and eat it too," or at least some part of it.

From a gender perspective, the discourse on poverty must be broadened from a economistic perspective to include these qualitative, less tangible aspects of life. In particular, it must look at women's pivotal role in production and reproduction from an historical and holistic perspective to uncover both the origins of women's (and family) poverty and the changing characteristics of the gender relations which inform it.

THE HISTORICAL CONTEXT OF GENDER RESEARCH AND EMPOWERMENT

In general, the holistic approach taken in gender research could and has contributed a great deal to understanding of poverty, and in particular the dynamics of poverty creation. Mainstream thought on poverty can also learn a good deal from the critiques of welfare, Women In Development and equity approaches which continue to form part and parcel of development approaches and programmes to alleviate women's poverty.

Research on gender in Tanzania has contributed and responded to many debates: the challenges of grassroots women struggling to maintain families and resist oppressive gender relations, government policies and practices, donor interests and the debates in global feminism. A small but significant body of data and information, analyses, and theory has been generated through (mainly) women's initiatives. The utilization of gender as an analytical variable in Tanzanian research has become significant only through a continuing struggle, particularly in the dialogue with policy makers and development managers.

From the beginning, sex has been regarded as a significant variable. In educational research, for instance, the sex of a student had specific correlation to educational access and the range of educational opportunities. The concept of gender was developed by feminist scholars to create scope to situate the sex variable in a wider socio-economic and cultural context. Gender as a social construct, rather than a biological category, allows researchers to focus on social relations which have different "engenderings" or articulations within different social, economic and political contexts.

Gender research as well as much research on women has been sensitive to poverty issues such as class/income differentials, as well as oppressive forms of relations, whether intra-household, intra village, national or, particularly for research informed in the leftist tradition, global/international. One characteristic which distinguishes various strands within this research is its stance and orientation. Some research does not take a critical stance towards development ideologies in general, but look at ways and means of incorporating women into the existing structures. Others, particularly Tanzanian women researchers and/or those grounded in Marxist/socialist frameworks, are critical of mainstream development approaches and ideologies and promote radical change in the *status quo*.

As a correlate of its critical stance, much of the critical gender research is also activist oriented: geared towards change at both policy and grassroots levels, and therefore committed to a participatory approach not only in grassroots research but also in the dialogue with policy makers and development managers.

This chapter will focus on research within this framework. Following Meena 1992 and other theorists of Southern and Eastern Africa, we will label this framework critical feminism because feminism referring to its commitment to change in oppressive gender relations, and critical because referring to its historical roots in the critiques of development ideologies. This framework not only characterizes the most progressive trends in Tanzania, but offers the most fertile ground for a new outlook on poverty alleviation as a development goal.

The Framework for Gender Analysis

Gender analysis takes as its starting point the different situations of men and women, which in turn generate different interests and priorities which sometimes coincide, sometimes conflict. In gender analyses, these differences are not based in biological differences, but because of a society's construction of what constitutes male and female roles and responsibilities, behaviour, values, cultures. Gender analysis also recognizes gender, as opposed to sex, as a social construct which varies in different historical and socio-economic contexts. Societies have given men and women different roles, activities, responsibilities and authorities and levels of power and value. These differences intersect with

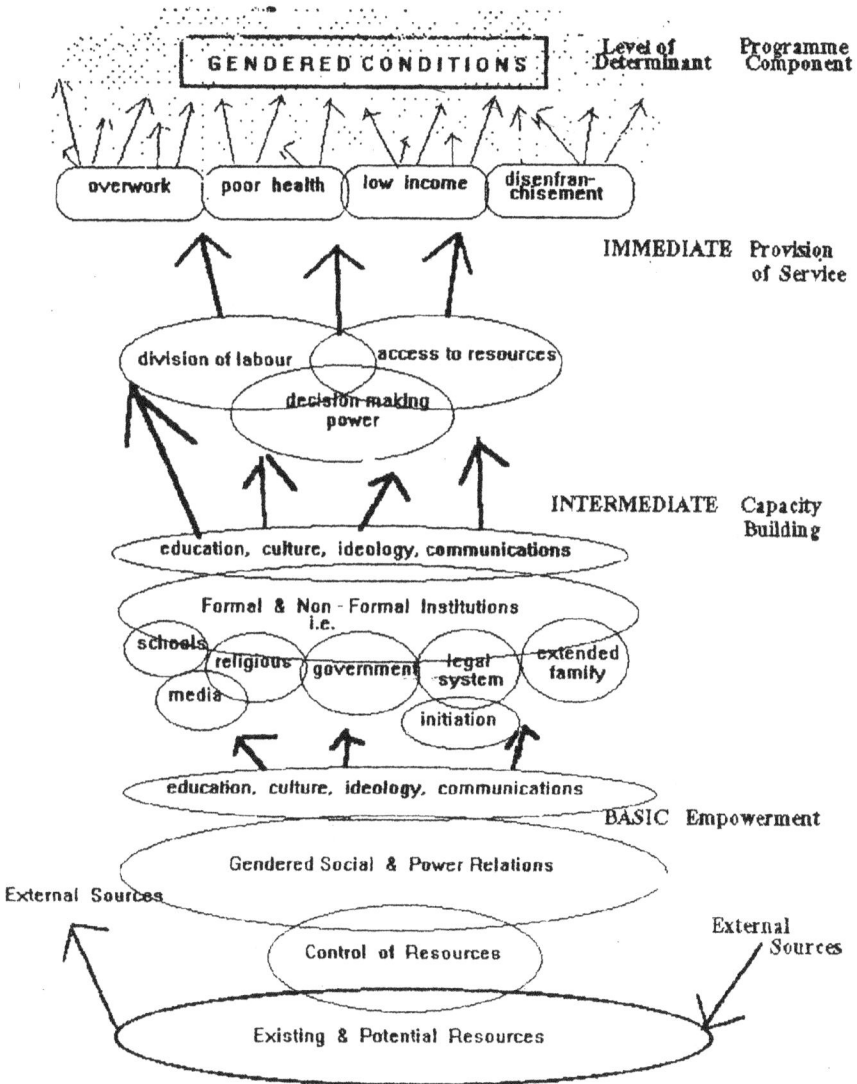

Adapted from UNICEF, Child Survival and Development Programme and TGNP,
Conceptual Framework for Gender Analysis and Action

Fig. 1: Conceptual Framework for Gender Analysis

other axes of differentiation such as age, ethnic group and urban/rural and global location to characterize the life situations and parameters of various women.

Gender differences, or differences based on gender constructs have been sites of struggle for Tanzanian women in everyday life: in particular three areas have been highlighted in the literature: the gendered division of labour, gendered access to resources such as land, credit, education and labour, and the more powerful control of men over decision-making processes. A fourth element is also gaining attention: the discourse on "tradition" or the ideology which legitimatizes and justifies this male control.

Critical feminists in Tanzania have developed an operational framework for analysis which allows differentiation of the various determinants which contribute to gendered conditions. At the top of the framework are the manifestations, conditions or characteristics of women vis a vis men. These usually include such indicators as poor nutritional status, maternal mortality, lower income, employment and educational levels. These are seen as related to the triad of division of labour, differential access to resources and decision-making processes, which in turn are mediated by various formal and informal social institutions such as the education system, legal system, marriage, religious institutions, as well as "traditional" socialization institutions such as the family and marriage.

Women in Tanzania have struggled for improvement of their situation at all levels of this framework. However, the key site and the hardest to open to change is the terrain, or, to use a macho word, "turf" of control over resources and the "traditions" or traditional ideologies which inform and legitimatize them.

UNICEF analysts have related a general empowerment framework to types of development strategies. This tool has been picked up by critical feminists in Tanzania. Strategies which target manifestations have often been labelled welfare programmes which target women's practical needs such as income, water, health facilities, labour-saving technologies. Strategies which target institutional formation and operations are termed capacity-building, while strategies which target control of resources and the traditions which legitimatize them can be classed as empowerment strategies. The critiques of past WID development approaches stemming from the Tanzania Gender Networking Programme (TGNP 1993) as well as Mbughuni (1989b, 1993a) among others, have focused on WID's lack of attention to root causes/determinants of women's oppression, and their concentration on short term welfare delivery. Approaches which address "practical" needs must also be accompanied by a capacity building or empowerment component. In operational terms, this means utilizing practical needs as an "entry point" for addressing women's strategic interests in bringing about what critical feminists have termed transformative change.

The ways in which Tanzanian critical feminists have aligned themselves with the empowerment approach and against what could be labelled short term or stop gap WID approaches can be seen in various sectoral analyses. The seminal work, *Education in Tanzania from a Gender Perspective,* utilized an early version of the framework to analyse the failure of the education system to bring about transformative change in gender relations and gendered conditions; in fact, the analyses points out how the educational process has ossified oppressive patriarchal relations. The TGNP has worked to popularize and develop critical gender analysis in the Tanzanian context, utilizing the expertise of transformative women in the NGO sector. This is yet another prime example of the appropriateness and relevance of the empowerment framework.

At this stage, gender researchers are looking in particular for ways and means of increasing dialogue with grassroots, including various forms of popularization such as popular theatre, workshops and pamphlets. TGNP has further developed a participatory research methodology utilizing facilitation and animation techniques. In this context, one of the important features of this framework is that it can be understood and contextualized by men at women at all levels of society, and has become an important tool for analysis and advocacy within a participatory research framework. In the field, the framework has been successfully utilized in participatory research on UNICEF's Child Survival and Development Programme (Mbilinyi 1992) as well as the *Gender Impact Study* for the domestic water programme sponsored by the Netherlands (Mbughuni 1993b and Nkebukwa 1993).

Critiques of Development and Women in Development (WID) Strategies in the Context of the Emergence of the Empowerment Framework

The following brief account of critical feminist critiques of development and women in development strategies relies on Moser's typology (1991) to place the global debate in a Tanzanian context. The analysis also draws on the work of contributors to the pioneering collection of articles on gender issues in Africa edited by Ruth Meena (1992).

WID Stage One: Developing Women, Developing Ladies, Developing Mothers

Within the Empowerment framework, initial post-independence approaches to improving women's condition can be classified as welfare oriented, addressing practical needs, and conceptualising women in her reproductive role.

From a critical point of view, this approach can also be seen as an albeit benevolent continuation of colonial policies which attempted to keep women on the farm by strengthening patriarchal forms of control. It is also part and parcel of the overall development approach which has generally been termed "modernization". Under this rubric, the state became the major change agent and channel of development with support targeted to "progressive" elements. In keeping with colonial and First World perceptions, "progressive" for men meant modern farming techniques, for women modern housekeeping. Women were brought into development not as producers, farmers, thinkers or managers, but through the back door as reproducers of the modern sector: in particular, as mothers and supporters of modern husbands. Bibi Maendeleo "Development Ladies" taught women domestic skills appropriate to the wives of civil servants and mothers of the future generation of vanguard leaders: sewing, cooking, household cleanliness, laundering and ironing.

The entrenchment of women in a supportive role was not exclusive to the progressive middle class. For the peasant woman, modernization meant more responsibility for family maintenance as cash crops of employment drew men out of the family labour pool (see agriculture sector for further discussion).

Even after the egalitarian rhetoric of the Arusha Declaration, development programmes did little to transform oppressive gender relations: Mama Maendeleo (Mother of Development) merely took the place of Bibi Maendeleo, and development programmes continued to entrench women in reproductive roles. Grohs (1985), looking at the potential for supporting women's income-generating projects in Tanga, for instance, found only limited and "traditional" projects in place. Under the Lushoto Integrated Development Project started in 1969, the Mabughai Training Centre offered 2 -3 week courses to women in topics such as home improvement, home management, food preservation, handicrafts, sewing, poultry keeping, vegetable gardening and the construction of smokeless stoves.

From a positive point of view, however, there were real gains in meeting women's practical needs through expansion of the social service sector: the provision of health services, including MCH clinics, the drive for adult education and later universal primary education facilitated women's capacity to improve her position.

WID Stage Two: Equity and Integrating Women

With the realization in the 1970s that initial "modernization" or "growth" approaches failed to eradicate poverty, but brought increasing differentiation among the populations of Third World countries, including Tanzania, development strategies turned to a "growth with equity" formula which included redistributive policies.

WID grew hand in hand with this approach, as it allowed room for making women visible and specific targets of development programmes. In Tanzania, the historical recognition of women's role and contribution to development was made visible in the forum of the BRALUP Workshop on Women's Studies and Development held in 1979, which brought together a large number of women and some men to exchange experiences on research on women. This Workshop also facilitated the formation of the Women's Research and Documentation Project and the seminal review of research on women in the bibliography by Mbilinyi and Mascarenhas (1983), which was later revised and translated into Kiswahili (Mbilinyi et. al. 1991). Women were now entering research and programmes as producers as well as reproducers.

The approach has also supported efforts "to make constraints to women's participation in development visible". In Tanzania, critical feminists used this opportunity to begin to uncover women's historical sites of struggle, particularly the changing sexual division of labour, its relation to commercialization and modernization, its legitimatizing ideology, and its repercussions in particular on health and the agricultural, education and employment sectors.

The Anti-Poverty Approach

One variation of the equity approach within WID is the anti-poverty or basic needs approach. The political legitimacy of such an approach cannot be questioned, however, it can be critiqued as maintaining a welfarist approach. In its economic form, the anti-poverty approach emphasizes the reduction of income inequities between men and women, thus opening the development parlance to women's income generation projects. According to Bryceson and Kirimbai's research in 4 regions, these projects were mushrooming in the 1970s in the form of cooperatives or women's groups (1980). In urban areas, projects emerged in the informal sector, and are now part and parcel of the urban and peri-urban landscape. As will be discussed in further detail later, the major shortcoming of this approach is its reluctance to facilitate change or "interfere" with traditional oppressive gender relations. The research by Mbughuni and Mwangunga (1989) has highlighted this situation: income-generating projects for women further entrench them in small-scale, traditionally feminine projects which often as not act as a stop-gap measure with long-term negative consequences. While income-generating projects meet women's real and critical need for cash income, Mbughuni (1989b) has argued that unless this approach also contains empowerment components and addresses women's strategic interests, it will continue to reinforce oppressive gender relations.

WID Stage Three: The Efficiency Approach

Although WID provided the opportunity for initial visibility of women, by bringing women as economic actors onto the development stage, it also led to the approach which focused on "capturing" or harnessing women's resources to development goals. As the currently dominant trend in WID and development thinking (it is efficient to address women as they are the major economic actors, particularly in the agricultural sector), this approach has emphasized opening access to women to the given development structures and resources. While gains in access are necessary, feminist critics argue that they are not sufficient to bring about sustainable change in gendered conditions as it takes an essentially uncritical stance towards the development process in general. As Sen and Grown ask (1985) who wants to become part of what has, historically, been a development process oppressive to women?

The Empowerment Approach: A Third World Alternative

In Tanzania therefore, the development of gender analysis has evolved from a discontent with both WID and general development approaches.

With the exception of the gains in health and education, research on the situation of women and later gender in Tanzania has offered a fairly consistent critique of development strategies as gender-blind, male-biased and negatively impacting on women.

The basic reason for this critique is the fact that earlier strategies avoided addressing the basic roots of women's oppression in patriarchal structures at the household/village level, gender-blind policies and implementation at national level, and the uncritical acceptance of biased development models originating in financial and donor institutions of the "unpoor".

Tanzanian feminists have also become acutely aware of the patriarchal hegemony of knowledge which has made them invisible in many past and present researches. Because of this situation, feminists are also acutely aware of the subjectivity of knowledge, have rejected the idea of "neutral" knowledge and are turning to research methodologies and subjects which acknowledge and make visible this subjectivity i.e life histories. Gender researchers are also making increased efforts for engagement of research in what might generally be called an activist perspective. Researchers are looking for ways of strengthening participatory or consultative methodologies in recognition of the interest in change of the status quo. At the same time, gender researchers are interested in creating favourable conditions for dialogues, in particular, on opening more room for qualitative research and frameworks which offer an alternative to the economic paradigm.

GENDER ISSUES IN THE CONCEPTUALIZATION AND MEASUREMENT OF POVERTY

General Issues

As stated at the beginning of this chapter, poverty is a relative concept, and may be perceived and experienced differently by men and women as well as by men and women of different classes. Critical feminists have therefore challenged traditional economic analyses of the economy in general. These criticisms hold major implications for the conceptualizing and measuring of poverty.

One major criticism of the economic paradigm is that focusing on production and marketed goods and services (with some room for subsistence) it has ignored the crucial role of the reproduction and maintenance of human resources as integral to the economic cycle. In particular, it has ignored women's behaviour as straddling both what is traditionally called productive and reproductive activities. We can join with Elson (1991a) in listing the consequences of the "male bias" : 1) women's substantial contribution goes unaccounted for; 2) that the "uneconomic" rationality that informs choices regarding inputs into human reproduction is labelled as "misbehavior" (after Buvinic 1986); 3) women's labour input is assumed to be "elastic" and immediately responsive to economic signals when it is not due to reproductive responsibilities.

Gender analysis has also revealed that macro-level statistics, so much a part of the economic paradigm, are not adequate indicators of the complex reality of change and struggle, and in particular they are inadequate to describe or analyse the situation of different women. Rather than revealing "real" situations, they often mask a complex process of conflict and negotiation.

A particular target for criticism among Western analysts such as Bruce (1989) and Young (1992) has been the neo-classical concept of the household and related data on households and income. Macro-level measures of poverty such as GNP, household level surveys of income and access to resources do not always make the particular situation of women's poverty visible. This is because intra-household dynamics are such that poor women are "more impoverished" than poor men. In particular, the parameters of traditional or patriarchal production and reproduction systems are such that women have less access to and control over resources available for household economy, and the scope for alternative strategies is eclipsed by the same patriarchal structures, in particular by their responsibility for the reproduction of human resources.

Measures of economic levels which look at the wage-price-welfare relationship assume that the household is a homogeneous economic unit, i.e. what comes in the household will benefit all members equally (Young 1992). Research in Tanzania, particularly in the area of nutrition and income-generation and budget studies, has indicated that some of the basic assumptions of such an approach are false (Koda et. al. 1987, Kerner 1988, Aarnink and Kigma 1991, Rasmussen 1986, UNICEF 1990): many researches have pointed out that households are not homogenous units but complex arenas of negotiation, compromise, acquiescence and resistance revolving around differing priorities, including differing priorities of men and women. The assumption, therefore, that pricing or other seemingly neutral interventions will alleviate household poverty or facilitate equitable distribution is false.

Implications of this critique for the conceptualisation and measurement of poverty can be summarized as follows:

(a) female poverty will remain invisible
(b) the dynamics of poverty creation will not be made visible
(c) women's utilization of resources outside the "economic" sphere will not be taken into account such as social networks, labour pooling
(d) women's creative responses to poverty will not be made visible, therefore strengths/opportunities specific to women are disvalued and unsupported
(e) women's rationales for the allocation of resources will not be considered or will be disvalued as "uneconomic"
(f) women's as well as other groups' perceptions and concepts of poverty and wealth will not become part of the dialogue on goals and strategies for poverty alleviation
(g) interventions will be treated as female (and male) "misbehaviour"

Characterizing Women's Poverty in The Tanzanian Context

There are at least four approaches to characterizing women's poverty: 1) characterizing women within households by measuring income and/or other socio-economic variables associated with income such as type of employment/economic activity, health and nutrition, educational levels; 2) characterizing women in general as poor and focusing on characterizing their position vis a vis men and 3) by characterising differences among women and 4) by examining a combination of the above i.e. the position of women vis a vis men, conventional class/income differences, and the position of women of various classes vis a vis each other.

Although gender research in Tanzania has always been sensitive to class/income differentials, it has tended to focus on the first two. In effect, it often classifies women as "poor" vis a vis men, leaving class characteristics as secondary consideration. In relation to the first approach, data on women's specific income is generally not available and also suffers from the shortcomings of income-reporting data. More work has therefore been done to relate women's position with other socio-economic indicators such as education level, type of employment, nutritional status, fertility, child welfare/survival.

There is also a general tendency in the early studies to locate women vis a vis men and to pay particular attention to highlighting general structural barriers. This tendency is in line with the WID research focus which does not differentiate among women but serves the important tactical purpose of making women's position vis a vis men visible (for example BOS, 1991 and Community Development 1989). Many other studies, such as those of Muro (1988) and Mnzava (1988) for the CCM Party and Government leaders, have documented gendered patterns in the division of labour, making attention to women's increasing work burden part and parcel of all research on women. Gendered patterns in employment (ILO/Jaspa 1985, Koda 1988), education (Mbilinyi and Mbughuni eds 1991) and in income generating projects (Bryceson and Kirimbai 1980, Mbughuni and Mwangunga 1989, Omari 1991), have also been made visible.

Wagao's study (1988) of the economic situation of urban and rural women exemplifies the tendency to view women as homogenous, to emphasize structural barriers and ignore the specific dynamics of household management or the intersection of class and gender. The study mentions some differentiation between "poor" and "rich" women, and although specific structural barriers such as the discrimination in intra-household allocation of resources, discrimination in the labour market and women's more restricted access to public services, are mentioned, these categories and barriers are not made significant operational variables. The study does not elucidate, for instance, how the different levels of income - "rich" "poor" - or class positions of women interrelate with their access to and control over inter and extra household resources.

From the perspective of the empowerment framework of gender analyses, poverty is gendered due to women's lack of access to and control over resources, and may differ significantly from her husband/partner's status in terms of income.

The analyses of Katapa (1993) has produced an interesting new framework and is one of the few researches which examines macro-level data differentiating among women. Using mother's marital status as a primary variable (married with husband absent/present, in consensual union, widowed, divorced, never married), she found that 1) single mothers were poorer than married mothers (single here meaning unpartnered whether by choice, widowhood, divorce), 2) the mother's wealth index differed from one marital status to another with those in consensual union at the top, followed by married women with husband present, and widows at the bottom. However, the index of wealth did not correlate with all variables relating to child survival and welfare. The mortality rate was generally high (11.7%), with the highest mortality rate among children of divorced mothers, the lowest among those never married (probably due to their relative youth). At the same time, illness incidence was highest among those never married and those married women with husbands absent in comparison with women with husbands present. Stunted children, on the other hand, were fewest among married women with husbands absent and highest among divorced mothers and mothers in consensual union. Severe stunting was significantly higher among all forms of single parents and women with husbands absent.

Married women with husbands absent were generally older than those married with husband present, their children had the highest survival probability, the lowest rate of stunted children, a better chance of attending health care including antenatal and immunization, but also a high rate of severely stunted children.

With the exception of severe stunting, the absence of the father was significant for child survival, i.e. the presence of the father had a significant negative impact on child survival. Why? Katapa suggests that the husbands' presence interferes with the allocation of resources within the household. The fact that these women also have a better incidence of receiving health care also affirms this conclusion. However, the higher probability of severely stunted (as opposed to the low probability of stunted) children, indicates that there are also variations among these households.

The research also confirms that women need to be married (or in consensual union) to gain access to basic resources for family survival. This is evidenced in the high survival probability of children in married (husband absent) households, as well as the poorer position of children of mothers who have become unparterned through death or divorce.

This research indicates the importance of differentiating among household headship as a significant variable for child survival. In examining the relationship between "single" and "partnered" households, she found few significant differences except in child mortality (136 for "single", 113 for "partnered"). However, significant differences were found among female/male headed households, including the factor of presence/absence of fathers.

Finally, it indicates the importance of further examining intra-household resource allocation management and the relationship of production and reproduction as significant areas to open research to the dynamics of poverty and family welfare.

At a micro-level, Katapa's analysis is enriched by the research of Aarnink and Kigma (1991), who looked at the different characteristics of female-headed, married in monogamous union and married in polygamous union households. As their research spanned an entire agricultural season and closely examined household management/allocation of resources in conflict situations, their work has brought to light both the constraints of the patriarchal farming system and women's creative responses (see section on agriculture for further elaboration).

PAST AND PRESENT RESEARCH ON GENDER AND POVERTY ALLEVIATION

Establishing a Base: Women in Societies under Colonialism

From the Empowerment perspective, correcting the image of passive, powerless and controlled women is just as important to improving women's position as more practical interventions. In this sense, many of the visions of the Tanzanian past need a recasting to look for the "pentimento" - the original image lost due to the artist's change of mind and heart.

Much of the past research on societies under colonialism stems from the empirical anthropological framework. Anthropological descriptions such as those of Jellicoe (1962) have provided detailed data on areas such as women's work burden. Raum's (1940) work on the Chagga examined childhood processes. Gulliver's (1965) research provided the colonial government with information needed to further entrench ideologies of male control. These researchers lack a critical analysis of gender relations of production and human production and the ideologies which inform them. In this sense women may be mentioned but their struggles invisible. There is also a tendency to regard the existing situation as ahistorical, fixing a "traditional" system at that moment in time. As a result, the dynamics of social change and particular social change in regard to women is not highlighted. Another problem with this research is that it focuses solely on male power systems (chiefs and sons of chiefs), whose legitimacy and efficacy were necessary to the colonial system. By ignoring women's different channels of power and communication, it reinforces the "traditional" picture of passive, powerless women.

In Tanzania, significance of correcting this picture has been recognized, and research which includes this owes a great deal to the original work of Mbilinyi (1979) One method she used was to "reread" the material in the light of gender and historical analyses, as in her critique of Feiermann's research on the Shambaa kingdom. Others have paid particular attention to women's channels, networks, power bases in the present context to throw light on the past. Mitzlaff's research on the Waparakuyu women, soon to be published in English, is a case in point. Archival information can be combined with life histories, stories or proverbs to uncover women's resistances and struggles. Mbilinyi's (1988b) work on runaway wives in Mbeya highlights women's resistance to male control of their productive and reproductive capacities. Wright's (1977) study of the position of women in Safwa society based on missionary accounts of life histories, points out how women's autonomy was affected by patriliny and migrant labour, and is one of the few studies which points out differences among women in an early colonial setting.   Still another approach is the use of life histories of living women to document women's struggles and strategies. The work of the Women's Research and Documentation Project in producing *Unsung Heroines,* (Ngaiza & Koda 1991) a series of life histories of "ordinary" women's struggles, is another contribution to research in this direction.

These researches can be seen as initial efforts to paint women into the historical landscape, in particular women's resistance, whether it took non-confrontational, go slow or more dramatic forms.

Women and the Colonial Economy

Critical feminist research on women in the colonial economy has looked at changing patterns of gender relations, particularly in agriculture, and often linked colonial and post-independence strategies. The negative impact of the commercialization of agriculture on the peasant economy and particularly on women has been its major focus. According to this analyses, the colonial economy relied heavily on women's labour in producing for family maintenance, including both productive and reproductive tasks. Through its policies instigating cash needs, labour migration and the movement of male labour from food to cash crops, the colonial government entrenched women on the farm in a subsistence economy parallel to and subsidizing the cash economy.

In Mbilinyi's analyses (1988a and 1991), post-independence policies have continued to demand increased commercialization and have geared support to the cash crop and larger-scale farmer. As a result, poor farmers and in particular, women farmers are becoming dispossessed, marginalized away from resources (including land, labour, credit and inputs). For women, she argues, the position is more acute as increases in agricultural output demand not only finance but intensification of agricultural labour. This research has been echoed in that of Tobisson (1986) on family dynamics among the Wakuria, and Vuorella (1987) in Msoga village, Bagamoyo.

Research has also been focused on the colonial education system of "adaptation" reinforced by a patriarchal division of labour and buttressed by "traditional" gendered stereotypes. Mbilinyi and Mbughuni (eds) (1991) argue that such forms of education ensured the continued subjugation of women to male control.

In general, research on colonial economy and education has explored the negative impact of colonial policies on women. These have:

(a) further increased women's work burden
(b) eroded her power base, channels of communication and organisations
(c) eroded access to resources needed to maintain family including fertile land, labour and finance
(d) subjugated women within the commercialization process

However, as stated in the previous section, there is only scant research which highlights women's resistance not only to colonial policies, but to increasingly oppressive gender relations which they berthed. More research is needed to document the specific ways in which the colonial experience impoverished women and their resistances. A related area which has remained almost untouched is the changing forms of patriarchal ideology. Huber (1973), for instance, examines how the Church fortified the dowry system. Such research could also unveil the selective highlighting and reinterpretation of cultural forms of expression to bolster patriarchy (proverbs, stories, songs).

Post-Independence Agricultural Development Strategies and Gendered Poverty Alleviation

The agricultural sector, as the backbone of Tanzania's economy, should become a driving force behind poverty alleviation. In fact, the majority of the population, and the majority of poor peasant households, are located in rural areas where agriculture is the main economic activity. There is available statistical evidence of increasing socio-economic differentiation between rural and urban areas. The recent joint household survey (BOS *et al* 1993) indicates that levels of income, education and health are all affected by location in a rural or urban context. It would be assumed, therefore, that improvement in rural agricultural production would be a main catalyst to poverty alleviation.

Micro-level studies such as that of Thompson (1985) indicate that in the process of differentiation, traders/government officials, waged persons at the top of the scale, followed by larger scale commercialized farmers, small-holders and, at the bottom, the landless, resourceless rural household. Given this situation, more attention needs to be paid to the nature of peasant or small-holder farming systems, here called patriarchal farming systems (after Mbilinyi 1991), and the position of women within them. Specifically, we need to examine how increasing differentiation affects different households and their strategies for survival.

Most research, however, places its emphasis on the negative impact of agricultural policies on the position of women.

Mbilinyi's work (1991) draws the broad outlines for examining changing gender relations in the agricultural sector. She takes a critical stance to agricultural development policies in general, draws the broad historical outlines of peasant women's poverty and places it in the context of general increased poverty in peasant households. She points out the increasing pauperization and proletarianisation of the peasant economy based in increased commercialization of agriculture linked to the interest of trans-national agri-business. In this context, women are the hardest hit as evidenced in the analysis of labour force participation. There is a dominance of women in the unpaid family labour category as well as increased presence of women in agricultural labour force in general and agricultural casual labour in particular.

Some critical feminist research has fallen within this context of examining changing gender relations in peasant households. For instance, Muro (1988) in her work and Tobisson (1986) have made the increase in labour burden and the narrowing of women's resource base central focii. Special mention should be made of the research on nutrition under the Tanzanian Food and Nutrition Centre and more recently UNICEF, which has provided a key focus for linking the productive and reproductive roles of women in a dynamic analyses of the allocation of resources.

Micro-level changes in the labor process have been documented, particularly the increased work burden for women under commercialization strategies (Mnzava 1989, Tobisson 1986, Grohs 1985, Muro 1988, Vuorella 1987, Mbilinyi and Kabalele 1982). As men moved into cash crop production or into towns, they removed their labor from the pool needed for family maintenance.

Earlier research on settlement schemes and Ujamaa villagization have also been criticized for negative impact on women. Brain (1975 & 1976) pointed out how settlement schemes dispossessed peasant women of access and control of land while entrenching the male household head as main controller of farm income. Giblin (1980) points out the increased labour demands and lower status of women due to villagization and cash crop production. Mapolu (1973) pointed out women;s increased labour burden under ujamaa villagization, where women are earmarked for donkey work in village development projects. Other researches point out increased distances to farms and firewood sources, increased competition for water resources, and even increased jealousy due to neighbor proximity as some of the negative consequences of villagization.

The impact of financial intensification of agriculture as been particularly negative for women. The purchase of inputs for cash crops, has worsened the lot of small-holders in general: inability to purchase input/input delays and subsequent losses/loss of fertile land/loss of soil fertility through monocropping are some of the indicated consequences. As documented by Thompson (1985) in Lushoto, poorer households have had to turn to casual or (male) migrant labor/outmigration to maintain family subsistence. Women, in particular poor women, with less access to financial and other resources, have few options but the intensification of their labour. In their study in Njombe, for instance, Mbughuni and Kaijage (1989) found women lamenting the withdrawal of all resources, including male labour, leaving them with the hoe and the land. The position of the poor peasant woman is further truncated by the fact that her livelihood and that of her family is tied into food crops. This allows her less scope to diversify and strategize for improvement.

Mechanization, including tractors and some oxen schemes, have also increased woman's labor, particularly in weeding. Although the negative impact of the migrant labor system under colonialism has been highlighted in some feminist research such as that of Mbilinyi (1991) on Southern Highlands, little research has actually documented the reasons for the *current* increased outmigration of women or the impact of current male outmigration and semi-residence.

The low resource base of rural women vis a vis men, their restricted access to productive resources to better their situation such as land, credit, technology, information and their own labour, has been documented in a number of micro-level studies such as that undertaken by the Women Expert Group for the Ministry of Education (1989), and the survey of women's income-generating projects undertaken by Mbughuni and Mwangunga (1989) for the Small Industries Development organisation.

Only a few researches in agriculture have explored differentiation among peasant women. Bader (1975), examined how women's class position affected the production process and her level of autonomy in Bukoba. Kirimbai (1981) found class/strata related to access to water. In keeping with the general sense that labour is the key input for small-holder farmers and women in particular, the main difference appears to be the ability to purchase hired labour. Another difference is access to off-farm forms of income generation, whether casual labour or petty commodity production which are crucial to the survival of poor households (Mbilinyi 1991). Even less explored as a focal point of research is the intersection of class and gender and their shaping of women's range of choices and strategies.

Women's resistance in struggles over cash and food crop production have been documented in some of the research. Mbilinyi (1988b) reports how women in Rungwe withdrew their labour from tea production demanding pay. Aarnink and Kigma (1991) report a Shinyanga woman's tactics to ensure first priority in labour to her food, rather than her husband's cash crop production.

Exposing the subordinated position of the poor and particularly women vis a vis the state and its arms of "extension", including petty officialdom and "extension" officers, has been another a focus of some of the research on rural conditions. Vuorella (1987) effectively illustrates the petty tyranny of officialdom in a series of women's recollections. Sumra (1985) cites the case of a uninformed official making meaningless directives, while Raikes (1987) argues that agricultural policy in general has become one of "eating the carrot and wielding the stick". Officialdom has generally been criticised for coercive measures and "top down" directive styles of communication. The ineffective role of agricultural extension in improving women's agricultural productivity has also been pointed out, particularly their traditional focus on cash crops and the male farmer. Muro (in WEG 1989) reports how one woman farmer in Kibaha complained that she continues to plant the same strain of cassava year after year; where are the new developments in her crop? In-depth research in Shinyanga also reveal the low level of contact between male extension workers and female farmers, and identified both constraints (lack of labour elasticity, lack of access to inputs, constrained decision-making powers, women's thinking on inputs and outputs) and opportunities (women's willingness to learn, use of group methodologies) for strengthening agricultural extension to women.

In general, more *current and particularly micro-level research is needed* which both documents and analyses the specific and changing position of poor women in agriculture and the opportunities, constraints and the conditions for improvement of their economic position. From the empowerment perspective, such research should pay particular attention to the changing power and resource bases of women vis a vis men and their strategies (negotiation, resistance, accommodation) for securing a livelihood.

The extensive work of Aarnink and Kigma (1991) is an example of new directions in research, new forms of analyses in the agricultural sector. Given their goal of strengthening women's agricultural production, they examine the dynamics of the patriarchal farming system as it relates to household resource management. Utilizing a framework which differentiates men and women but also differentiates women by the nature of their household headship and composition: female headed households, households with married women in polygamous and monogamous marriages. Significant differences were found in the division of labor, the access to and allocation of resources (including labor, land, finance and social networks) and decision-making power among the households. Other significant factors affecting these patterns were the presence of co-resident female adults and the size and age composition of the household. They conclude that women's agricultural productivity can be strengthened but through a series of supports which include strengthening women's position in vis a vis men, in particular women's access to agricultural resources and her control over their allocation, greater decision-making power for land and input use and purchase, greater command of her own time, a freedom to decide how to use her time. These conclusions have strategized on the basic oppressive nature of patriarchal farming which constrains women's parameters for manoeuvring to secure a livelihood. This research is unique in:

(a)   linking issues of agricultural productivity to reproduction by examining women's multiple roles and wide range of choices for resource allocation,

(b)   highlighting the practical consequences of differing priorities of men and women,

(c)   recognizing social networks and other forms of resource mobilization as part of women's strategies (barter, labor exchange, kinship),

(d)   its focus on differentiating among women, and

(e)   its attention to women's perceptions of their activities and their goals.

The increased reliance on patron-client/inter-household relations during times of crisis, particularly among poor households, is also underlined in Bryceson's (1990) work on food security.

In differentiating households, particular attention should be paid to female-headed households, including those affected by temporary male out-migration. The characteristics and nature of female-headed households has as yet been poorly documented in research. The above study can be taken as a starting point. It noted that female headed households allow more room for female decision-making, but access to land is limited. Labor is identified as a major constraint for agricultural improvement or expansion in all households, but particularly for female-headed households. Katapa (1993) also noted that female headed households have a different socio-economic make-up which bears a relation to child welfare. Her study places these as poorest households. There is a need to establish the frequency of female-headed households, their opportunities and production dynamics.

The phenomenon of male migration or semi-residence should also be taken as a significant variable. Periodical male absence was typical of the poorer research location in Shinyanga (Aarnink and Kigma 1991). Thompson has put outmigration of children of current residents in Lushoto at a staggering 69%. According to Mbughuni and Kaijage (1987), women in Njombe complained of effectual abandonment by their husbands, who returned only to "take the child off the breast", i.e. to make the wife pregnant. How widespread is this pattern? Given the real constraint of labor in agricultural production and the pressing need for off farm income to maintain the family, what does this pattern mean? Are rural men abdicating their role as responsible patriarch? What are the consequences?

Research on Constraints and Opportunities for Women in the Strategy of the Self-Employment/The Informal Sector

The importance of the informal sector as an alternative form of income-generation in Tanzania is evidenced in its increasing size in the economy. Maliyamkono and Bagachwa (1990) placed the contribution of the informal sector to national GNP at between 20% and 30%; Sarris and Van den Brink placed it as high as 60% (quoted in Bagachwa et al 1992). In a household survey of informal sector activities in Dar es Salaam by Tripp (1989), it was found that informal earnings make up nearly 90% of household income. In their survey of urban small scale enterprises, Bagachwa et al (1992) outlined general characteristics of these enterprises as: small capital investment, small labour input, low wages and constraints in capital. This study also found that sex was not a significant variable in relation to type of enterprise/industry or size, and that there were fewer women managers (13% of all managers) but with a higher percentage of female managers in Dar es Salaam (44%).

Other research in the 1970s by Bryceson and Kirimbai (1980) and later in to the 1980s by Mbughuni and Mwangunga (1989) and Omari (1991), which looked at women's income generating projects in urban as well as rural areas, has pointed out not only the increasing participation of women, but gendered differences. Specifically, women's projects are of a smaller-scale, with less capital investment, lower returns, utilizing traditionally skills, and are service-oriented and traditionally "feminine" types of projects.

Women in rural areas are increasingly turning to individual micro-enterprises to fill livelihood gaps. In 1980, 60% of women were estimated to be participating in group or individual projects. By 1989, according to Tovo (1991), the figure had risen to 90%, with women often undertaking multiple "miradis" or strategies for increased income. According to Tripp (1989), urban areas have a similar pattern: indications are that women's participation has risen from 7% of women in 1971 to over 65% in the late 1980s.

Research also indicates the poor returns and gender-typing of women's projects. Tripp's research (1989) on urban women's projects indicated poor women were most likely to be involved in food-processing industries or retail selling of petty commodities such as charcoal or kerosine. The same study also indicated that men's starting capital was 4 times greater than that of women, and their returns 5.4 times higher.

Current rural women's projects are headed by beer brewing (56%) followed by sale of cooked food (41%) and sale of agricultural produce (40%) (Tovo 1991). According to the analysis of Mbughuni and Mwangunga (1989), women have experienced history of a negative experience with group and/or cooperative projects. This backlog of negative experience is most likely the main reason for the current preference for individual projects.

There have been a few generalized attempts to characterize the impact of class on participation in the informal sector. Kassungu (1990) and Wagao (1989) point out that better off urban women have more access to "free" time for income generation as well as to capital resources, which might make their projects more capital intensive, larger scale and with higher returns. Omari's (1991) research would seem to back up this sense: poultry keeping, dairy farming, horticulture are the domain of the better-off women, while poorer women engage in sales of petty commodities and agricultural produce.

The study by Mbago et al (1989) of low income urban households found that household used strategies of multiple income with main sources in wage employment, farming and small business. It found that a greater proportion women depended on farming and small business, while men dominated waged income. It also found that farming was the main rural source of income, wage income the main urban source.

Constraints to women's more effective participation identified in the literature include a *higher degree* of constraint than men in reference to access to capital, financial institutions, raw materials, skills and technology (Mbughuni and Mwangunga 1989, Omari 1991), as well as gender specific constraints such as lack of free (non-elastic) time and restricted mobility and hijacking/misuse of enterprise resources by husbands or, particularly in the case of rural group projects, various forms of officialdom. The historical context of women's projects as necessarily group and welfare-oriented and dependent on grants has also acted as a constraint in the earlier period (Mbughuni and Mwangunga 1989). Another complaint is the misappropriation of funds meant for poorer women by the well-connected and their husbands.

Critical feminists have viewed the movement of women into the informal sector as both and opportunity and as a stop-gap measure. Viewed in a positive sense, self-employment may open the way to greater self-esteem, economic independence. However, the opportunities for rural and poor women are greatly restricted by the low resource and time base. The increase of women's contribution to family maintenance may mean men's opting out of family responsibility, or become a source of increasing marital friction. These issues have been mentioned in the analyses of women's projects such as Koda et. al. (1987), and are a frequent issue raised by women entrepreneurs in seminars/workshops (the reference is to various workshops held for women entrepreneurs by SIDO). This issue needs further documentation and analyses. It is usually assumed, for instance, that women have moved into self-employment due to a crisis in family survival; it is not an option, but a necessity. The capacity to generate long-term growth or social benefits such as self-image and esteem, may be minimal. As a result, some critical feminists have pointed out the necessity of building capacity-building and empowerment components into support programmes (Mbughuni 1989b). An in-depth research of case studies of women's initiatives/income-generating projects by a group of feminist researchers (Koda et. al. 1987) came to similar conclusions.

Research by Bagachwa et. al. (1992) indicates that women employed in the informal sector (as opposed to "the women entrepreneur" in the informal sector) receive less pay than male employees. The TGNP (1993) analysis also pointed out the nature of this sector (unregulated, lower pay, no formal contracting) means less employee income and security. As women (one would suspect poor women) are increasingly seeking employment through this sector, there is a danger of increasing polarization through this sector.

These researches indicate the need to further analyse the informal sector from the viewpoint of *multiple sources of income* as well as *gendered, class and locational patterns*. Particular attention should be paid to those employed in this sector. We also need to know women's own goals and strategies for negotiating access to resources (finance, raw materials and her own time) and for overcoming patriarchal forms control. Hopefully such research would provide a base for strategizing on strengthening women's opportunities in this sector. There is also a need to explore the possible limitations of the informal sector for sustainable improvement/transformation of poor women's position.

Research on Constraints and Opportunities for Women in the Strategy of Formal Employment

Waged employment is an option open to few females: according to the 1988 Population Census only 3% of women were engaged in waged labour as opposed to 10% of men. Research has also indicated gendered patterns of employment within the formal sector: women form 27% of high and middle level employees, and are concentrated in traditional service fields such as nursing (69% of the total employed), clerical work (31%) and teaching (27%) (BOS, 1992).

Research has also indicated that women earn lower pay for comparable work (Knight and Sabot 1981). There are very few women managers or women in scientific/technical fields. Micro-level data in the industrial sector carried out by Meghji (1977) and Mgaya (1976) also indicates women hold lower paying positions with less potential and real training opportunities.

The reasons for this situation have been suggested in some of the literature but not fully documented or explored. One set of reasons is structural: women's generally lower educational levels and gender-streaming limit women's options. On a micro-level, Mukurasi (1986) documented the impact of negative employer attitudes towards women as another problem area; men are reluctant to hire women due to increased costs. Husband's attitudes towards allowing women's employment and/or mobility in the informal sector has also been a negative influence (Nkebukwa 1993). The role of patriarchal ideology which devalues the successful woman outside the home, as well as the desire to control women's productivity by keeping her at home or on the (his) farm, may well be another crucial factor. Sexual harassment in the workplace is also more widespread and under-reported than assumed (Shaidi 1993). Women's own self-image and the cultural stake she has in ensuring successful reproduction may generate a form of self-limitation whose parameters are set by the patriarchal ideology.

Finally, one could hypothesize an increased female participation in the sex industry due to high unemployment and depressed formal labour market. Given the tight economic conditions, more men may prefer buying casual sex to marriage. We know little about the extent and roots of the commoditization of sexual relations in Tanzania. There are, however, a number of studies (particularly on *women's* fertility) which blame women for their increasing "misbehaviour." Studies such as those of Lupilya (1992) and Kapinga (1988), for instance, blame adolescent fertility on the breakdown of traditional socialization processes. In effect, they are bemoaning the breakdown of "traditional" male management and control of female sexuality. An example of a more forward-looking new direction is the work on teenage pregnancy currently reaching completion under the Women's Research and Documentation Project.

General Observations on Future Research on Economic Activities

In view of the prevalence of a discriminatory pattern - in agricultural as well as formal and informal economic activities, further analyses is needed to bring the causes of these patterns to light. In particular, the role of patriarchal gender relations, its control of female resources, mobility, and options, needs to be brought into the research terrain.

A central area for further research and action is to characterize the inter-relationship between production and reproduction activities as affected by class/location. How do women of different classes/locations negotiate and juggle these responsibilities? What are their goals, priorities and strategies?

The research in Shinyanga by Aarnink and Kigma (1991) would suggest that for poor rural women, food production and security is their main priority. How do they reach this goal given often different male priority for cash income? How do they manage responsibility for child care given their crucial role in food production and off-farm income generation? What are the strategies of poor urban women? Despite the early government and donor push for the establishment of day care centres, they are few and not always acceptable to mothers. Poor women may have fewer choices; they may well rely on unpaid labour of family members or neighbors, or send children to grandparents.

Increased information and knowledge in these areas would help effective strategizing for change and empowerment.

The New Crisis: Structural Adjustment and its Implications

The limitations and negative effects of structural adjustment as a development strategy which will eventually alleviate poverty has been widely discussed in critical feminist literature outside Tanzania, particularly in Britain in the work of women such as Elson (1991a and b) and the Commonwealth Secretariat. In Tanzania, criticism has been levelled at Structural Adjustment policies both in terms of their inefficacy and their negative impact on women. The TGNP analyses, for instance, points out that the expected positive returns of increased output have not yet materialized in all agricultural export crops, and the greater volume of some crops may be due to larger output in large-scale rather than small-holder farms. Research in Iringa on the impact of Structural Adjustment showed that main beneficiaries of Structural Adjustment were better-off traders (TADREG 1991).

For the Tanzanian household, particularly the poor and middle levels, Structural Adjustment policies have augmented the crisis in survival. Devaluation, removal of subsidies and price controls has meant a decline in real income due to rising costs of production and consumer goods. At the same time, cost-sharing policies are eroding their access to social services in health, education and water.

The negative impact of these policies will be particularly felt by women. In rural areas, women continue to form the backbone of agricultural labour, and their main and often only resource for increased productivity and income is their labour, their main strategy intensification of their labour in agriculture and securement of off-farm employment. What will be the cost to their own and their family's well-being?

Another possible negative impact is the increased entry of men into commercialized production of food crops and/or the augmentation of struggle over allocation of resources to food versus cash crops. As the TGNP analyses points out, food crops are cheaper to produce and rate of returns higher. Historically, men have moved into controlling such "traditionally" feminine areas in the past, particularly when it comes to sales. Mnzava (1988) reports on research which indicates that men control 100% of the sale of paddy in Morogoro. In Kilimanjaro, Muro (in WEG 1987) points out that men have taken control of milk sales in Arumeru, once a "traditionally" feminine domain. This situation may lead to the erosion of one of rural women's major sources of income. On the other hand, the push for "switching" of agricultural production from food to export crops, or the exportation of food crops, will most likely also erode women's resource base. Not only will her labour be in increasing demand for "export" crops, but she will have little control over the proceeds. The drive for export can even lead to the selling of basic food staples for export. In

Mtwara, for instance, cassava is being sent to Europe to feed livestock, posing a threat to food security which has necessitated action by the authorities (personal communication with the author, Mtwara January 1992). In urban areas, women's survival strategies focus on employment/self-employment in the informal or private sector, where various forms of gender-stereotyping limit their opportunities and are further reinforced by institutional barriers to accessing productive resources such as credit and technology, as well as wage discrimination. Their advancement is further hindered by child-care responsibilities.

Cost-sharing policies will most likely impact differently also on men and women. Women, whose access to cash is less than that of men, will have to increase negotiation for cash to meet their own priorities, whether education of children, health care or water. Alternatively, they will opt out or intensify labour. Increased cost-sharing in water and health in particular, mean an increased work burden for women in an already tight situation. It will be women, for instance, who care for the elderly/sick whose access to health services has been eroded by increased expense, or who will "pay" for truncated hospital services by providing food and care for hospitalized patients.

This brief discussion points to *the importance of analyzing and making visible the gendered and class implications not only of Structural Adjustment, but of all of macro-level and global policies.* As discussed earlier, this has been a major trend in critical feminist literature, in particular literature in the agricultural sector. A new direction is increased emphasis on making these implications and impacts be made visible not only to development managers and policy makers, but grassroots actors who can opt to mobilize critical voices, pressure groups.

OTHER FACILITATING/CONSTRAINING FACTORS

Education

Education has traditionally been seen as the major avenue to improving individual levels of income. Research has indicated that the common-sense correlation of education and wage differentials holds also for women in the formal sector and the informal sector as well as casual labour (ILO/Jaspa 1985, Mbilinyi 1991). Several researches have corroborated the point that completion of primary schooling is a dominant characteristic of those currently working within the informal sector (Mbilinyi 1991, Bagachwa et. al. 1992, Omari 1991).

Other researches have indicated that education has a positive "spill-over" effect on other areas of major concern to women such as child nutrition and mortality (UNICEF 1990, BOS 1989) and the educational attainment of children (TADREG 1990). Other less directly causal relationships could be postulated between the emergence of women leaders in rural and urban areas and increased levels of education for women.

Certainly, there is obvious evidence that institutions of higher learning are crucial to fostering the development of transformative women's groups and individuals (for example, Women's Research and Documentation Centre, Institute of Development Studies Women's Studies Group, Women and Education, Women's Science and Technology Group, to name those only at the University of Dar es Salaam).

Given the current crisis in primary education with enrolment levels dropping as low as an estimated 55%, according to one TADREG study (1993), research needs to explore the reasons for this situation with gendered/class patterns within the overall trend. To date, research has uncovered a number of factors: withholding of children from school for labour use elsewhere, high cost of schooling, parental dissatisfaction with school management of funds, and quality of schooling (including forced labour, sexual abuse of girls and future employment opportunities).

It could be hypothesized that poor rural children, already disadvantaged through lower quality schooling, are hit harder in this crisis.

Early research by Malekela (1985) clarified gendered and class patterns of education at the secondary level. Post-primary educational opportunities for girls are expanding mainly in the private secondary school sector, and researchers have often pointed out that the main beneficiaries are children of the urban and better-off families (see Mbilinyi and Mbughuni eds 1991).

These patterns suggest that education is contributing to increased differentiation between urban/rural and poor/rich groupings, and therefore needs immediate strategizing to improve access of the poor.

The report on *Education in Tanzania with a Gender Perspective* analyses the important role of education, not only in increasing women's productivity, family welfare and income levels, but also as an alternative arena of socialization, a place where gender relations can be transformed. Given the current nature of the educational system, however, it is more likely that it will continue to reinforce conventional norms. The report points out major qualitative problems within the education sector which need further research, including affects of gender-streaming, gender stereotypes in teaching materials, classroom discrimination, copycopy pedagogy, and the "macho" environment of the teaching and learning process. The research also uncovered the role of the transformative teacher in strengthening girls' educational careers.

These qualitative aspects of the educational process need further documentation and analysis. The Faculty of Education has already undertaken some work on patterns of classroom interaction (Mbunda et al eds 1990). However, the analysis of gendered and class patterns lacks depth. One example which could be followed in other areas is the work of the Women's Expert Group's post-literacy programme, which brought research to its practical fruition. The work of this group involved 1) field research on women's strategic interests and priorities 2) re-orientation of a basically "patriarchal" curriculum which kept women in the kitchen (Domestic Science) or on the farm (Agriculture) without addressing basic problems in the division of labour and allocation of resources 3) re-writing of texts to remove gender-typing 4) introduction of more guided discovery teaching methodologies and animated learning 5) workshops for tutors for familiarization with the materials coupled with gender-awareness raising.

Another problem area which is inadequately understood is girls' generally poor performance vis a vis boys. Possible reasons suggested point to the gender stereotype of women: a heavier burden of post-school domestic chores, classroom discrimination, and conflicting self-images of school/employment/achiever versus nurturing mother. More research needs to be done on the reasons for girls' poor performance in order to facilitate their chances for further education.

Legal Issues

Legal issues are a concern to poverty alleviation not only because they influence the accumulation of capital and regulate economic enterprises, but because they could form a major source of redress for women whose economic, social or political well-being has been threatened.

Critical feminists in Tanzania have long called for both legal literacy and legal reform. According to a prominent lawyer leading the reform efforts as critical feminists, specific areas identified for change are 1) the operational existence of a discriminatory customary legal system alongside statutory law 2) laws dealing with marriage and child care/custody 3) inheritance 4) sexual abuse/harassment 5) discriminatory employment regulations (drawn from Msumi 1988 and Women, Law and Development Workshop, Kunduchi Beach 1989).

Given the fact that the Law Reform Commission has slated many of these laws for possible reform, there is a need to make their negative impact clear. More research is needed on, for instance, the dispossession of widows by the husband's family, child neglect and abuse or abandonment, as well as all forms of sexual and marital violence or harassment. Research needs to focus not only on the letter of the law and case histories or purely legal issues. Issues of gendered access to statutory law, its administration and the prevalence and scope of the "mischief" which gave birth to the original law.

Specific reference has also been made in the literature (Mbilinyi 1991, Tripp 1989) to legalized forms of harassment of women in such issues as enforcement of licensing and health regulations for small-enterprises, the development levy and mobility (Human Resources Deployment).

In order to achieve further documentation, the field needs to be opened up to feminist researchers from other fields as well. There are a number of groups of women lawyers and activists working for change. They have focused their attention on legal aid/crisis clinics, which are situated in urban areas. Women lawyers, particularly practising lawyers, are extremely few and feminist research in law/legal issues minimal. One exception is the M.A. thesis of Sherbanu Kassim (1993) on violence against women in Dar es Salaam and rural Iringa. She researched domestic violence using a legal framework but also investigated the extent of domestic violence and the constraints to seeking legal redress. She found that 50% of the respondents, both male and female, had experienced domestic violence. However, women preferred to seek redress in traditional conciliatory fora such as extended family, rather than the courts. This trend made it difficult for them to provide evidence of mistreatment when applying for divorce. This field needs to be opened up to researchers from other disciplines.

There is also a need to open up the issue of male violence against women in general: why do men beat/abuse women? Under what conditions? What is the contribution of the socialization process to negative male attitudes and general societal devaluation of women? Such issues should also investigated how, why and under what conditions women undervalue or misuse each other, and under what conditions solidarity can be nurtured.

Cultural Issues

Cultural forms of expression such as proverbs, songs, theatre, mass media, popular literature, are, like education, possible arenas of change. Initially, researchers such as Mbughuni (1982) and Matteru (1982) argued that the image women is skewered by patriarchal ideology which labels women of "good" as mothers and subservient wives but "bad" as powerful temptresses. As a patriarchal ideology, it does not reflect reality but plays a role in shaping its parameters. Current research could focus more on both men and women, i.e. gender relations, and how they are portrayed in cultural forms of expression.

The area of socialization also needs new research and analysis from a gender perspective. Such research would not only identify and characterize mechanisms and instruments which effect acceptance/internalization of a patriarchal ideology, but also various forms of resistance and negotiation.

Health Issues

The poor health status of women and their children has been documented in various researches. UNICEF (1990) in particular has undertaken extensive analysis of the situation of women and children, and provided a framework to identify determinants of this situation. Although there is no known research on the impact of health care responsibilities on productivity, it is assumed that this situation constrains women's capacity to bring about sustained improvement: she carries the practical burden for family health care as well as preventive sanitation and nutritional measures.

UNICEF's (1990) analysis of the causes of child malnutrition have located root causes in the gender discrimination in the allocation of productive resources (land, labour, credit), as well as discriminatory patterns of consumption and distribution. Given women's responsibility for children under a patriarchal system, child health status is a critical factor interacting with women's position. Care, provision and production for child survival is also the major priority of rural women and forms the basis of their positive self-image (Mbughuni 1993b). Given this situation, strengthening the position of women vis a vis control of resources would seem a key element in improving health and well-being. Accessing women to resources as a discrete or singular intervention can no longer adequately sustain, improve or strengthen family well-being.

Maternal mortality and morbidity may also be due to gendered distribution and consumption, participation in labour and control of resources. Much research in maternal mortality stems from the medical profession and stresses "clinical" causes (Rukonge 1988). Underlying and basic causes have not been adequately analysed.

Given the inability of the health sector to decrease maternal mortality rates over the last 15 years, this area needs further research and analysis.

Institutionalized Barriers: Attitudes and Approaches

Male Misogyny

One of the major difficulties faced by critical feminists trying to bring about change is the male bias institutionalized in government and other powerful structures. This bias is expressed not only in the gender-blindness of policy formulation and implementation, but the recalcitrance of those in power to advocate change in oppressive gender relations. Tactics for "putting off" change are many, and have been documented in international contexts (Rogers 1980, Longwe 1990). In Tanzania, the case of the struggles of the Women's Expert Group called in by the Ministry of Education is a case in point: men's (and women's) lip service was mandatory in the face of donor power, but halfway and informal exchanges threatened future reprisals. These struggles should be documented.

To date the major strategy to combat male recalcitrance on national as well as grass roots level, has been "awareness raising" workshops. The effectiveness of such workshops is unknown, particularly the sustainability of any impact. More research is needed to locate and characterize the roots of male misogyny in the changing gender relations, its varied forms of cultural expression (popular literature, songs, stories, proverbs) and practices. Such research could be linked with the cultural and socialization issues mentioned above. Positive, fruitful and supportive gender relations should also be identified and analysed. How and under what conditions do men prove supportive allies for changing gender relations?

Hierarchical Structures and Procedures

The brutalizing effect of top down and directive approaches of extension, leading in extreme circumstances to coercion, were often mentioned in earlier discussions of state/citizenry relations, particularly in the peasant economy (Vuorella 1987, Sumra 1985) but also in the informal sector (Tripp 1989) and financial institutions (Virji and Meghji 1987, Mbughuni and Mwangunga 1989). It has been suggested that these tendencies further limit the accessing of the poor and particularly poor women to these resources and reinforce oppressive patriarchal relations. There is a need to seek ways and means of further encouraging the breakdown of these structures.

The discussion on "top down" procedures was also part and parcel of the development of participatory research in Tanzania (particularly the *Jipemoyo Project*). The discussion is now being and developed with particular emphasis on how to reach empower women. Changing strategies as discussed in TGNP (1993) and enriched through field experience such as that in UNICEF's social mobilization strategy (Mbilinyi 1992), and participatory researches (Mbughuni 1993b and Nkebukwa 1993) could provide a framework and basis for further operationalizing of the empowerment approach.

Also of particular interest in developing a new framework is the work of participatory or popular theatre as articulated by Mlama (1989) and Lihamba and Mlama (1986), who have managed to catalyze the assessment and analysis and action process at the grass roots level. Some research (particularly by UNICEF Communications Section) has also indicated that many of the "normal" channels of communication - radio, newspapers, town meetings, are not effective for women and are disempowering. The same may well hold true for all the poorer people in village/urban settings. There is a need to identify and further development of channels of communication which are not one-way and disempowering.

SUGGESTIONS FOR A RESEARCH AGENDA

General Observations and Recommendations

The preceding discussions have indicated a number of areas of research critical for facilitating a strategy for poverty alleviation which will also benefit women and strengthen their position in production and reproduction. Prerequisite to such research is a gender conceptualization and analysis which allows room to explore the interrelationship of productive and reproductive roles and allegiances of women, their range of resources (including the "symbolic" or social resources) and their strategies.

The discussions have also pointed out the importance of utilizing gender-sensitive concepts, instruments and tools in undertaking macro and micro level research, and has highlighted the significance of participatory research and animation to research within the empowerment framework.

Specifically, the chapter has indicated that more attention needs to differentiating among women, i.e. the intersection of gender and class with special attention to poor women (as opposed to women) as a significant analytical variable. Further directions include focus on household resource management at the micro-level (what might be called negotiation/juggling) situations, and implications of macro-level policies theoretically as well as how they are played out on the micro-level in specific situations.

Special attention should be paid to areas generally unexplored such as changing patriarchal ideologies, forms of control, and forms of cultural expression as well as women's resistances.

It should also be pointed out that after the extensive field research in the 1970s and early 1980s which "made women visible", particularly the negative impact of various policies, there has been a paucity of intensive and long-span field research on gender issues. This trend may be part of the overall trend of donor driven research which is tied to specific projects, as well as the lack of priority and funding given to basic research by Tanzanian institutions.

Given the newness of the empowerment and gender frameworks, as well as the rate of rapid differentiation and acceleration of economic hardship, more basic research is needed to feed new analyses. At the same time, theoretical thinking and conceptualization needs refinement and rethinking within the Tanzanian context.

While basic research may take a longer time framework, targeted research also has a useful contribution to make and can "dialogue" with longer term research. Mentioned below are the major areas identified in the preceding discussions which may be subjects of research.

Areas for Research

1. Changing gender/power relations as they interact with class and regional variables: characteristics of gender relations in various classes/regional groupings/types of households within a global context.

2. Nature, scope and determinants of women's poverty; how women and men experience poverty differently; differing perceptions of self, priorities, goals; poor women's goals, priorities and strategies for maintaining a livelihood (urban/rural).

3. Household management strategies including labour and resource allocation and control, time use, food and income paths.

4. Men's and women's priorities and strategies in times of crises such as drought, food shortage, erosion of resources and their relation to class.

5. The relationship between economic improvement and gender transformation/empowerment; does having a better income change gender/power relations? If so, under what conditions?

6. The implication and impact of macro-level and global policies, focusing on structural adjustment policies, both on a theoretical level and as played out in daily experiences and times of crisis.

7. Gendered and class patterns of resistance to state/bureaucratic/ patriarchal control.

8. Opportunities and constraints in utilizing/strengthening forms of women's cooperation.

9. Characteristics/strategies of female headed households vis a vis other forms of households, including those with periodic absence of male head, to be linked to issues of defining the household in the Tanzanian context.

10. Poor women's juggling of productive and reproductive allegiances and responsibilities, and how they affect their productivity in various sectors (agriculture, self or informal employment).

11. Patterns and sources of (poor) household resource mobilization and their parameters, strengths and constraints as shaped by gender/class, to include also consideration of "non-economic" resources (social or symbolic capital).

12. Non-economic forms of resources and how they are utilized and

accumulated by women (various forms of networks, mutual obligations, and other forms of social capital).

13. The experiences of poor unpartnered women widows, divorcees.

14. Poor women's strategies to access land, labour, finance; constraints and opportunities.

15. Detailed studies of labour shortages in small-holder production, periodicity, reasons, and strategies used to overcome them.

16. The impact of male migration and semi-residence on small-holder production, both negative and positive.

17. Reasons for increased female migration to urban areas in relation to decreasing opportunity/patriarchal control in rural households (could also be studied in relation to youth); life courses of migrants.

18. The extent and nature of poor women's participation in the informal sector; types of enterprise, returns, constraints, life courses of women's enterprises or employment.

19. Women's strategies for resource mobilization and control in the informal sector.

20. The history, nature and gendered patterns of participation in the sex industry.

21. Characteristics and determinants of gendered patterns in the formal labor market.

22. Determinants/reasons for low primary school enrolment.

23. Determinants/contributing factors to girls' school performance, particularly poor performance in primary schools.

24. Qualitative problems in the education sector from a gender perspective: gender-typing, gender-streaming, classroom interaction, curriculum.

25. The experience with family life education to date and how to improve its potential for gender transformation, including issues of adolescent ' pubescent sexuality.

26. The impact of transformative teachers on girls' educational careers.

27. Causes of maternal mortality and poor maternal nutrition in the context of the allocation and distribution resources; how do women maximize "stretch" resources, what are the costs?

28. The nature, scope and roots of male misogyny in the context of changing gender relations.

29. The characteristics and extent of violence against women in the context of changing gender relations.

30. Changing gender relations as presented in cultural forms of expression.

31. The socialization process from a gender perspective.

32. Investigation and dissemination of information on positive role models - not the "big shots" but ordinary women's struggles, strategies and successes, life histories, struggles and successes in various forms of bureaucratic or hierarchical control.

33. Identification and development of appropriate channels of communication to the poor, with particular emphasis on women.

REFERENCES

Aarnink, Nettie and Koos Kigma (1991). *The Shamba is Like a Child: Women and Agriculture in Tanzania Vol. 1.* Leiden: Women and Autonomy Centre of Leiden University.

Alloo, Fatma (1988). *Report of the Seminar on Portrayal of Women in the Tanzanian Media and in the Language,* Seminar organized by Tanzania Media Women Association and held at the Institute of Finance Management Dar es Salaam, 29-30 January.

Bader, Zinnat (1975). *Women, Private Property and Production in Bukoba District.* University of Dar es Salaam unpub. M.A. diss.

Bagachwa, Mboya S.D., A. H. Sarris P. Tinos (1992). "Small Scale Enterprises in Tanzania: Results from a 1991 Survey." Paper for Cornell University Food and Nutrition Policy Programme and the Economic Research Bureau University of Dar es Salaam, Collaborative Research Programme.

Brain, James L. (1975). "The Position of Women on Rural Settlement Schemes in Tanzania." *Ufahamu,* Vol. 4, No. 1, pp. 40-59.

Brain, James L. (1976). "Less than Second Class: Women in Rural Settlement Schemes in Tanzania." in N. Hafkin and E. Bay eds., *Women in Africa.* Stanford: Stanford University Press, pp. 263-282.

Bruce, Judith (1989). "Homes Divided." in Caren A. Grown and Jennifer Sebstad, eds., *World Development,* Vol. 17, No.7, pp.979-992.

Bryceson, Deborah Fahy (1990). *Food Insecurity and the Social Division of Labour in Tanzania 1919-1985.* London: Macmillan.

Bryceson, Deborah and Mary Kirimbai eds. (1980). *Subsistence or Beyond? Money-Earning Activities of Women in Rural Tanzania,* University of Dar es Salaam, BRALUP Research Report No. 45.

Buvinic, Marja (1986). "Projects for Women in the Third World: Explaining their Misbehaviour." *World Development,* Vol. 14, No. 5, pp. 653-664.

Elson, Diane ed. (1991a). *Male Bias in the Development Process.* Manchester: Manchester University Press.

Elson, Diane (1991b). "Male Bias in Macro-Economics: The Case of Structural Adjustment." in Elson ed. (1991a), pp. 164- 190.

Giblin, Marie J. (1980). "Women Peasants and the Transition to Socialism in Tanzania." Paper for Political Science Course, Columbia University, N.Y.

Grohs, Elisabeth (1985). "The Identification of Assistance to Self-Help Projects of Rural Women in Tanga Region." Paper prepared for GTZ Eschborn.

Gulliver, P. H. (1965). *Social Control in an African Society: A Study of the Arusha Agricultural Masai of Northern Tanganyika.* London: Routledge and Kegan Paul.

Huber, H. (1973). *Marriage and the Family in Rural Bukwaya* Freibourg: OUP.

ILO/JASPA (1985). *Women's Employment Patterns, Discrimination and Promotion of Equality in Africa: The Case of Tanzania.* Report prepared for ILO/JASPA by M. Mbilinyi. Addis Ababa: ILO/JASPA.

Jellicoe, M.R. (1962). "An Experiment with Mass Education among Women: Singida District, Tanganyika." *Occasional Papers in Community Development*, No. 1, pp. 1-45.

Kapinga, Damas (1988). *Adolescent Fertility in Tanzania: A Case Study of Dar es Salaam.* University of Dar es Salaam, unpub. M.A. diss.

Kassim, S. (1993). *Legal Provision against Domestic Violence with Special Reference to Criminal Law: A Critique.* University of D'Salaam, M.A. diss.

Kasungu, Halima Y. (1990). "A Situational Analysis of Women in Employment." Paper for A Day of Action on Health Hazards of Working Women, Tanzania Women in the Media Association.

Katapa, Rose (1993). *Mother's Martital Status as a Correlate of Child Welfare in Tanzania: A Research Report.* Dar es Salaam: unpub. mss.

Kirimbai, Mary (1981). *The Impact of Domestic Water Supply Projects on the Rural Population.* University of Dar es Salaam, unpub M.A. diss.

Kerner, Donna (1988). *The Social Uses of Knowledge in Tanzania.* City University of New York, unpub. Ph.D. diss.

Koda, Bertha et. al. (1987). *Women's Initiatives in the United Republic of Tanzania: A Technical Cooperation Report.* Geneva:ILO.

Koda, Bertha (1988). "Elimu, Mafunzo na Ajira katika Maendeleo ya Wanawake." Paper for Joint Seminar of CCM National Executive Committee, Ministers of the Union Government and Members of the Revolutionary Council of Zanzibar on Women in Economic and Social Development in Tanzania, Dodoma.

Knight, John B. and Richard H. Sabot (1990). *Education, Productivity and Inequality in the East African Natural Experiment.* Oxford: OUP.

Lihamba, A. and P. Mlama (1986). "Women in Communication: Popular Theatre as an Alternative Medium: The Mkalabalani Popular Theatre Workshop." Dar es Salaam.

Longwe, Sara Hlupekile (1990). "From Welfare to Empowerment: The Situation of Women in Development in Africa." *Women in International Development Working Paper No. 201*, Michigan State University, East Lansing.

Lupilya, Charles Paul (1992). *Trends in Women's Age at First Marriage and Associated Factors: A Case Study of Dodoma in Tanzania.* University of Dar es Salaam, unpub. M.A. diss.

Malekela, George A. (1985). *Access to Secondary Education in Sub-Saharan Africa: The Tanzanian Experiment.* University of Chicago, Ph.D. diss.

Maliyamkono T.L. and M.S.D. Bagachwa (1990). *The Second Economy in Tanzania.* Athens: Ohio University Press and James Currey.

Mapolu, Henry (1973). *The Social and Economic Organisation of Ujamaa Villages*. University of Dar es Salaam unpub. M.A. diss.

Mascarenhas, Ophelia and Marjorie Mbilinyi (1983). *Women in Tanzania: An Analytical Bibliography*. Uppsala: Scandanavian Institute of African Studies/SIDA.

Mascarenhas, Ophelia, Marjorie Mbilinyi and Patricia Mbughuni (1991). *Wanawake wa Tanzania: Harakati za Ukombozi Wao*. Dar es Salaam: Dar es Salaam University Press.

Matteru, May L. Balisidya (1982). "The Image of Woman in Tanzanian Oral Literature: A Survey." *Kiswahili*, Vol. 49, No. 2, pp. 1-32.

Mbago, M.C.Y., H.R.K. Bamwebuga and P.P. Namfua (1989). *Final Report on Survey of Socio-Economic Conditions in Urban Areas in Tanzania*. Dar es Salaam: Eastern Africa Training Centre.

Mbilinyi, Marjorie (1979). "The Changing Position of Women in Petty Commodity Production: The Case of the Shambaa Kingdom." Paper presented to the Symposium on Women and Work in Africa. University of Illinois at Champaign-Urbana.

Mbilinyi, Marjorie (1988a). "Agribusiness and Women Peasants in Tanzania." *Development and Change*, Vol. 19, No. 4.

Mbilinyi, Marjorie (1988b). "Runaway Wives in Colonial Tanzania" *International Journal of the Sociology of Law*, Vol. 16, No. 1.

Mbilinyi, Marjorie (1991). *The Big Slavery*. Dar es Salaam: Dar es Salaam University Press.

Mbilinyi, Marjorie (1992). "Social Mobilization/Animation and the Child Survival and Development Programme: An Overview." Paper prepared for UNICEF, Dar es Salaam.

Mbilinyi, Marjorie and Mary Kabalele (1982). "Women in the Rural Development of Mbeya Region." Mbeya RIDEP Project Report No. 10. Dar es Salaam.

Mbilinyi, Marjorie and Patricia Mbughuni eds. (1991). *Education in Tanzania with a Gender Perspective: Summary Report*. Stockholm: SIDA Education Division Documents No. 53.

Mbughuni, Patricia (1982). "The Image of Woman in Kiswahili Prose Fiction." *Kiswahili*, Vol. 49, No.1, pp. 15-24.

Mbughuni, Patricia and Elizabeth Kaijage (1989a). "Njombe District Report." in WEG/SIDA/MoE (1989).

Mbughuni, Patricia and Shamsa Mwangunga (1989b). *The Integration of Women into Small-Scale Industrial Sector*. A Report prepared for SIDO and SIDA, Dar es Salaam.

Mbughuni, Patricia (1989c). "Strengthening Women's Position in Economic Activities." Paper prepared for UNICEF Workshop on Gender Sensitization,

Dar es Salaam.

Mbughuni, Patricia (1993a). *Country Gender Analysis: Tanzania.* Stockholm: SIDA.

Mbughuni, Patricia (1993b). *Gender Impact Study for the Domestic Water Supply Programme: Morogoro Region.* Report prepared for the Royal Netherlands Embassy, Dar es Salaam.

Meena, Ruth ed. (1992). *Gender in Southern Africa: Conceptual and Theoretical Issues.* Harare: SAPES Books.

Meghji, Zakia M.H. (1977). *The Development of Women Wage Labour: The Case of Industries in Moshi District.* University of Dar es Salaam, unpub. M.A. diss.

Mgaya, Mary Hans (1976). *A Study of Workers in a Factory.* University of Dar es Salaam, unpub. M.A. diss.

Mkurasi, Laeticia Theresa (1986). "Tanzania: Women, Socialism and the Government's Basic Industrialization Strategy."   Paper prepared for Workshop on *Women and the Industrial Development Decade in Africa,* African Training and Research Centre for Women, UNECA.

Mlama, Penina (1989). "Women and Communication for Development: The Popular Theatre Alternative (The Naimonga CSD Project, July 6-20 1989)." Report prepared for UNICEF, Dar es Salaam.

Mnazava, E.M. (1988). "Wanawake, Nishati na Chakula: Gurudumu la Maendeleo Tanzania." Paper for Joint Seminar of CCM National Executive Committee, Ministers of the Union Government and Members of the Revolutionary Council of Zanzibar on Women in Economic and Social Development in Tanzania, Dodoma.

Moser, Caroline (1991). "Gender Planning the Third World: Meeting Practical and Strategic Gender Needs." in Tina Wallace ed. *Changing Perceptions: Writings on Gender and Development.* London: Oxfam, pp. 158-171.

Msumi, H. (1988). "Wanawake na Sheria." Paper for Joint Seminar of National Executive, Ministers of the Union Government and Members of the Revolutionary Council of Zanzibar on Women in Economic and Social Development in Tanzania, Dodoma.

Mukangara Fenella E. (forthcoming). *Annotated Bibliography on Women and Gender Issues in Tanzania.*

Muro, Asseny (1979). *The Study of Women's Position in Peasant Production and Training: A Case Study of Diazole I Village in Bagamoyo District.* University of Dar es Salaam, unpub. M.A. diss.

Muro, Asseny (1985). "Women Commodity Producers and Proletariats: The Case of African Women." in Fassil Kiros, ed. *Challenging Rural Poverty,* Trenton: Africa World Press, pp. 61-80.

Muro, Asseny (1988) "Wanawake na Maendeleo ya Uchumi na Jamii." Paper prepared for the Joint Seminar of National Executive, Ministers of the Union Government and Members of the Revolutionary Council of Zanzibar on Women in Economic and Social Development in Tanzania, Dodoma.

Ngaiza, Magdalena and Bertha Koda eds. (1991). *Unsung Heroines.* Women's Research and Documentation Project Publications. DUP, Dar es Salaam.

Nkebukwa, Anna (1993). *Gender Impact Study for the Domestic Water Supply Programme: Morogoro Rural District.* Report prepared for the Royal Netherlands Emmbassy, Dar es Salaam.

Omari, Cuthbert K. (1991). *The Social Dimension of Women in the Informal Sector.* University of Dar es Salaam Professorial Inaugural Lecture.

Raikes, Phil (1986). "Eating the Carrot and Wielding the Stick: The Agricultural Sector in Tanzania." in Boesen et. al.eds. *Tanzania: Crisis and Struggle for Survival.* Upsaala: Scandanavian Institute of African Studies, pp. 105-142.

Rasmussen, Torban (1986). "The 'Green Revolution' in the Southern Highlands." in Boesen et. al. eds. *Tanzania: Crisis and Struggle for Survival.* Upsaala: Scandanavian Institute of African Studies, pp. 191-206.

Raum, O.F. (1940). *Chagga Childhood.* Oxford: Oxford University Press.

Rogers, Barbara (1980). *The Domestication of Women: Discrimination in Developing Societies.* London: Tavistock Publications.

Rukonge, Anatole D. (1988). "Afya ya Mama na Uhai wa Mtoto." Paper prepared for the Joint Seminar of National Executive, Ministers of the Union Government and Members of the Revolutionary Council of Zanzibar on Women in Economic and Social Development in Tanzania, Dodoma.

Sen, Gita and Caren Grown (1987). *Development, Crisis and Alternative Visions: Third World Women's Perspective.* New Feminist Library. London: Monthly Review Press.

Shaidi, Joyce (1993). *Sexual Harassment of Women in the Fornmal Sector The Case of Tanzania,* draft report, Dar es Salaam.

Sumra, Suleman A. (1985). *Primary Education and the Transition to Socialism in Rural Tanzania.* University of Dar es Salaam, unpub. Ph.d. diss.

TADREG (Tanzania Development Research Group) (1990). *Girls' Educational Opportunities and Performance in Tanzania.* TADREG Research Report No. 2, Dar es Salaam.

TADREG (1991). *Structural Adjustment in Socio-Political Context: Some Findings from Iringa Region* by David Booth. TADREG Research Report No. 3, Dar es Salaam.

TADREG (1993). *Parents' Attitudes Towards Education in Rural Tanzania.* TADREG Research Report No. 5, Dar es Salaam.

TGNP (Tanzania Gender Networking Programme) (1993). *Gender Profile of Tanzania.* TGNP: Dar es Salaam.

Thompson, Graham (1984). *The Merchants and Merchandise of Religious Change: the New Orthodoxies of Religious Belief and Economic Behaviour amongst the Shambaa People of Mlalo, North East Tanzania.* Cambridge University, unpub. Ph.D. diss.

Tobisson, Eva (1986). *Family Dynamics among the Kuria: Agro-Pastoralists in Northern Tanzania.* Gothenburg Studies in Social Anthropology No. 9. Gotenburg: University Press.

Tovo, M. (1991). "Microenterprise among Village Women in Tanzania." *Small Enterprise Development: An International Journal,* Vol. 2, No. 1, pp.20-31.

Tripp, Aili Marie (1989). "Women and the Changing Urban Household Economy in Tanzania." *Journal of Modern African Studies,* Vol. 27, No. 4, pp. 601-623.

UNICEF (1990). *Women and Children in Tanzania: A Situation Analysis.* Dar es Salaam: UNICEF.

URT/Bureau of Statistics (1992). *Women and Men in Tanzania.* Varnamo: Falths Tryckeri.

URT/Bureau of Statistics/Planning Commission/Macro- International (1993). *Tanzania Demographic and Health Survey 1991/1992.* Columbia Maryland: Macro-International.

URT/Ministry of Community Development, Culture, Youth and Sports (1988). *The Situation of Women in Tanzania.* Dar es Salaam: Government Printer.

Vuorella, Ulla (1987). *The Women's Question and Modes of Human Reproduction: An Analysis of a Tanzanian Village.* Monographs of the Finnish Society for Development Studies No. 1/Transactions of the Finnish Anthropological Society No. 20. Helsinki.

Wagao, Jumanne H. (1988). *Analysis of the Economic Situation of Urban Women and Children.* Report prepared for UNICEF, Dar es Salaam.

Wallace, Tina ed. (1991). *Changing Perceptions: Writings on Gender and Development.* London: Oxfam.

WEG (Women's Expert Group)/Ministry of Education/SIDA (1989). *A Report of the Evaluation of Adult Education Post- Literacy Materials from the Point of View of their Relevance to and Impact on Women.* Dar es Salaam, mimeo.

Wright, Marcia (1977). "Family, Community and Women as Reflected in 'Die Safwa' by Elise Kootz-Kretschmer." in Bengt Sundkler and Per-Ake Wahlstrom eds. *Vision and Service: Papers in Honour of Barbro Johansson.* Uppsala: Scandanavian Institute of African Studies, pp. 108-116.

Young, K. (1992). "Household Resource Management." in Lise Ostergaard ed. *Gender and Development: A Practical Guide.* London: Routledge, pp. 164.

Virji, Parin and Zakia Meghji (1987). "A Study of Credit Facilities to Women in Tanzania." Report prepared for NORAD, Dar es Salaam.

8

Social and Cultural Factors Influencing Poverty in Tanzania

C.K. OMARI

INTRODUCTION

The United Nations is convening a summit on social development for the heads of governments on March 11th-12th 1995. This conference, to be held in Copenhagen, Denmark, is to concentrate on three main issues related to poverty. These are:

(a) alleviation and reduction of poverty,
(b) expansion of productive employment, and
(c) enhancement of social integration, particularly of the more marginalized and disadvantaged groups.

The UNICEF report on the State of the World's Children (1994) says the poverty situation in the world affect the development of the children, hence efforts geared towards poverty alleviation are a priority in its programmes and projects (1994: 22-38).

This chapter aims at describing and analyzing the socio-cultural factors that will enhance the achievement of the above set of objectives. It will take Tanzania as a focus of its discussion. In the course, examples from other parts of the world will be cited for the purpose of strengthening of the theme under discussion. By and large, the presentation has a sociological orientation.

The Problem

Sociologists have had difficulties in defining what is poverty. The history of the development of societies shows how various governments have had difficulties in dealing with the problem of poverty due to the definition problem. It is, however, now agreed that we can distinguish between *relative* and *absolute* poverty situations in a society.

The two words can be used to explain the situation based on the quantitatively available information, or can be qualitatively applied to analyse and present the situation under discussion. *Absolute* poverty applies to the state of affairs where a population or part of it fails to receive sufficient resources to support minimum health requirements like nutrition and calories intake. *Relative* poverty is defined in relation to general standards of living in a particular society or country. It is related to what is accepted as poor in the socio-cultural setting, rather than an absolute level of deprivation. This definition, then varies from one country to another, and from one time to another depending on the general standards of living being enjoyed by other people in the community/country, and what is generally accepted as the poverty line.

Researchable questions may be raised here: Is poverty in one country the same as in another? Can we use the same variables in measuring people's poverty line?

Another distinction worth noting is between the "poor" and "poverty". While "poor" is an adjective explaining the population where the "poverty" situation is found, poverty is a noun explaining the state of affairs indicating the low status of the people. But the question is: Are the two words synonymous when they are daily used by the people? The concept of poverty has been developing historically and culturally and it is related to a class definition (Bernard 1973:139-142). According to this definition, given the economic development and social relations that exist in a society, there will always be "poverty" in a given country and at any given time in history. It is out of this concept that some economists have developed the level of incomes, which help to draw the line between the poor and the well-to-do people in society. If the general income of the people is below that line known as "poverty line", then the concept of "poverty' is applied to those people. Even with the quantified data, it is not that easy to draw the "poverty line" in a society for it is always drawn in comparison to what other countries or societies are experiencing.

The World Bank Report (1990:26) describing the concept of poverty, uses the consumption - based measures of poverty. This definition involves two major elements:

> The expenditure necessary to buy a minimum standard of nutrition and other basic necessities and a further amount that varies from country to country, reflecting the cost of participating in the everyday life of society. (World Bank Report 1990:26)

In order to establish a global poverty line, the report admits that it has to be arbitrary and employs two figures based on the 1985 *purchasing power parity* - PPP - dollars. The figures are $275 and $370 per capita per person a year. According to this report, such figures are derived from the studies carried out in several low income countries like Tanzania, Bangladesh, Kenya, Indonesia, Morocco, the Arab Republic of Egypt and India. Thus $375 was the upper poverty line while $275 was the lowest poverty line.

Following the above methodological procedures and analysis Sarris and van den Brink (1993) made a study of the Tanzania poverty situation and come out with some interesting conclusions. Using the ILO study of 1982 and Household budget survey of 1976/77, they say that 56.3% of the Tanzania households would be classified as poor and 67% as poor (Sarris and van den Brink 1993:113-114).

On the other hand Ensminger and Bomani (1980:19) say that people can identify themselves as poor when they compare themselves with others. They say:

> ...The people living in poverty can see for themselves the disparity between their way of life and the life-style of those who control the production resources.

In another statement, Ensminger and Bomani (1980:14) say: "Most of the developing countries poor are rural residents and thus limited to earning their living from agriculture."

Thus poverty as a way of life can be described and analysed at an international, national, as well as at community level.

Using the poverty line index used in the World Bank Report (1990:28), it is noted that roughly one-third of the estimated people in developing countries live in poverty. These were estimated to be about 1,115 million in 1985. Of these 630 million people (18%) of the total population living in the developing countries were considered to be extremely poor. UNICEF (1994:23) says approximately one-fifth of the world's population live in absolute poverty.

The above figures will definitely change with the introduction of *Structural Adjustment Programmes* (SAPs) which have led so many developing countries to lay off its people. The "retrenchment" process as it is called in those countries with the SAPs, has produced a new class of poor people. These "new poor" belong to the laid-off people who have some kind of knowledge/skills and experiences, but have been thrown into the world of a "free market" to seek employment on their own. How far are they poor, will be elaborated below.

The income per capita as an index for measuring the level of poverty, hence being able to distinguish between the poor and non-poor is subjective and culturally conceived. As a country develops economically and becomes wealthier even the poverty line index changes. In capitalist thinking, the aim is to have all the people lead their lives above poverty line through job-creation so that all the people have what is called "gainful employment". Financial institutions like IMF and the World Bank financially support poor countries to achieve that objective. (Bernard 1973:139-142; Landell-Mills, 1992).

Within this general discussion on the concept of poverty, it would be useful to make a distinction between poverty and inequality for both terminologies are socio-culturally perceived, and defined in many instances. Poverty has been defined as the life situation in which people do not enjoy the minimum requirements in their lives according to the accepted set standards.

The concept of equality is a complex one. The complexity is not because there have not been some people who have studied and defined it, but various aspects of inequalities that manifest in the society make it very difficult to deal with the problem. For example, inequality in income is the most known and discussed in a lot of literature. But inequalities exist between the sexes (females-males relation), between people of different religions, colour, regions, or zonal differences such as rural vs urban.

SO WHO ARE THE POOR?

How can we, therefore, identify the poor in the society? Rehnema (1993:10) says it all depends on what you mean by the concept of poor. The consumption based poverty line index discussed above cannot help us much, especially when we consider the socio-cultural aspects. So we need, at least, some other indicators to be able to establish who are the poor in a society. This will help identify some strategies for alleviating poverty in society.

In the process of developing the criteria of distinguishing the poor from the non-poor, descriptive analysis has been employed. The analytical method has been developed and employed by those who deal with welfare services in the society. Such people have been able to distinguish between "worthy" and the "unworthy" poor (Bernard 1974:139). It must be clarified clearly from the beginning that such terms were associated with the development of the welfare state, especially in the developed capitalist countries.

The "unworthy poor" in America, for example, antedated the industrialization epoch and continued to the post-industrial times. From about seventeen century these have been the of poor law administration process. There were people who were not-work-oriented even though they were capable. These could not achieve the level of development in capitalist societies as the "Protestant Ethic" demands according to Weberian definition and analysis (Weber 1948). They were generally considered as unsuitable for competitive industrial work and were associated with immoral social acts for they were ill-regulated (Booth 1902).

On the other hand, we had the "worthy poor' who were the target of philanthropic programmes and actions. These were expected to develop and pass from "worthy poor" to "non-poor" social class. For example, in 1964 a war was declared against poverty in the USA. This policy was specifically designed towards the "worthy poor" and not "unworthy poor".

Although the concepts of "worthy poor" and "unworthy poor" are no longer used in describing the poor people of the world, we have assumed other analytical tools like "class position" analysis. Terms like "under class" or other economic and statistic quantitative data reflect the same positions. By using this analytical approach, people like Djurfeldt and Lindberg (1975) could develop consumption indices to measure the poverty level in a Tamil village in India.

In the Malthusian paradigm, the poor were associated with excessively high birth rates which affected the pay rise and consumption levels. People become poorer as they reproduce excessively. In the Darwinian paradigm, it was believed that the poor were the incompetent, unfit in the struggle for survival. These belong to the group of creatures who have been weeded out in the process of struggle for their existence. The fittest are the well-to-do people. They have survived the struggle.

When theories like "culture of poverty" was developed and applied in the studies of poverty it was believed that the poor are the result of the socialization process from the family level (Bernard 1973:141). The socialization process could work both negatively and positively in the society. This depends on how the process is accepted and put into practice on one hand, and on how one analyses the process on the other. Positively, it prepares the poor to endure their class position, and makes life something worthwhile. Negatively, the process makes it impossible for the people to escape the situation. They come to "like it" and use their time creatively, one of which has been the reproductive power.

Whatever theories and concepts that have been developed over time to describe and analyse the poor living conditions of a group of people, all talk about those who find it difficult to survive in the society (Gans 1962:268; Sandbrook 1992; Midgley 1984). One thing is clear, all these theories and concepts, describe and analyse the situation of life of the people "out there" and not "among us".

This distinction is very important at this juncture for when we come to the strategies for poverty alleviation in the later part of the chapter, the differences will come out clearly. It is worth mentioning here that most of the concepts on who is poor and who is not, originated in developed countries where the indices to measure the poverty line were developed and applied to those societies for a long time (Midgley 1984: Ch. 2).

HOW DO WE MEASURE THE POOR CULTURALLY

The way people live tells much about the poverty of the people. But this leads to the comparative analysis of which sometimes is not an easy undertaking.

Whom do we compare with so that we can get sufficient data to enable us make some kind of comparison between the poor and non-poor socially and culturally? The economic indices are insufficient in this case as has been argued above.

The Quantitative Indices

The above line of argument is very important for unless we know who are the "poor" and which criteria used to identify them; any policy directed towards them will not succeed. For example, in the World Development Report (1990:28) it is said that by using consumption level indices, Sub-Saharan Africa has one-third of the world population as poor people. Sarris and Brink (1993) have used the same to measure Tanzania poverty situation. Midgley (1984:44) says that in matters of those who are absolute poor, only 21 percent lived in Africa. But how about in relation to its regional population? Can it also be said that the population of the poor is as high as that? Midgley (1984:44) would surely say it is. Let us take another case. Based on general observation, it is said that 89 percent of the salaried people in Tanzania live below poverty line. (Sarris and Brink 1993:114). Are the 11 percent non-poor, and at what level? And by using what criteria? Or take the ILO report of 1982 which estimated that only 15 percent of the households in urban areas might be considered as living below poverty line, while rural household of the same class are estimated at 25-30 percent. The poverty line for the whole country stands at 25 percent.

It is, therefore, very important that we establish methodological procedures for the identification of the poor class before we can identify the socio-cultural factors in the alleviation of poverty.

It is generally accepted that the poor are heterogeneous, and data about them are difficult to obtain. In a country like Tanzania where per capita income is just an estimate, and probably the exact income of the people is not known (Yeats 1990), we depend very much on unreliable and inconsistent official statistics (Bagachwa 1993:1; Sarris and Brink 1993:48). Normally, the low income, the level of purchasing power at households and consumption level among the people are good indices to identify who are the poor. But what do you do when the majority of the people live below the poverty line? In Table 2:1 of the World Bank Development Report (1990:29) by using the headcount index, 30 percent of the people in the Sub-Saharan region are said to be extremely poor. So other social indices have been developed to describe the poverty situation in Africa. For example, high rates of infant mortality (IMR) and under-five mortality rates (U5MR) are used to explain poverty situation. Life expectancy, the longevity of life among the adults population; maternal deaths, access to the social services, adequate food intakes, and the problem of malnutrition in both adults and children are used to measure poverty.

These are generally accepted as good social indicators which lead to a reasonable measure of the well-being of the people (Sen 1986). Other indicators are lack of education for the whole society or part of it; a substandard housing situation, and living in areas liable to environmental hazards. These are deprivations within the list of the basic needs which everyone in a society should enjoy. Short of that, they are considered as poor people for it is "deprivation for the many and affluence for few". (Chambers 1984:36; Hardiman and Midgley 1982: Chpt. 2).

Within the same country, distinction between poor and non-poor can be made in relation to rural and urban differences. It is, however noted that more studies have concentrated on the urban poor than on the rural poor partly because indices of poverty in urban areas are more conspicuous. But more important it is because of the class nature of the urban poor communities (Sandbrook 1982; Sarris and van den Brink 1993). It is generally agreed that although the urban poor may have high incomes in some countries than the rural poor, the urban poor suffer more than the rural poor due to lack of basic needs and poor social service delivery systems (World Bank Report 1990:30). The nature and morphologies of urban communities, together with the bad utilization of available resources may breed "special poor social groups" than the "general poor of rural people" whose general life style, may be studied more easily than the urban poor. It is for thid reason thet many scholars tend to focus more on wage and unemployment problems when researching on the poor (Ishumi 1984).

The gender aspects in poverty analysis is also relevant. In an African society whereby the division of labour and inheritance is according to sex and age, in many instances women belong to the poor class. (Omari 1989b). Male domination is prevalent in that they control the household and family properties, as well as the productive forces. Being part of the household labour force, women do not own the means of production, in this case land and animals (Mbilinyi and Omari, 1993). As a result, they belong to the lower strata of the society. Studies in many instances have concentrated on the generally poor rural households without discerning the plight of poor women at household level resulting from socio-cultural practices and orientation.

Surely poor rural families lack capital to invest in the general improvement of their small plots of land, hence the low level of productivity; they lack "human capital" (World Bank Report 1990:32) they lack technology (Ensminger and Bomani 1980: Chaps 7-9); and they lack general education which is an asset in development. But women are more disadvantaged in this case for they cultivate the land which they do not own (Omari and Shaidi, 1992) and in many cases their educational level is low due to the very same socio-cultural reasons and background (Mbilinyi, 1972). In patrilineal societies, land usually belongs to the male kinship. Women have no right to own or transfer it to their daughters. Suffice it to say that all available variables used to measure the poor in society show that women are very much at the lower stratum of many communities (World Bank Report 1990:31).

Research agenda No. 1

Ensiminger and Bomani have made a point in relation to the poor which I believe needs more research. According to them, the development of developing nations has been looked at from the industrial and Western point of view - which is materialistic in nature. So even the concept of poverty has that connotation. Research topics which need our attention are: Who are the poor in Tanzania given that incomes are not realistically reported at interview time?

Sarris and Brink (1993) have concluded that it is the middle income group who have been hit by the economic crisis. The lower income group has remained the same. Let us find out who are the poor in the Tanzanian context.

Second research topic could be the whole area of the priority values of the people who live in poverty.

Demographic Characteristics of the Poor

Demography is the study of population trends in a particular society. The factors that influence population growth are, however, socio-cultural in nature (Omari 1989a). The poor in many societies tend to have large families or large number of economically dependent members. In Africa where fertility rates among the women are generally high, the family sizes are large too due to cultural practices. Generally, therefore, the picture that we find is that many households compositions tend to be large.

For example, according to the 1988 Tanzania Census Report, household average size was 5.2 people. There has been a systematic increase of the average since the 1967 census. In 1967 there were 4.4 people in a household; in 1978 it increased to 4.9 members, and the 1988 census shows that increase. Such members may not necessarily belong to the same parents biologically. The nature of the family structure may influence the household size as well.

The increase of household members in Tanzania may be attributed to the high birth rates brought about by uncontrolled fertility levels. Such trend influence poverty also. It could be a result of inter-regional population movement for when closely scrutinized, there are regional and district differences as well on this issue.

High fertility rates among women may be culturally dictated in relation to poverty. On one hand the couples may need many children as culturally determined. On the other, there are high infant mortality rates in many poor communities. Thus in order to compensate for the lost children, and since the parents are not sure whether the children born will survive, they always try to have many children so that the natural selection through deaths is allowed to take its course.

Children are very highly susceptible to diseases in many developing countries. In communities where there are no proper health care systems, the environment is bad, housing situation is unbearable, and the parents are unable to meet the basic needs of the members of their families, more infant mortalities - especially under-five mortalities - will be on the increase.

From the foregoing, therefore, there is a close correlation between demographic trends and poverty levels in a society.

Research agenda No. 2

*There are two topics which I believe need our attention since we have very little information available. First, the whole area of **adult mortality**, especially in relation to the "new poor" and the rural families need further research. Second, we need some anthropological studies on the impact of economic crisis to the attitudes among couples towards the need for children. In this case we would like to see the social cost impact to the poor households both in rural and urban areas.*

Dynamism in Household Economic Activities and the Poor

The majority of the poor in the world live in rural areas. Tanzania is no exception to that rule. Rural areas in Africa, and Tanzania for that matter, are the basis for national economies because agriculture contributes significantly to the national income. Yet the majority of rural areas in Tanzania (85%) own less than one acre of farming plots, and use low level technology.

These smallholders, important as they may be in the national economy, through their small plots of farms cannot earn sufficient income to help them raise their standard of living. As a result, rural small-holder farmers engage themselves in various other economic activities to help increase their incomes. That is where the dynamism of rural people's economies begins. It is, therefore, not surprising that poor households combine several economic activities to enable them survive. They cultivate, have chicken (free lance), have goats/sheep, have cattle and may be involved in one or more informal businesses as well. Since many of the Tanzanian rural farmers carry out their economic activities within the family land, the non-farm activities are either carried out within the family land or nearby. These may include small stores which sell basic essential commodities at village level like salt, kerosene, matches; and some food items like maize flour, beans and rice. It could also be a beer selling business which belong to a family. This can either be carried out within the family land or outside it, in which case it is hired for that purpose only. The good case here is the *mbege* selling business in Kilimanjaro region.

The non-farm economic activities are of a different nature depending on the socio-cultural factors of the communities. The same applies to animal husbandry. For example, one does not expect beer selling or piggery business in a predominantly Muslim community. But such business can be carried out very safely in other communities where there are no clashes between the business and the existing religious beliefs.

The non-farm economic activities among the rural poor families/households in Tanzania depend very much on the family labour force. Roles are assigned to the individual according to sex and age. These economic activities may include crafts, selling of used clothes, and beer brewing. Women and children are the main participants in such activities. (Omari 1989b). In urban areas too, women and children are involved in non-monthly salaried jobs. The activities include the making and selling of cakes, and the commonly known *mama ntilie* business which is very effective in providing food to poor workers. The income generated in such activities help the poor households to survive economically. In the wake of economic crisis and the superimposed SAPs to Tanzania society, the trend for many poor families to get involved in these various economic activities (non-farm and informal) will continue for these are strategies for survival. (Koda and Omari, 1991).

We have the whole areas of open market or roadside business popularly known as "*machinga culture*" in an urban centre like Dar es Salaam. These are activities mainly carried out by youths. The relationship between such businesses and the household economy needs to be established.

The tendency is for poor households to get involved in several economic activities simultaneously. These may be a kind of strategic plan for their own economic survival. However, the process has negative effects towards their development. Most of these non-agriculture economic activities are carried out without skills or education. Sometimes these are established just as a means of keeping someone busy, and not for any economic gain at all. Thus such economic activities do not help poor households get into the path of economic vertical mobility, and to escape poverty. They are trapped. But sometimes this may be a cultural phenomenon. Some people have the tendency to get contented with the little income they get. When someone says "I own a business," what does that entails? A few oranges on a stall outside the house?

Of course there are other socio-cultural and socio-economic variables which contribute to this trap. Things like the inability to control the market prices of their produce, the unreliable weather, and bad policies contribute greatly to the trap. We need to know more on how many households have remained poor in a specific period so that if any social policy is to be instituted, the obstacles towards vertical mobility are known. We would also want to know more about which households have remained poor for a long time; and which managed to move out of poverty, at what rate, and by what level in terms of income. Also the socio-cultural factors that have facilitated such social mobility are worth studying.

Research agenda No. 3

The relationship between the roadside business (the machinga) and the poverty alleviation on one hand, and government/state interference on the other needs to be documented and analysed. Has the government failed to help the poor youth in their effort to creatively organize themselves as an economic social class? What has the Machinga culture to do with the overall government objective in industrial development and production? Where are we heading to with the machinga culture of selling imported products without selling our own products?

SOCIO-CULTURAL FACTORS FACILITATING THE ALLEVIATION OF POVERTY

Earlier, we dealt at length with the problem of the definition of both what is poverty, and who are the poor in a given socio-cultural context. In this concluding sub-section I specifically deal with the socio-cultural factors that may help to hasten the alleviation of poverty in a society, taking Tanzania as a focus for our discussion.

The Limits of Quantitative Indices

It is very revealing to note that "the substantial increase in consumption per capita in the developing world as a whole has not led to an equally impressive reduction in poverty" (World Bank Report 1990:39). This statement is a conclusion arrived at after the analysis of survey data collected from eleven countries for a period of at least ten years. These countries represent 40 percent of the total population from developing countries, and 50 percent of the poor countries (World Bank Report (1990:40). One of the problems encountered in such a survey has been unreliable statistics. The report, however, notes that Tanzania was one of those countries in Sub-Sahara Africa where systematic large scale urban and rural surveys have been carried. It is noted that the living standard of the people of Tanzania has declined at an annual rate of 25 percent between 1969-1983. It further noted that in the urban areas of Tanzania the decline was more dramatic than in the rural areas.

Real wages fell by about 65 percent during the same period, and real private consumption per capita fell by 43 percent since 1973. (World Bank Report 1990:42). But such figures do not give us the real picture of the poverty situation. If the figures were speaking the reality, no one in Tanzania would have survived to this day.

Such trends of decline of standard of living however, has effected more the poor families especially in their budgeting process and eating habits. People have moved away from meat and other dairy products and vegetables to cheap starches and beans. As a result many people have developed the "big belly culture" signifying the well to do aspects of their lives!

In the past some scholars have suggested stages of economic development as a way to get out of the poverty situation (Rostow 1960). They have also developed theories like "trickle down' to explain how the wealth can spread from the few to the majority of the people; or distributive and egalitarian theories to explain how to get out of poverty situations (Midgley 1984). Yet these have not brought the desired results. Or have we understood differently the concepts of equality, egalitarian and other concepts used to explain poverty?

There was time when poverty was seen as a transition period to a better future (Bernard 1973). It was believed that all the people would move out of poverty if they take the economic opportunities and facilities availed to them. The World Bank and IMF have been involved in this process in the developing countries for a long time now trying to eradicate poverty among the poor (Kiljunen 1988; Landell-Mills 1992). The whole thrust in the programmes initiated by these financial institutions - and others which are very sympathetic with the plight of the poor in developing countries - is that if credit institutions and banking facilities are developed and are available to the poor, the money invested will help the poor come out of the poverty situation. But the results have been disappointing, and/or in a slow pace. Are we looking for a *utopia* situation, or are we wrong in our approaches towards poverty alleviation?

Research agenda No. 4

*Some quantitative researches are needed to show **the contribution of informal business to the household income among the civil servants** so as to establish the real GNP in the country.*

The Socio-Cultural Factors

On the drawing board things look great and one can make some suggestions on how to eradicate poverty. One can work out the input-output correlation - in this case the money invested and the anticipated and expected economic growth - and see how the poverty situation is flown out of the window. But very rarely have such suggestions been discussed or thought of in relation to the socio-cultural factors related to the investment pattern and set of priorities in the financial and management process among the poor.

Money economy and "free market" oriented businesses demand a certain type of culture. That culture is not well-known to many of the poor people. We know the anthropological studies on the traditional marketing systems, trade exchange, and investment patterns. Such information is on the non-monetary economic systems in our societies. The peasants and the poor in Africa have already been integrated in the money economy not by their own choice and design, but as the direction in which the whole world economic system is moving. One would like to know the spending culture among the poor. For example, what would a poor person do with a big loan or subsidy given to him/her? In many cases I have observed poor people getting into a drinking spree or marrying more wives out of money they got from a lottery or pension fund at the end of their working years.

How about investment for the future? The culture of spending and not worrying about the future will put more people into a poverty situation.

Research agenda No. 5

Investment patterns among the poor needs research. This could be combined with agenda No. 1 above on the set of priorities in life among the poor.

Also the culture of being satisfied easily with the little one has needs to be eradicated from the many households whose "Uswahili culture" dictates that one gets satisfied with the little that one has. A small plot of land is called a farm which will produce enough to satisfy the family needs. The subsistence economy in the world economy will only increase poverty among the people instead of eradicating it. Peasants have to cultivate to feed themselves and the urbanites.

The New Poor

In Tanzania we are now getting a new class of poor people. The "new poor" are all those who will be involved in the retrenchment exercise as recommended by the IMF. At this moment we do not know exactly how many people will be laid off or retired as part of the retrenchment exercise. It is only estimated that about 80,000 civil servants and parastatal employees will be laid off by the end of 1994. One thing is clear: they will get some money, a substantial amount in the poor person's standards, when they are laid off. One would like to know what plans do they have on how to spend such money. I have seen some of them getting into drinking and enjoying themselves with friends out of the money they have been given. They are celebrating rather than planning for their old age years.

The "new poor" are different from the "general poor population" in that these are people who have got used to certain life-styles which have influenced their cultural behaviour; they are better educated, and they are more skilled and experienced. They are now going to be thrown into   "the free market" to struggle on their own for survival. Their skills and knowledge gained over the years while working in the government system may not be useful and relevant in the "free market" economy where the private sector is still in its infancy, and the informal sector - though flourishing - is still facing some problems (Bagachwa 1993). After all, the new poor are not familiar with the survival strategies which the general poor have developed through experience over the years. The survival strategies which the general poor have developed for some time and are now useful to some households in making them survive in the wake of economic crisis (Koda and Omari 1991), may not be practical to the new poor. These were developed within the socio-cultural factors which these new poor may be unfamiliar with. How then will the new poor utilize their skills and knowledge in their new situation to survive?

The new poor are culturally poor for they have been moved out of their working environment which they were used to. Materially they may look alright. But being put in a new environment they become poor culturally. Hence they are a new social group of poor people.

Research agenda No. 6

The new poor are people who will have to be reoriented into new life. **Some surveys using tracer studies on the individuals and what they are doing after the retrenchment exercise given the state of affairs in old age benefits** *(Nijanga and Omari 1991) would be of great importance both to the Tanzania government and the international community given the high hopes one has of usefulness of these people in societal development. Past studies on the retirees have shown that the majority die within the first two years of their retirement age. How about the new poor?*

Business-like and Hard-working

One would like to study more the emerging African entrepreneurship among the poor, and how they stay in such business. The study would trace for how long a person has remained in the same business and if he/she has dropped out, and the reasons for dropping out. The *mama ntilies* and their "hilton hotels" should be one of the areas for more studies so as to know exactly their income pattern; their investment pattern; and their social responsibilities at the household level. Studies on gender relations carried out in other contexts (Mbilinyi and Omari 1993) have shown that the more these women control and manage their own incomes, the more the responsibilities that are added to them at household levels. Their husbands or male partners run away from their parenthood responsibilities because the women are now considered to be more capable of taking care of the household responsibilities financially. The researchable question is: Do the Women engaged in the informal business help the poor households get out of the poverty situation or is the increase of the responsibilities on them as the result of their involvement in the informal business make them able to escape from the poverty syndrome? We would like to know how many women entrepreneurs have developed from this kind of business. This may be a challenge to *The Association of Tanzania Business Women* and other social scientists concerned with the studies and plight of poor women and gender relation in general.

It has been revealed in many studies that many of the people engaged in the informal business do not posses good and adequate formal education, skills or certificates of recognition. At the same time it has been recognized generally that education and skills are a great asset in the improvement of standards of living among the poor. People with skills and education have the possibilities to acquire new technology which in turn will help improve the performance in economic development. This will further help develop appropriate technology rather than import technology for development (Swantz 1989). As a cultural process, technology cannot be imported; it has to be developed by the people themselves taking into consideration the socio-cultural factors that operate and influence such a process in a society.

It has also been noted in many studies dealing with the rural poor that due to the low level of technology they use, their productivity is also low. We cannot expect to transform the rural poor through the use of "Adam's hoe". Technological development is a must. Technology and skills that will directly raise the productivity among the agricultural oriented economies, while at the same time reducing the heavy burden that fall on the peasants - especially the women - would be worthwhile studying among the rural poor.

One would like to know more about the existing training manuals geared towards the education of peasants and the "new poor", especially as propounded by some NGOs in the country. What are the contents of these materials and syllabi developed for the poor in matters of skills and education? There are several NGOs and UN institutions involved in the retrenchment process, and all these talk about training: what is it? What do we know about the NGOs and the poor in Tanzania? In the process of capacity building, one would like to know whether such a process increases people's self-sufficiency or leads to the dependency syndrome which does not solve the problem of poverty. Studies in the past (Omari, 1991) have shown that programmes and projects introduced in the name of the poor, are actually bureaux for the employment of expatriates and the bourgeoisie class in Tanzania.

Of very great importance to us at this juncture is to try to understand the cultures that operate behind various ethnic groups in Tanzania. For example, some ethnic groups in the country have accepted self-reliance activities as part of their development process, while others have to wait for the government to initiate development programmes and projects for them. In other ethnic groups begging is part of their culture, and so they flock to towns; while in others it is the other way round. What makes them different, and how can we alleviate poverty among such social groups? Definitely the process will take different paths depending on the cultures that operate among them.

Research agenda No. 7

One would like to study more about the aspirations of the "machinga" business people, and to establish why machinga are males and "mama ntilie" are women. Are these businesses based on some traditional division of labour? It is also useful to establish their investment patterns and development economically. It is said that the poor operate economically in the traditional and informal sector. The whole area of interaction between formal and informal economic development in Tanzania needs research so as to establish the economic culture of the people who are actively engaged in the development of the country.

Ownership of Development

The ownership of development by the people themselves will help to shape the destination that the poor are heading to. Many of the policies developed and initiated to alleviate poverty have been externally conceived and planned. The poor people who are supposed to benefit from such policies have not been involved in their formulation. It is generally observed that most positive and effective policies in changing people's poor lives have been those in which the people themselves participated in the conception and planning process. So the ownership of the developmental process needs to be assessed, especially in those projects and programmes initiated to raise the living standards of the poor.

The whole concept of sustainable development needs more information especially as related to the programmes and projects among the poor. Poor people are tired of many experimental projects and programmes initiated in their names but which do not give them their entitlement.

Research agenda No. 8

A lot of researches and evaluation reports have been produced on programmes and projects that have been introduced to the poor communities and failed. In many cases the failures have been attributed to the lack of ownership by the people who are the beneficiaries of the programmes and/or projects. Indepth studies could help sharpen the theoretical formulation on participatory development, and how we can overcome top-down development both among the NGOs, the government, or the UN system.

Decision-making Process and Gender in Cultural Context

Division of labour and the development of labour force at household level is another problem in the alleviation of poverty among the people. There is a need to alter the division of labour drastically at household level where some basic decision making related to the alleviation of poverty take place. The decision making process and gender relation in matters related to resource allocation in poor households in the wake of economic difficulties needs more research. For example, a system like *upatu* (traditional credit system) needs to be studied in details to establish what women buy with the money they get from this system. This system seems to have created a culture of subsistence in Tanzania urban areas (Trip 1988b). Does this traditional credit system help to alleviate poverty or does it just enlarge the operation of poverty business? One would also like to know more on how investment in the education of children is being allocated at household level in the wake of the cost-sharing in social services; and how such decisions affect girls more than boys. Decisions on budget allocation at household level, and who gets what in view of scarce resources available also needs more research.

These are areas which deserve more research so as to identify socio-cultural factors that influence or inhibit the alleviation of poverty at household level. Since many of these areas are related to socio-cultural factors in the alleviation of poverty at households level, we need up-to-date and comprehensive information about them. These will enable policy makers to devise social policies which will affect changes at household level for the better.

Research agenda No. 9

The whole area of traditional and the emerging credit system among the poor people needs to be systematically explored. Upatu is just one of the traditional credit systems. Can we uncover other systems and how do they work among the poor? Are there private money lenders in Tanzania? And if there are, how do they operate?

Religious Beliefs and Poverty

Religious belief systems in Tanzania manifest in various ways. In one way or another they reveal some aspects of Tanzanian cultures. At one level we have had witchcraft accusations whereby several people have been killed, especially elderly women in Usukuma areas (Omari 1993). The witchcraft accusations in Usukuma and other areas in Tanzania are a manifestation of underdevelopment. Masanja and Mesaki (1983) have documented some evidences on how this belief system is counter-productive in Usukuma.

The effects of such accusations is that people live in fear and mistrust among themselves. Development efforts are directed at trying to eradicate such belief systems instead of alleviating the poverty of the people. In some places beliefs in witchcraft and superstition have been used in explaining the causes of poverty as revealed in infant mortality rates and diseases (Omari, 1971).

There have been some researches on this issue in Tanzania. But there is a lot to be done especially in medical sociology and anthropology. We need to know more about health care utilization process among the poor. We need to know more about the situation the poor people are facing in the wake of economic crisis, the introduction of SAPs and the introduction of cost-sharing in health care system in Tanzania.

At another level, especially among the Christian religious belief systems which have been used to pacify the poor so that they do not see and rebel against their misery (Nyerere, 1968) a close analysis of the poor in relation to their belief system is necessary. The revival and fundamentalist movements of "born again" regimes in the country have led poor people to accept their poor positions in the world for they are told that they will inherit the kingdom of heaven. They are encouraged not to deal with the "evils of poverty" that they are experiencing. To them the "evils of poverty" are associated with the power of the devil. To get out of these evils is to accept Jesus as saviour and be "born again".

This "side tracking" of the poverty situation which in turn affects the poverty alleviation efforts. Once people have been misdirected in their attitudes towards poverty problems, whatever efforts are done to alleviate poverty will be rejected.

The millennium religious movements seem to attract poor people more than the well-to-do although even at the University of Dar es Salaam we see substantial numbers of youth belong to these movements. We would like to know more about the fundamentalist process in the country, especially when we see that Muslim fundamentalists attract the poor politically. Why do the poor resort to these fundamentalist belief systems rather than the liberal belief systems?

As a social control device, traditional belief systems created a kind of an egalitarian society of its own kind. The social development level in which such societies found themselves living in allowed them to practice a kind of economic equity relation. Obligation to others, especially among the members of the kinship group, was a part of the expected roles to be played effectively by all the members of the kinship and households.

In trying to explain this kind of relation, Hyden (1981) termed it as "the economy of affection". In the money economic system, and especially in the wake of the weakening of the family structures and the economic crisis, we would like to know more on how the salaried people in urban areas still carry on their obligation by remitting some money to the rural areas to support their parents, especially the retired and the old. We would like to know more about the rural life of the elderly poor people whose children are working in urban areas. Are the moral fabrics that united the extended families collapsing, and what other forms of relationships and networking are emerging in our society to replace them?

Research agenda No. 10

*Religion is a powerful agent in people's perception and idea formation. A large scale comparative study on the influence of religion on poverty in Tanzania needs to be carried out; **the relation between religion and economic development** needs to be documented and correlated properly.*

CONCLUSION

This chapter has been selective in its choice of socio-cultural variables in relation to the alleviation of poverty process. There are other socio-cultural factors which could be dealt with. For example, the whole area of the relation between poverty and environment could be developed into a good researchable topic. We put emphasis on more production among the peasants. What has this do with the environment around them, and how do the poor respond? What does the concept "exploitation of natural resources for development" mean to the poor rural agriculturist? What has the liberalization process in the country got to offer the poor whereby the natural resources are exploited by few a people who have the money, while the poor who own the earth have no power to control and manage them? What is social justice and entitlement to the poor people in the wake of liberalization, and what has the market forces to do with the poor of Tanzania?

These and other questions need our thought and deliberations. If by doing so we can make a meaningful step in the process of alleviation of the poverty situation in our country, we would have achieved one of the most important step in research enterprise.

REFERENCES

Bagachwa, M.S.D. (1993)"Estimates of Informal Parallel and Black Market Activities in Tanzania". Paper presented at *International Conference on Development Challenges and strategies for Tanzania: An Agenda for 21st Century*, October 25th - 29th 1993.

Bernard, Jessie (1973) *The Sociology of Community* London: Scott, Foresman and Co.

Booth, Charles (1902) *Life and Labour of the People in London,* London: MacMillan.

Chambers, Robert (1984) *Rural Development: Putting the Last First* London: Longman.

Djurfeldt, Goran and Staffan Lindberg(1975) Pills Against Poverty Land: Curzon Press.

Ensminger, Douglas and Paul Bomani (1980) *Conquest of World Hunger and Poverty* Iowa-Ames: The Iowa State University Press.

Gans, Herbert J. (1962) *The Urban Villagers,* New York: The Free Press.

Hyden, G. (1981) *Beyond Ujamaa in Tanzania: Underdevelopment and uncaptured Peasantry,* London: Heinemann.

Hardiman,M and James Midgley (1982) *The Social Dimensions of Development:* Chichester: John Wiley.

International Labour Office (ILO) (1982) *Basic Needs in Danger: A Basic Needs Oriented Development Strategy for Tanzania* Addis Ababa: JASPA.

Ishumi, A.G.(1984) *The Urban Jobless in Eastern Africa* Uppsala: SIAS.

Kiljunen, Kimmo (1988) *The World Bank and World Poverty* Helsinki: Institute of Development Studies (occasional Paper No. 2.

Koda, B.O. and C.K. Omari (1991) "Crisis in the Tanzania Household Economy: Women's Strategies in Dar es Salaam" in (ed.) Mohamed Suliman, *Alternative Development Strategies for Development* Vol. 2, London: Institute or African Alternatives pp. 117-131.

Landell - Mills Joslin (1990)ing the Poor: the IMF's New Facilities for *Structural Adjustment* Washington: IMF.

Masanja, P. and S. Mesaki (1983) "Witchcraft and Homicide in Usukumaland: a Sociological Background" *Research Report* University of Dar es salaam.

Mbilinyi, D.A.S. and C.K. Omari (1993) "The Evaluation of Gender Sensitivity in Church Development Programmes in the Church Province of Tanzania". *Report* Dar es Salaam.

Mbilinyi, M.S. (1972) "The Decision to Educate Girls" *Ph.D. Thesis* University of Dar es Salaam.

Midgley James (1984) *Social Security, Inequality and the Third World,* Chichester: John Wiley.

Nyanga, Ayub K.T. and C.K. Omari (1991) "Old Age Insurance in Tanzania" in (eds) Tracy, Martin B. and Fred C. Pampel *International Handbook on Old Age Insurance* N.Y. Greenwood Press. pp. 175-182.

Nyerere, J.K. (1968) *Freedom and Socialism* Dar es Salaam: Oxford University Press.

Omari, C.K. (1971) "Matumizi Mabaya ya Utamaduni". *Report* University of Dar es Salaam.

Omari, C.K. (1989ª) *Socio-cultural Factors in Modern Methods in Family Planning* New York: The Mellen Press.

Omari, C.K. (1989b) *Rural Women, Informal Sector and Household Economy in Tanzania* Working Paper No. 79 Helsinki: WIDER.

Omari, C.K. (1991) "Social Dimension in Women in the Information Sector" *Inaugural Professorial Lecture* University of Dar es Salaam.

Omari, C.K. (1993) *Uchawi na Ushirikina* Mwanza: Inland Press.

Omari, C.K. and I.P. Shaidi (1992) "Women access to Land in Pare" *Research Report* IDRC/Dar es Salaam.

Rahnema, Majib (1993) "It depends what you mean by Poor" a bridged version of a paper presented at *International Workshop on Environment and Poverty* Dhaka, and appeared in Family Mirror second Issue November 1993, p.10.

Rostow, W.W. (1960) *The Stages of Economic Growth* Cambridge; CUP.

Sandbrook, Richard (1982) *The Politics of Basic Needs; Urban Aspects of Assaulting Poverty in Africa* London: Heinemann.

Sariss, A. H. and R. van Den Brink (1993) *Economic Policy and Household Welfare During Crisis and Adjustment in Tanzania*, N.Y., New York Press.

Sen, Amartya (1986) *Food, Economics and Entitlements* Working Paper No. 1: Helsinki: WIDER.

Swantz, Marja-Liisa (1989) *Transfer of Technology as an Intercultural Process;* Helsinki, Finish Anthropological Society.

Trip, A.T.(1988a)"The Politics of reciprocity; Urban networks and the Informal Economy in Tanzania" Paper presented at the Meeting of the Finish anthropological Society, February 1988.

Trip, A.T.(1988b) "Defending the rights to subsist: The State vs the Urban Informal Economy in Tanzania" Paper presented at the African Studies Association Annual Meeting, Chicago, Illinois, 28th-31st October 1988.

UNICEF (1994)*The State of the World's Children* New York: OUP.

Weber, Max (1948) *The Protestant Ethic and The Spirit of Capitalism* London: Allen and Urwin.

World Bank (1990) *World Development Report 1990* New York: OUP.

Yeats, A.J."On the Accuracy of Economic Observations: Do Sub-Saharan Trade Statistics Mean anything? in the *World Bank Economic Review*, Vol. 4, No. 2 (May 1990) pp. 135-151.